BEHIND the BADGE

STORIES AND PICTURES FROM THE DMPD

BEHIND the BADGE

STORIES AND PICTURES FROM THE DMPD

STAFF

Creative Director
Steve Peglow

Research Editor
John Zeller

Designer / Art Director
Steve Peglow

Production Editor
Suzanne Stander-Peglow

Copy Editors
Anna Kingery, Pam Shapiro, SPO Frank Scarcello,
Suzanne Stander-Peglow, Jim Zeller

Writers
Tom Alex, Linda Banger, Mary Brubaker
Richard Crook, Tom Suk, Jan Walters, John Zeller

SPO Cynthia Donahue, SPO Charles Guhl,
Willis Bassett, Lt. Ben Bishop, Capt. W. L. Johnson,
Anna Kingery, Asst. Chief Bill McCarthy,
SPO Michael McDermott, Capt. Jim O'Donnell,
Chief William Moulder, Peggy Schleuger, Pam Shapiro,
Capt. Dale Patch, Robert Wright Sr.

Photographers
Marty Boyd, Deb Barber, Christina Lynch Jones,
John Zeller, Dan Belt, Steve Peglow

Illustrator
Steve Peglow

Jacket Illustration
Mark Marturello

Printer
Garner Printing, Des Moines, Iowa

Book Committee
SPO Frank Scarcello, Sgt. Michael Leeper,
Asst. Chief William McCarthy, SPO Charles Guhl,
Anna Kingery, Marye Dusenbery,
Peggy Schleuger, Pam Shapiro

Steve Peglow, Suzanne Stander-Peglow,
John Zeller, Richard Crook, Mary Brubaker

Produced by
PEGLOW ART & DESIGN PUBLISHING
836 Hull Avenue, Des Moines, Iowa 50316-1169

Published by
THE DES MOINES POLICE BURIAL ASSOCIATION
Copyright 1999 All Rights Reserved
Published in 1999 in the United States

ACKNOWLEDGEMENTS

A book like this would be impossible without the help of the many community members who gave of their time and resources.

We would like to take this opportunity first to thank *Des Moines Register* Editor Dennis Ryerson for allowing us access to the files and photo archives of the *Des Moines Register,* and for permission to reprint stories and photos. Also, the staff of the Cowles Library at Drake University, who gave us open access to their microfilm newspapers and film copy machines, often into the early morning hours.

Members of the committee who deserve special mention are John Zeller for being a walking book of Des Moines and Iowa history; Sgt. Michael Leeper for his collecting and organizational skills, not to mention the far-sightedness to save old photos and equipment when others would have thrown them away; Marye Dusenbery for an uncanny ability to put names to faces, no matter how many years have faded the photo; Frank Scarcello of the Des Moines Police Burial Association, who took the heat; Carla Bierman who tackled the task of compiling a complete employee list; Paul Stigers, Elston Hardenbrook, Sheila Vorwaldt, Bob Baggs, Dale Cowden, Dale and Judy Cox, Sheri McDanel, Maybelle Brain, Antoinette Dell'Aquila, St Louis Jail Co. and the dozens of family members and friends who loaned us photos and told us stories. Space does not permit us to list everyone by name but we deeply appreciate all contributions.

Finally, this would never have happened if it weren't for the determination and drive of Assistant Chief Bill McCarthy, who joined the force in 1970 with the dream of there one day being a printed history of the Des Moines Police Department.

Steve and Suzanne Peglow

In the 150-plus years covered by this volume, many things have changed; among them, the methods of addressing women and a person's racial or ethnic background. In all cases, we have chosen to refer to such people using the terms common at the time. ✪

ISBN 0-9674157-0-5

INTRODUCTION

Several hundred well-dressed people mill about in a large room at the Des Moines Convention Center. The Chief of Police is there, the mayor, often large groups of uniformed officers from other jurisdictions in central Iowa.

At last it's time to begin. Everyone finds a seat, a few welcoming remarks might be given from the lectern. Then silence falls. All heads turn, all eyes are focused on the back of the room as briskly up the aisle march two lines of straight-backed, solemn officers wearing for the first time the dark blue uniforms in which they will spend a large portion of the next two decades of their lives. It's graduation day: tomorrow, or maybe even tonight, a new class of recruit officers will be on the streets.

More speeches, a benediction and several awards later, the moment arrives. The graduates are called, one at a time, to the front of the room to receive their badges.

Each officer has asked someone special to perform this honor. It might be mother or father, especially if Dad happens to be a cop too. It might be a proud wife, but often a son or daughter gets the call, and as those tiny fingers fumble with the clasp, more than one recruit has been thankful for the handkerchief they tucked into their pocket.

There are many things that set a police officer apart. The uniform. The gun. The black-and-white with the flashing lights. But more than any other single thing, the glint of gold on the left breast pocket tells everyone that here is someone different.

The badge is a symbol of the job. And it is a strange job. It requires patience, integrity, and sometimes, courage. It requires the ability to deal on an almost-daily basis with things most people will never see. For seventeen Des Moines officers, it required them to lay down their lives in the performance of that job.

It is that fact that truly sets this job apart: the chance that it could happen again. Every officer who pins on a badge knows that, and they do it anyway because they meant it when they swore to protect and serve. They chose this job not because it will make them rich or famous. They chose it because they want to try, in some small way, to affirm the ancient belief that we are each brought into this world to make it a better place.

There is a reason why Des Moines police officers wear their badges on the left side of their uniform. Behind every badge is a beating heart. Behind every badge is a story.

Here are a few of them.

—*Pam Shapiro*

***Sgt. Michael Leeper
with one of the first police
photographs saved by the
Police Artifacts Committee***

BEHIND the BADGE

STORIES AND PICTURES FROM THE DMPD

CONTENTS

CHAPTER SIX 1980-1999

*Ed Mellon and
daughter Mary, 1895*

*Badge, Handcuffs and
Police Roll Call Book, 1885*

Pash-e-pa-ho, "The Stabber," Chief of the Sacs and Foxes who were removed from their territory by the Dragoons in 1845, one year before Iowa became a state.

Fort Des Moines No. 2 as seen by an artist in 1844

Captain James Allen, whose 52 Dragoons arrived at the Des Moines and Raccoon Rivers followed by a company of 46 infantrymen, bringing the force at the Fort Des Moines No. 2 to nearly 100. Dragoons kept the peace along the frontier from 1843-1846.

POLICING THE FRONTIER

BY LINDA BANGER

Iowa was a rich land of sprawling prairies and thick timber. For centuries it had been the home of the Sac and Fox Indians, as well as the Pottawattomie and the Sioux.

The Louisiana Purchase of 1803 brought white settlers to the land. Fur trappers, traders and a few missionaries were already familiar with the territory.

In 1842, the U.S. government purchased the area, which included the part we call Des Moines, from the Sac and Fox tribes. It sent in a contingent of soldiers to prepare the Indians for resettlement in the west and protect them from the intrusion of whites before the region was opened to settlement.

On an early spring day in 1843, Capt. James Allen and a detachment of dragoons, or mounted infantry, were following the Des Moines River from the Mississippi near Keokuk, and arrived at the junction of the Des Moines and Raccoon rivers. The soldiers' destination was called "Raccoon Forks," or simply, "The Forks."

The soldiers crossed the river and came to a place where today the Court Avenue bridge stands. They immediately set about cutting trees and trimming logs to make barracks, and named the military outpost "Fort Des Moines."

Barracks were built along the north side of the Raccoon River for enlisted men and along the west bank of the Des Moines River for officers. The settlement stretched from Vine Street on the north down to the Raccoon River, and from the Des Moines River west to near present-day Southwest 8th Street.

Willows and poplars lined the banks of the river. Nearby timber on the bottom ground of the river and on the hills overlooking the valley provided plenty of fuel and building materials. Large bluffs to the north and to the south across the Raccoon River towered over the fort. Across the river on the east side, the land was low and prone to frequent flooding. It was covered with trees and thick brush and backed with steep bluffs on the northern part of the valley.

In 1846, Iowa became a state. The dragoons, whose job was now over, pulled out and settlers began to arrive in the area. The barracks and other buildings abandoned by the departed soldiers were soon filled with the families of the hardy pioneers who settled Des Moines. They had scarcely moved in and created a loose form of local government when winter arrived early.

It began snowing the first part of November and didn't stop until the end of December. Along with the heavy snow came driving winds and fierce cold. The pioneers were poorly prepared for cold weather, let alone a prairie winter. They used

Stacked Dragoon Sabres

**Jail Key and
Wooden Police Whistle,
1890**

the canvas from their prairie schooners on the interiors of the cabins to keep out the wind and snow.

Luckily, there was still plenty of fuel in the area. Food, however, was scarce. There were no settlements nearby or a mill to grind grain (assuming the settlers even had grain). Fairfield and Oskaloosa were the nearest grist mills.

Hunting in cold weather proved to be poor—the usually plentiful game went to ground in the deep freeze. That is, all except the wolves that prowled around nearby. Tales were told in later years of the boldness of the wolves poking their noses in between the loose chinking of the primitive dwellings. At the time, fewer than 100 people lived in the town. Life was hard and dangerous for those early Des Moines settlers.

Barlow Granger was one of them. In 1849 he would establish the first newspaper, *The Iowa Star*—now called *The Des Moines Register* (he was going to name it *The Fort Des Moines Star*, but he did not have the correct letters in large type). He settled on the south side on what is today appropriately named Pioneer Road, not far from (of course) Granger Avenue.

Wilson Alexander Scott also went through that first rough winter. He owned 500 acres on the east side of the river. Ten years later, his tireless lobbying and donation of a building site brought the State Capitol to the east side of Des Moines. Scott eventually went broke and headed west in the 1859 Colorado gold rush. He died of cholera while en route, and his body was returned to be buried where he had requested: on the grounds of the State Capitol. His grave south of the capitol building overlooks the Des Moines River.

One of the settlement's first physicians, Dr. Francis Grimmel, and his family spent the long winter in the old garrison. The family, with few supplies for such a harsh spell, was saved when another settler, Dr. Brooks, provided them half a side of beef.

Grimmel's daughter married another pioneer, Judge Phineas Casady. Their descendants would found banks and a large insurance company, Banker's Life, today called The Principal. The judge would found The Equitable Insurance Co.

with F.M. Hubbell, who had arrived here in 1857 at age 16.

For three years, soldiers had lived in the area and patrolled it. They had been the recognized authority, the enforcers of law and order. With their departure, it was up to the early pioneers to establish a government in the fledgling town, make laws and enforce them.

This, then, was the beginning of Des Moines, Iowa. ✪

DES MOINES POLICEMEN, 1878

Standing, left to right: **Capt. Albert Jarvis, Otto Kilbaum, Cormick McCauley, Billy Smith**
Front row, left to right: **Charles Shafer, Frank Collins, George Gray, Chas Mingus**

The full Des Moines police force display to a local photographer their first complete police uniform. The proud patrolmen showed off their new regalia to taxpayers on September 26, 1878. In a rare extravagance, the city council voted 9-2 to spend $35 for each of the eight handsome outfits consisting of a blue serge hat embellished with the officer's number, jacket with brass buttons, belt, baton and shiny policeman's badge.

Police Dagger 1890

"Skinny-dipping was against the law . . .between sunrise and one hour after sundown . . . ."

UPHOLDING THE LAW IN THE EARLY YEARS

BY LINDA BANGER

It was the nosiness of James T. Stoutenburgh that resulted in the discovery of the long-lost original charter of Des Moines.

Stoutenburgh was the city's purchasing agent and known for his snooping around in out-of-the-way city buildings.

That's what he was doing in the basement of City Hall that April day in 1927, when he noticed a bundle in a shadowy corner. Pulling it out and dusting off the dirt and cobwebs, he held in his hands the original 1853 charter of the Town of Fort Des Moines carrying the signature of Governor Hempstead. The crumbling, leatherbound book had been shuffled around and then lost for years.

The charter, written in the spidery scrawl of the time, included the street plans and ordinances for the frontier settlement which numbered over 500 souls. At the time, riverboats still plied the tricky depths of the Des Moines River, while stagecoaches cautiously navigated the swampy ground of the Skunk River bottoms on trips between the town of Fort Des Moines and Iowa City, then the state's capitol. The railroad would not arrive in the central part of the state for another 13 years.

When the charter was drawn up, the town's western boundary was 8th Street, about where the stables had been located for the horses of the Army Dragoons when the town was a military compound.

The early charter provided that the streets Elm, Market, Cherry, Mulberry, Court and Locust be a chain, or 66 feet, in width. Vine and Market streets, however, were to be 25 feet wider.

The town had four wards and eight councilmen. The wards had been determined by bisecting the town along 6th Avenue and Locust Street. The only law enforcement was a town constable who administered the law with vigor.

One of the first financial crises of the city occurred when the council was forced to seek additional revenue to pay the constable's fees

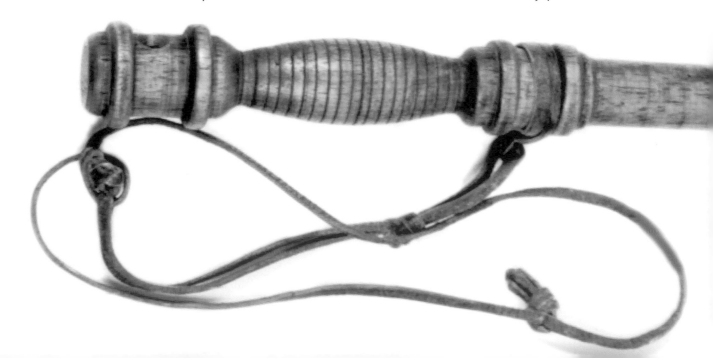

for burying an unknown man in a potter's field and removing a dead cow from a pond. Each of those duties netted $10 for the lawman.

Other laws or city ordinances in the city charter of 1853, and amended in later years to keep stride with changing times—as well as crimes—included:

• *Prevention and regulation of "…the rolling of hoops, playing of ball, flying of kites, or any other amusements or practice having a tendency to annoy persons in the streets or on the sidewalks or to frighten teams and horses."*

• *Regulating the keeping and sale of gunpowder.*

• *Prohibiting hogs, cattle, horses, and all other animals from running at large.*

• *Fining any person for "…leaving a horse or mule or team of horses or mules alone and unsecured upon any street, alley or other public ground while the animals are attached to any vehicle. The animals and/or vehicle would be impounded by police and the owner would have to pay costs and expenses to recover the property."*

• *Selling anything on Sunday was prohibited.*

• *Speeding violations were also enforced: "Any person who shall ride or drive any horse or other animal immoderately, or shall drive any horse or other animal attached to any carriage or vehicle in a careless manner or at such a rate of speed as to endanger life, limb or property shall be subject to fine."*

• *"Kite-flying, firecrackers, torpedoes or*

"…riding horses…over any bridge…within the city at a rate of speed or gait faster than a walk," was prohibited.

other explosive fired, thrown or exploded upon public streets or grounds, or any sport likely to scare horses, injure passengers or impede the passage of vehicles shall be subject to fine."

• *"Driving or riding horses, mules or other animals over any bridge over the Des Moines or Raccoon rivers within the city at a rate of speed or gait faster than a walk," was prohibited. A $20 fine if convicted of speeding on bridges could result.*

• *Horses or other animals could not be hitched to fences, railings, ornamental*

or shade trees.

• *The early city fathers covered all bases when dealing with sins of the flesh: "Any person who shall appear in a public place in a state of nudity or in a dress not belonging to his or her sex, or in an indecent or lewd dress, or shall make any indecent exposure of his or her person, or be guilty of any lewd or indecent exposure of his or her person, or be guilty of any lewd or indecent act or behavior, or shall exhibit, sell, or offer to sell any indecent or lewd book, picture, or other thing, or shall exhibit or perform any indecent, immoral or lewd play, or other representation, shall be subject to a fine."*

• *Skinny-dipping was against the law: "Every person who shall swim or bathe when naked or insufficiently clothed in the Des Moines or Raccoon rivers in view of any house, shop, bridge or frequented street or road between sunrise and one hour after sundown, shall be subject to fine."*

• *Breeding animals in public was frowned upon: "Any person who shall indecently exhibit or let to service any stallion, jack or bull within the city, shall be subject to fine."*

• *Seining or the use of a net while fishing in the Raccoon or Des Moines rivers was prohibited.* ✪

"THE FOULEST JAIL IN IOWA"

BY JOHN ZELLER

Catching horse thieves, apprehending murderers and running in confidence men, easy women and drunks are all good deeds for a lawman to do. But afterwards a policeman needs a jail to finish the job, and the only calaboose in town—until 1883 when Des Moines built its own—was the infamous Polk County jail.

When the dragoons quit pioneer Fort Des Moines for the Mexican War in 1846, they

Prisoners were lowered by rope into the 1850 jail.

left a log guard house at 3rd and Vine Street. But in 1849, the county was busy building its first county courthouse on Cherry Street (south of the present courthouse), and wanted the jailhouse next door.

In 1850, they completed the two-story gem. The dimensions were 24 x 16 feet, with a nine-foot ceiling in the ground floor jail. The jail was stout, built with double walls of one-foot-thick squared timbers with six inches of rock hammered between them. It was nice, roomy and airy, with windows on the north and south ends. A prisoner could enjoy a pleasant panorama of the Raccoon River Valley to the south, for as long as his arms held out while he dangled from the bars of the high-set windows.

When jailer "Pap" Hewitt put a rascal in jail he would say, "He's there to stay b'gosh." Indeed, no one ever picked the lock or crashed the door because there wasn't a lock or door in the place. The prisoner was marched over from the courthouse and up the stairs to the jailer's quarters, where they opened a trap door in the floor and dropped him down on a rope.

The jailer's wife provided the meals, which were sent down via the "rope telegraph." When nature called, there was a handy bucket which left by the same route. The first county jail did service for a dozen years, but by 1862 *The Register* was calling for its extinction, advising visitors "to retain a vigorous grasp on their noses as their only means of fortifying themselves against the delicate odors exhaling from the old rookery!"

That year Polk County was finishing work on a "monster" courthouse in the present-day courthouse square. Five years in the making, the new courthouse was a marvel of bad workmanship, shoddy materials, cost overruns and crooked contracts.

The courtroom, at 60 feet square, could seat 1000 people and was the largest public hall in Des Moines at the time. The inaugural event was a political speech given by the Missouri Democrat spellbinder, Henry Clay

Dean on March 31, 1863. Dean set the stage for the future reputation of the building in two ways. First, as always, Dean smelled—bad. "Dirty Dean," or "The Great Unwashed" lived up to these monikers, as would the jail. Secondly, the "Copperhead" followers of Dean, who were locked out of the proceedings by the Republican county clerk, breached the barricade by hoisting one member through the door transom, who then removed the iron that barred the door. Later, leaving the jail by unusual means became not so unusual.

After the Civil War, the county dolled up the big barn. New architectural plans included such decorative touches as a mansard roof, a teetering clock tower, faux-marble pillars, two alabaster statues of Liberty and Justice flanking the door, and four wooden graces atop the roof. The

Polk County Courthouse and Jail of 1850

courthouse yard sprouted new grass, an ornamental iron fence, a two-story bandstand, and a fountain where four iron geese floated in the basin spraying water from their long, graceful necks.

Unfortunately, the cosmopolitan air was mixed with the redolent stench wafting from the old county courthouse. Was it "Dirty Dean?" No, it was the county jail, which in 1863 had been moved into the bowels of the building. In April of that year, they put out bids for an "iron cage," and by August the first prisoners, six army deserters, were "cozily luxuriating within its walls."

Over the years, the county made necessary improvements to the jail. In 1868, they enlarged it to two main rooms east and west with a corridor dividing them. The west room held the iron cage and the privy vault. At the end of the hall to the north were three "dungeons," pitch-dark solitary caverns, and to the south a new cell for female prisoners. In 1887, they built a north addition to the courthouse, including more jail space beneath. But, for the entire 40-year span of the courthouse jail, its newspaper reviews always read the same:

"A disgrace to the state and a reproach to the civilization of the county."

"A perfect cesspool of vile smells."

"Justice does not require inhumanity to prisoners, it is wrong to stink them to death."

"Polluted by the elluvia from the noxious hole."

"More odors than a July war dance in Guinea."

"An old blue bottle without a stopper."

"Not fit for a hog pen."

Unfinished Polk County Courthouse of 1868

"Dirty, dingy, damp, dank, dark, decomposing, dribbling, dreary diabolical old hole."

And simply, "the foulest jail in Iowa."

Unsurprisingly, prisoners wanted out. Happily for them, the temple of justice was a piece of catch-penny economy. The foundation walls were of soft-fired brick or porous stone of a "rotten condition." The soil outside was loose with sand and gravel. The prisoners became happy gophers. They dug out using iron bars, knives and drills passed to them by confederates through the iron bars of the jailhouse windows. (One industrious fellow sold prisoners pints of whiskey that he poured down a long funnel poked between the bars.)

Polk County Courthouse, 1871

Escape attempts were innumerable and at least 15 successful "jail deliveries" freed perhaps 50 prisoners over the years. On a busy night the jailer could have 40 "guests," most of them too drunk to be interested in escaping a night's lodging. However they could be encouraged into loud drunken singing to cover up the sound of the digging.

On July 19, 1872, Jailer Wise rose at dawn to run a mooing cow off the courthouse yard when he found the smiling face of one Mr. Duff peering out of a newly-excavated hole in the wall. When queried by the jailer what he might be doing that fine morning, Duff wiggled a hand free, pointed it toward the far gate, and replied, "looking at that fellow run."

Four prisoners had escaped. Hardin, an arsonist, led the four out, and they eluded the posse for two days. By then the posse was cold, hungry, miserable and in a mood to hang Hardin for their discomfort. Hardin lived to declare that he never before "realized

Jailer Wise discovers Mr. Duff in the midst of a jail escape, 1872.

the benefits of a jail."

Poor Charles Howard was not so fortunate. In 1874 a mob broke in the jail, dragged Howard outside by a noose and hung his body from a lamp post. Henceforth, Howard's ghost was said to inhabit the jail.

Disgusted, *The Register* wrote "that old rattletrap is about as safe a place for the confinement of villains as to lock them in hollowed out pumpkins." To stem the flow, the county lined the walls with boiler plate, which only tested the prisoners' ingenuity, and strung barbed wire across the courtyard to keep friends away from the windows.

When breaking "out" got harder, they changed direction to going "up." They burned holes in the ceiling through the county treasurer's or auditor's office floor, and then jumped out the window. Once in 1889, while the guard was off buying a toothache remedy for one moaning inmate, 15 prisoners took this route to freedom. Escapees tended to hightail it out of town and the county seldom pursued unless they were foolish enough to steal from someone important. In 1893, they chased poor Frank Forsythe down the Mississippi to Missouri and brought him back to spend two years at hard labor in Ft. Madison for stealing Barlow Granger's chickens.

By 1901, the old county courthouse and jail were removed to construct the present courthouse. The wreckers started off using dynamite, but then slowed the pace when they learned of a "priceless" 40-year-old jug of whiskey rumored to be hidden in the foundation. If it existed, some lucky escapee must have found it years before.

There was one discovery in the building rubble. One worker single-handedly captured the last court house fugitive: enormous "Convict Sam," the pet jailhouse rat, identified by the tiny bell lovingly tied around his neck by an unnamed prisoner long ago in the good old days of the Polk County Jail. ✪

CHIEF ADAM HAFNER

BY LINDA BANGER

MAYORS		POLICE MARSHALLS, CHIEFS
1852	T. Bird	J.Youngerman
1853	B. Luce	P. Bowers
1854	L.P. Sherman	J. Youngerman
1855	B. Granger	J. Harter
1856	W. DeFord	T. Hall
1857	C.C. Nash	S. Noel
1858	H.E. Lamereaux	J.T. Moore
1859	R.L. Tidrick	R. Hedge
1860	P.H.W. Latshaw	L. Jones
1861	Ira Cook	Jester Hedge
1862	T. Cavanaugh	A.N. Marsh
1863	W.H. Leas	S. Noel
1864	"	"
1865	G.W. Cleveland	W. Lowry
1866	"	S.H. Carson
1867	"	"
1868	"	
1869	J.W. Hatch	F.M. Smith
1870	"	S.H. Carson
1871	Martin Tuttle	M.T. Russell
1872	J.P. Foster	
1873	G.H. Turner	W.M. Patchen
1874	A. Newton	Adam Hafner
1875	"	"
1876	G.H. Turner	J.S. Davis
1877	"	George Christ
1878	George Sneer	J.H. Bryant
1879	"	"
1880	"	John Smith
1881	W.H. Merrett	"
1882	"	A.H. Botkin
1883	"	Adam Hafner
1884	P.V. Carey	"
1885	"	"
1886	"	A.H. Botkin
1887	"	"
1888	J.H. Phillip	"
1889	"	Alfred Jarvis
1890	W.L. Carpenter	S. Stutsman
1891	J.H. Campbell	Fred Johnson
1892	C.C. Lane	"
1893	"	"
1894	Isaac Hillis	"
1895	"	J.H. Ford
1896	John MacVicar	Fred Johnson
1897	"	"
1898	"	"
1899	"	"

There probably could not have been a worse time to be a Des Moines policeman than when Adam Hafner hired on in 1869.

Born in Germany, young Hafner arrived in the United States with his family in 1854. At that time young German men were subject to mandatory military service. His mother did not want any of her six sons to become targets and persuaded her husband to take the family to America.

Once in the states, Adam Hafner decided dollar-a-day factory work was not for him. At about the same time he was bitten by the traveling bug. He worked with harvesting crews near St. Louis and in lumber camps in Pennsylvania and New York. He traveled to St. Joseph, Missouri, and then to Atchison, Kansas, where he worked on a wagon train taking supplies to Fort Laramie, Wyoming. He was excited at the idea of seeing the Great American Desert, which he imagined being populated only by Indians and buffalo. Hafner soon had enough of Indian Territory, though, and got a job breaking horses and herding cattle on the plains of the west.

He came to Des Moines in the spring of 1860 and found a job helping build a dam at the foot of Center Street. But adventure called, and a year later he went to Denver, where he spent the summer taking wagon loads of supplies to the mining camps in the mountains. Upon his return to Des Moines, a flour mill had been built at the dam near Center Street and he got a job there.

After his travels and adventures such an ordinary job soon grew old, and in 1869 he joined the city's police force. At the time there were less than half a dozen men on the force to

oversee a town of 15,000. The crime rate in the frontier town had greatly increased following the Civil War. Robberies, burglaries, murders and other mayhem brought on in part by returning war veterans, as well as a growing population, kept the members of the department busy.

In 1874, Hafner was elected to the first of two terms as city marshal. It was during that time the worst epidemic of law-breaking and criminal behavior in the city's history occurred.

Much of the crime wave happened insultingly close to the Des Moines Police Department, which was at the time headquartered in the Sherman block at 3rd and Court. The older buildings there were havens for thieves, thugs, prostitutes, gamblers and assorted low-lifes. South of the railroad tracks was "below the Dead Line," a region so dangerous that the police advised citizens that they were on their own if they were foolish enough to venture there. At night the most dangerous of the criminal element were going about their business on poorly illuminated streets patrolled by only three or four policeman.

In 1874 also came the lynching of Charles Howard, convicted murderer of the popular tailor, John Johnson. No member of the lynch mob was ever found, nor did anyone ever admit to being part of the mob that stormed the jail, overpowered the jailer, and dragged Charles Howard out to be strung up from a lamp post.

This was followed two months later by the sensational murder of Ella Barrett, purportedly a seamstress, but more likely a prostitute with a flair for needlework. Four black men were arrested for the murder of Ella

12

ILLUSTRATION BY STEVE PEGLOW

Baggage train of the 8th Cavalry, 1864 photo taken from the Sherman Block at the northeast corner of 3rd and Court Avenue, first home of the Des Moines Police Department. View looking west on Court Avenue

Barrett. Strangely enough, abundant money for the defense of the men came from somewhere, enough money to hire the finest lawyers. Two of the men were acquitted.

Adam Hafner always felt that the trials and acquittals had cost somebody a lot of money. By the time it was all over, he'd had enough of police work. He moved out of town in 1876 following his purchase of a farm in Warren County. There he stayed for two years until 1878, when he accepted a second appointment as deputy marshal and returned to the capital city. He was later chief of police and continued in law enforcement during the '80s when prohibition was introduced to the city and the liquor laws were enforced.

During Prohibition, police carried out raids where they were confronted with clubs, knives and revolvers. One officer, Logan, was shot to death during a liquor search.

Weary of it all, Hafner returned to his farm south of Des Moines where he remained three years, only to return once again when he was elected to the city council in 1894.

In 1910, the veteran policeman retired to Florida where he died in 1918. ✪

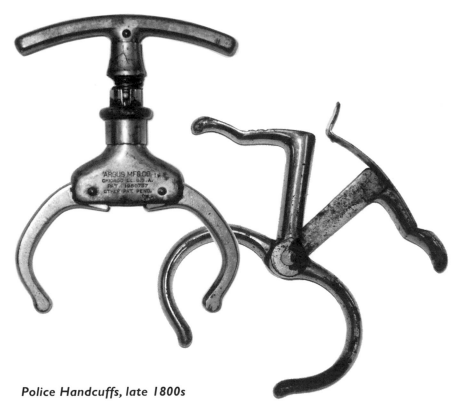

Police Handcuffs, late 1800s

13

Editor's Note: The old police blotter found in 1944 has disappeared in the past 54 years. Our only view today of these interesting records came from this story printed in **The DM Register**, February 23, 1944 by Pulizer Prize-winning reporter Clark Mollenhoff.

About 1870
Police Turn up Big News

BY CLARK MOLLENHOFF

Desk detectives at the Des Moines police station Tuesday found some interesting reading in an age-stained record book of police arrests covering the period of 1871 to 1878.

The frankness of the "author" of the book, the jailer who kept the records, makes the book much better reading than modern police records.

Madame X.

On June 21, 1871, the jailer noted the arrest of one Madame X whose occupation was given as fortune teller. She was charged with vagrancy and the following notation was made:

"A wolf in sheep's clothing, a hag of the first water, has the impudence of the d----l, is saint or sinner as circumstances require. Was defended by ————————————for $25 but no services rendered."

A majority of the arrests in 1873 were for prostitution or resorting to a house of ill fame.

The jailer frankly referred to the woman's occupation as a prostitute. Most of the women now brought in from vice raids are listed as "housewives" by occupation.

Sometimes the jailers in the seventies referred to loose women as "sporting lady" or as "sporting woman."

Other Occupations.

Other occupations listed on the records were: Lamp lighter, gas fixer, loafer, refuser of labor, drummer, cooper, pottery man, old woman, miller, thief, counterfeiter, brickmaker, hosteler, bruiser, ladler, wood sawyer, ex-policeman, fast horseman, saddler and capitalist.

Although prostitution charges were in a majority during 1873, there was a generous sprinkling of charges of assault and battery, intoxication and disturbing the peace and quiet. One or two murders were sure to show up on each month's records.

Traffic charges which constitute a majority of today's arrests, were in a minority in the seventies with only a few charges of fast driving, fast riding and fast driving on a bridge. One person was charged with hitching a horse to a tree in a cemetery.

One ordinance forbade driving a horse across a bridge at a faster pace than a walk and another provided for moderate speeds.

Saloon Keepers.

Saloon keepers of that day were charged with keeping open after hours, selling malt liquor (beer) and selling liquor in violation of the law.

In 1877 the fall of one policeman was noted briefly. The man, whose occupation was given as policeman, was arrested for being disorderly. An arrest a few days later listed the same man as a former policeman, when he was charged with threatening to commit a public offense.

On March 23, 1877, a man whose occupation was listed as mayor was arrested for intoxication. City records show that the mayor's office was vacated shortly after the arrest.

Working on Sundays violated the "Blue Laws"

The sad fate of a merchant—let's call him Jones—was traced by the jailer in his frank listings of occupations. Jones first was arrested and charged with intoxication in 1871. He then was listed as a merchant.

Jones, by overimbibing, visited the jail periodically and his occupation from 1871 to 1877 went through this cycle: Restaurant owner, eating house keeper, deadbeat, vagrant and bum.

Another individual, a drayman, was a steady customer at the jail on charges of larceny, intoxication, assault and battery and resorting to a house of ill fame. But he apparently didn't end up on the barroom floor for later he was listed as a manufacturer and the jailer started referring to him only by his initials.

The records were fairly complete as to names but they do show the arrest of "Chicago Jack," "The Swede," and "Two Indians."

The record of nativity showed that a majority of the early Des Moines "jail-birds" were foreign born. The Irish dominated the assault and battery field.

A livery clerk was charged on July 25, 1871, with insulting a woman. Other arrests of the period showed that a woman, listed as a "lady," was charged with adultery; a farmer was accused of selling diseased horses; a school teacher was found in a house of ill fame; and a man listed as a "capitalist" was charged with disturbing the peace.

Another "capitalist" was accused of contempt. Four waiters were charged with violation of a bathing ordinance.

Those arrested apparently paid fines equaling the exact amount of cash they had on them when taken to jail. The records frequently showed that a man paid a fine, without indicating the exact amount. Detectives speculated that the fine might have been an extra bonus for the desk sergeant.

65¢ TO $15.60.

Over the period from 1871 to 1878, the intoxication fines ranged from 65 cents to $15.60, with such odd sums as $1.30 and $7.25 paid by some persons. In the column of the record entitled "effects" of the prisoner, the record uniformly carried the word "none."

One group arrested in a raid on a house of prostitution paid fines varying from $4.50 to $12 apiece but each faced the same charge.

There was juvenile delinquency even in those days. The first month that records were kept, March of 1871, found three minors listed among the 20 arrests. An 18-year-old girl was charged with larceny and two boys—15 and 17 years old—were accused of vagrancy. In 1874 a 16-year-old girl, after her third arrest for prostitution, was sentenced to leave the city. ✪

LOCAL HISTORY

Charlie Shafer, 1878

	Des Moines Population	Des Moines Police Force
1850	502	1
1860	3,965	1
1870	12,035	4
1880	22,408	15
1890	50,039	39
1900	62,139	58

CANNONBALL TOSSER
CHARLIE SHAFER

BY LINDA BANGER

During the early years when the city's police force numbered less than half a dozen officers, none was more colorful than Charles Shafer.

He was appointed to the police department around 1873, at a time when members of the force were hired by the mayor.

They called him Charlie, the same nickname he'd had for years when he was a performer with the renowned Orton Circus, headquartered near Adel.

Charlie Shafer was a "cannonball tosser," a juggler of heavy iron balls. His strength and muscle-bound physique were formidable. He was considered preeminent in his particular profession and was a regular of the sawdust ring, not just a fly-by-night performer who worked a season only long enough to get paid and then disappear. He entertained audiences around the country for 13 years.

One night in 1872, he amused them in a way that had not been advertised on the show bill. One of Charlie's fellow performers was a man by the name of Burr Robbins, who made a habit of beating his young apprentice. He often took out his frustrations and temper on the small boy in a brutal and cruel way, which was considered the scandal of the circus.

Usually a man to mind his own business, Charlie Shafer decided one day that he had had enough of this. He told Robbins if he touched the boy again, he'd have to answer to him, and promised to whip the man.

Two weeks later, Robbins again began to beat his apprentice. The boy's cries of pain could be heard in the dressing room while performers were preparing for the show. The audience was already seated and waiting for the entertainment to begin.

They didn't have to wait long. Hearing the child's cries, Charlie raced through the dressing room and outside to the horse stalls where the small boy was being beaten. Just as Charlie was about to grab him, Robbins spotted him and bolted for the show ring.

The circus performers dressed in glittering costumes watched in amazement as their two colleagues dashed past them. Charlie was gaining on his quarry who saw that he had only one avenue of escape from the wrath of the burly cannon ball juggler, and headed for the center pole. The agile Robbins made a desperate leap, grabbed hold of the netting, threw himself onto the center pole and shinnied up it like a monkey.

With no head for heights, Charlie was left at the bottom of the pole, shaking his fist at the man and turning the air blue with swearing—all in front of a stunned audience.

Perhaps Charlie first found his zest for correcting wrongs that day as he stood in the sawdust of a circus ring. It was not long afterward that he retired from the show and pinned on a policeman's badge. ✪

THE MURDER OF
ELLA BARRETT

BY LINDA BANGER

Ella Barrett was an attractive young woman, well-dressed and wearing fine jewelry, who arrived alone in Des Moines on an afternoon train in the spring of 1874.

She appeared respectable, and the first few days she was in the city, she stayed at the Savery Hotel at 4th and Walnut (it later became the Hotel Kirkwood). However, the hotel manager soon realized that the woman's character left much to be desired and she was asked to leave.

Miss Barrett found rooms three blocks away at 7th and Walnut, in the apartment above McFarland's Store. She told the landlord she was a dressmaker and would have her business in her apartment. She bought furniture and paid for it from a large roll of cash she carried with her.

Her landlord became suspicious about exactly what kind of business Miss Barrett was involved in. There was a steady stream of men going up her stairs, particularly at night. The landlord realized that his new tenant's conduct was on the shady side, and ordered her out.

A few days later, having seen no evidence that she had left, he decided to investigate thinking maybe she was sick. There was no answer when he knocked on the door at the bottom of the stairs. He cautiously opened the door and noticed something on the steps. Taking a closer look, he saw that it was blood; pools of blood, more blood than he had ever seen.

The landlord called out across the street to a passing city councilman to come help him. Together they climbed the steps and when they got

to the top, found the lifeless, blood-soaked body of Ella Barrett lying in a heap.

A coroner's examination showed she had been struck savagely in the head and neck numerous times by a hatchet. Any one of the half-dozen wounds would have caused her death, and her skull was crushed to powder in places. She had been dead several hours.

She had probably been in bed when she was called to the lower door by a knock. She had grabbed some clothes to put on; when her body was found she was wearing only her dress and slippers, but no stockings. Opening the door to her unknown caller, she was struck down on the spot. Her body was dragged up the narrow stairs and left on the landing while the intruder rummaged through her luggage, taking jewelry and items from her wardrobe.

Numerous arrests were made in the sensational murder case, and four black men were indicted. Two were acquitted, and two, Bert Graves and Andy Smith, were convicted. Smith was later released on appeal. Bert Graves, who had been a well-known and popular porter at the Savery Hotel, was sentenced to the Fort Madison Penitentiary, where he died of tuberculosis.

Before he died, Graves asked to speak to the warden and admitted he had killed Ella Barrett with a hatchet. He said he had two accomplices and was ready to name them when he was overcome with a coughing spell. "Tomorrow," he gasped to the warden.

Tomorrow never came for Bert Graves. He died before sunrise and the mystery of who helped him murder Ella Barrett died with him. ✪

THE LYNCHING

BY LINDA BANGER

When Miss Alwilda Smith found the length of old rope in 1904, she was in the middle of cleaning house and preparing to move. The rope had been hidden away for 30 years, but Miss Smith knew immediately what it was.

Her brother, Ed, was a deputy sheriff when he brought the rope home late one night, hidden under his coat, and told his sister what had happened a little before Christmas in 1874.

It all began in June when the body of John Johnson, a quiet, unassuming tailor, was found murdered on 2nd Street near a bordello operated by Annie Groves. While no arrests were made, it was suspected that Johnson's demise came about in Annie Groves' house and that she knew something about it. Although a large reward was posted, no arrests were made and police appeared in no hurry to solve the crime. The apparent indifference by the police was a ruse to throw off the guard of whomever had murdered John Johnson, while the detectives quietly carried out an investigation.

This continued for two months, until August, when Annie Groves married Charles Howard Nelson, also known as Charlie Howard, a bartender and banjo player. Since he was much younger than his bride and looked more respectable, police suspected Annie had knowledge which compelled Howard to marry her to keep her quiet.

They became suspects in the Johnson murder, but there was still little evidence against them, so the police continued to bide their time. During the last part of August they came into possession of a few facts which enabled them to arrest the newlyweds and put them in the basement jail of the Polk County Courthouse.

Charlie Howard was tried for the murder of John Johnson and found guilty. He was sentenced by Judge Maxwell to life

By the time the vigilantes arrived at the lamppost on the northeast corner of the courthouse square near 5th and Mulberry, Howard, wearing nothing except a nightshirt, was already badly battered, and either dead or mortally injured.

Polk County Courthouse

in prison in Fort Madison. As Howard was led out of the courtroom following his sentencing, activity was afoot which would become the talk and the shame of the town for years to come.

Late that night, men began to gather around the courthouse square. A number of them broke into the courthouse, over-powered and tied up the jailer and took his keys. They opened the cell and pulled the convicted murderer from his screaming wife, who shared his cell while awaiting her trial.

A rope was brought out and placed around Howard's neck. "Wait," he pleaded, "Give me a minute or two with my wife."

His request went unheeded. He was roughly dragged from the cell by the rope, along the entire length of the hallway, and up the stairs out of the basement. By the time the vigilantes arrived at the lamppost on the northeast corner of the courthouse square near 5th and Mulberry, Howard, wearing nothing except a nightshirt, was already badly battered, and either dead or mortally injured.

The mob which filled the streets was anonymous—their faces blackened, covered or otherwise hidden. A few of the men quickly hoisted the rope holding Howard's body up over the lamppost and there he was lynched. They left his body there, his feet dangling a few inches from the ground.

As the sun came up the next morning, December 15, thousands of people came to the square to view the body of Charles Howard hanging from the improvised gallows.

Nobody ever boasted about their activities that night, and the identities of members of the mob that hung Charles Howard were never known.

After his body was cut down, the lamppost was removed and never replaced.

The rope was quietly tucked under the coat of a young deputy who took it home and hid it. When his sister found it 30 years later, she knew its sinister history and turned it over to police officer Charlie Shafer.

It may even yet be resting in some dark, hidden place, a remnant of a night of terror and shame. ✪

BEHIND THE BADGE

BY LINDA BANGER

By 1880 when the U.S. Census was taken, Des Moines was officially 29 years old. The citizens of the town of Fort Des Moines, as it had been called in its early years, had voted to incorporate as a town in 1851, an act which was ratified by the Legislature in 1853.

Four years later, Des Moines was incorporated as a city without the prefix "Fort."

Des Moines was becoming one of the leading cities west of the Mississippi. Wholesale trade and manufacturing were booming. Pork processing was another prominent industry. Coal mined at various sites around the area amounted to 125,000 tons. The average annual salary of a Des Moines resident was $485.

With all the industry and even though its population had reached over 22,000, it still resembled a frontier town. Des Moines consisted of 12 square miles and except for two blocks on 4th Street which were gravel, none of its 200 miles of streets were paved. Brick or wood sidewalks, however, kept pedestrians out of the mud and gutters were paved with stone. Along the streets, trees provided a park-like vista and offered welcome shade in the summer.

Members of the police force expected to maintain law and order in the town were appointed and controlled by the mayor. The city council's role consisted of fixing the number of men and the wards from which they came.

The 1880 Census listed one chief of police, who was paid $55 a month. There were also one captain and eight patrolmen who were each paid $50 a month. Their distinctive navy blue military-style uniforms cost about $35 each, which the officers were expected to provide. Other law enforcement officers included a marshal with an annual salary of $800, two deputy marshals who were paid $50 a month, and two special marshals from each ward who served on an on-call basis.

Police officers equipped with revolvers, clubs and whistles walked their 12-hour shifts from 6 to 6. Each walking beat was two miles in length.

In 1879 they made 1,037 arrests, principally for drunkenness, assault and battery, larceny, keeping or frequenting houses of ill-fame and disturbing the peace. Property valued at nearly $1,500 was reported either lost or stolen—more than half of that was recovered and returned to the owners.

Those given jail time courtesy of the city for various crimes numbered 298 in 1880, which was 51 more lodgers than 1879. Crime was on the increase and the annual budget of the police force was less than $10,000.

Besides patrolling the streets, policemen also cooperated with the fire department by protecting property at fires, and if necessary, enforcing regulations for fire protection. They also aided the health department by abating nuisances and seeing that streets and alleys were kept clean and sanitary.

Listed under the duties and responsibilities of the marshal were taking care of defective sewers and street cleaning, as well as removal and burial of any dead animal within the city limits.

Street cleaning was usually performed by prisoners. Most people agreed it was not a good system because as a rule, prisoners didn't like to work (this was often the cause of their troubles with the law).

Confusion and conflict frequently reigned between the city's police department and the marshal and his deputies, both answering to the mayor. This was a situation Mayor William H. Merritt commented on in a report attached to the statistical data of the 1880 Census:

"My observation teaches that cities are best governed where there is but one police department. In cities of the first class in Iowa, the law provides for marshal and deputies, whose duty it is to see that the ordinances are executed, streets and alleys cleaned, nuisances abated, order preserved during sittings of the council, and mandates of police court executed. This could all be done by the regular force at less cost and avoid unprofitable jealousy and rivalry between two departments." ✪

*Ed Sunberg,
1895*

The POLICE STATIONS

The new Sherman Block in 1857 became the first home for city government and the Des Moines Police Department. Hoyt Sherman built the three-story building on what was then the north end of downtown on the northeast corner of 3rd Street and Court Avenue. Sherman and Benjamin Allen located the new Equitable Life Insurance Company of Iowa there in 1867. The top floor meeting hall hosted the first stage and musical entertainment in pioneer days. The city rented space there for 25 years until 1883, when they moved into their own city hall. The black walnut timbers fell to the wrecking ball in 1924.

City Hall on northwest corner of 2nd and Locust, 1883-1911

BY JOHN ZELLER

On New Year's Day, 1883, Mayor P.V. Carey and nine councilmen formally opened Des Moines' new combination city hall and police station. The mayor presided over the dedication from his elaborately-carved black walnut "throne" on a beautifully carpeted dais. The large, second-floor council chamber (25 by 57 feet) of the building was light and airy.

The councilmen were happy as well with their "nobby" East Lake-styled desks of black walnut and cherry wood, the oilcloth floor coverings and the massive walnut railing that divided their sanctum from public seating. When the council was not in session, Mayor Carey could retire to his own private office and admire the fancy Brussels carpet ".....a bewildering combination of flowers and vines with maroon as the standard color and variegated with white, violet and purple."

On the portico above the steps that led to the front door at 2nd and Locust, bold letters spelled out simply "City Hall." The architecture was described as "modern gothic... stately and massive in appearance." Compared to the old city rooms in the Sherman Block, it was a palace. This kind of glamour came from the genius of local architect William Foster and cost the city $30,000. At 80 feet long by 60 feet wide, with two stories, a complete basement, an attic, 12-foot ceilings, four vaults and surmounted by an artistic clock and bell tower, the city got its money's worth.

The Des Moines Police Department really came of age in its new quarters. The ground floor provided the police an assembly room, marshall's office and judge's chambers. Immediately below was Des Moines' first city jail, with a kitchen, toilets and a separate cell for women. The police even had private entrances on both floors that kept prisoners away from the good citizens visiting city hall.

The jail needed two more weeks' work before it was formally accepted on January 14, 1883. Plans by architect Foster for round jail cells were scrapped in favor of conventional square ones. The city also complained that the cell bars were too flimsy and that openings in the walls for water and heat pipes provided weak points. They debated whether walls three bricks thick would secure desperate men.

In the meantime, one John Rutherford was allowed an early peek at the city jail on January 5th. Officer Clay Smith had found him drunk, asleep and nearly frozen in an east side coal yard. This first arrest was probably a good deed by Officer Smith. The long and lanky Rutherford was "so stiff indeed that Officer Smith was alarmed that he would break in two before being thawed out."

The jail was officially inaugurated with its first real bad men on January 15. *The Register* declared the four, Bob Hathaway, Jim Reynolds, Sam Bell and Bruce Martin, "the hardest quartet that ever roamed the city." As jails go, it was nice enough that within the year the police had

Police Station, 1883-1893

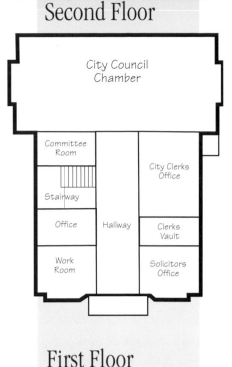

Second Floor

City Council Chamber

Committee Room

Stairway

Office

Work Room

Hallway

City Clerks Office

Clerks Vault

Solicitors Office

First Floor

Police Court Room

Judges Chamber

Stairway

Mayor's Inner Office

Mayor's Outer Office

Police Assembly Room

Marshall Office

Auditor's Office

Hallway

Vault | Vault

Treasure's Office

Basement

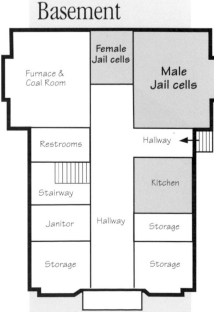

Furnace & Coal Room

Female Jail cells

Male Jail cells

Restrooms

Hallway

Stairway

Janitor

Hallway

Kitchen

Storage

Storage

Storage

Floor plans of City Hall and Police Headquarters, 1883

The combination east-side City Hall, Fire and Police Stations was erected in 1883. It was located west of the alley between East 4th and East 5th streets on the south side of Walnut Street. For the fire department it was Fire House #2. They used the building for an astonishing 92 years until 1975. For a few years the building fell into anonymity as a storage site. The police used the building just briefly, installing a jail cell in the basement. When during demolition the iron cage was rediscovered, it was the cause of some puzzlement.

to install a work yard where prisoners broke stones, in the hope of discouraging freeloading "tenants."

Ten years later, the police moved into new headquarters as the other city offices scrambled to grab the department's vacated space in the crowded city hall.

In 1912, the city completed its present-day city hall on the river front. The old building with its many small rooms and hiding places had become associated with corrupt ward politics and secret deal makings of the past. The new building was a symbol of the fresh "Des Moines Plan" of civic reform and honest government.

They praised the old building in 1883, but when they tore it down in 1912 to erect the new city market, there wasn't a sentimental tear shed in this town.

THE NEW CONVENIENCES, 1893

On March 25, 1893, the policemen of the Des Moines Police Department said farewell to city hall as they lined up and filed out.

Their parade was a short one—the new combination police station and fire department lay just 25 feet north of city hall at the corner of 2nd Avenue and Grand Avenue.

The building was designed by local architect George Hallett and built by Conrad Youngerman

for $29,990—$10 cheaper than city hall in 1883.

The police marched to the 2nd Avenue entrance under a monumental Romanesque arch and climbed the 12 steps of the broad stairway into their new "model police station."

The building reflected the increased specialization of police work. It not only had an office for City Marshall Johnson, but also one for the captains and another for the desk sergeant equipped with telephones and the police alarm system.

The new conveniences included an apartment for the jailer, bedrooms for policemen on overtime duty, and a stable for the four police dray horses complete with a garage for the paddy wagon.

On opening day, the daily papers inspected the building. *The Leader* extolled that the headquarters was "not excelled in elegance and convenience in any city in the West." *The Register* concurred: "the new quarters are commodious and elegant, Brussels carpets adorn the floors and hardwood desks and all the elegance of the effete East abound."

Police Court Judge Eggleston inspected his new office and the spacious, oak-trimmed courtroom. At 9:00am, the first morning session of the police court would determine who would be honored as the first to enjoy the new jail, "so luxuriously furnished that it will draw crooks from miles around

MAPS BY STEVE PEGLOW

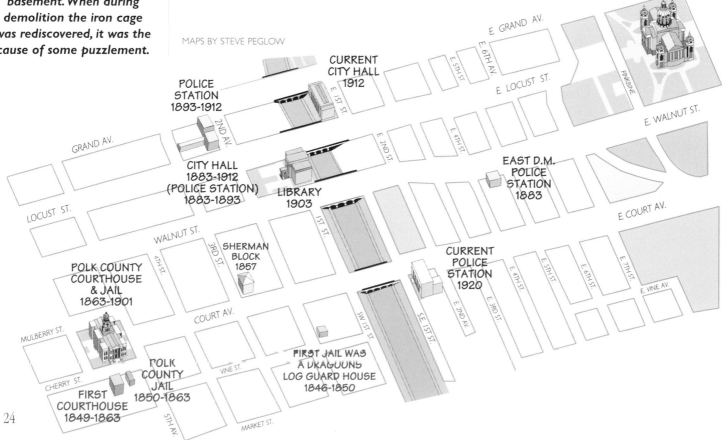

*Far left, **1883 City Hall**; middle, **1893 Police Station**; far right, **1893 Central Fire Department***

and will even make respectable citizens rob their trunks simply for the chance of spending a night in it."—*The Register.*

First on the docket was Alonzo Robinson, who was fined $10 for intoxication and released. Next came one Calvin Chase, who was ordered held on vagrancy and robbery charges. Officer Shafer escorted the prisoner downstairs to the new cala-boose, which he christened "Chase's Retreat."

In March 1920, the police department assembled for the last time in the building. They formed ranks and marched out of the building down the same 12 steps they had marched up 27 years before; now the stairway was well worn by the tread of thousands of wrongdoers. "The way of the transgressor is hard"—on an old building. ✪

Reprint: ***The DM Capital***, March 27, 1920

The photograph of the steps leading up to the old police station shows that the thousands of feet that have trodden the stone approach have chewed away the steps as much as two inches in several places. In the 25 years that the old station was in use, all classes of folks from wayward youngsters to heartless murderers did their bit toward knocking the corners off the steps. Undoubtedly most of the work was done by the plain drunks who, in the good old wet days used to line up two dozen at a time before "hizzonner."

25

The Des Moines policemen with Police Chief Fred Johnson, front row center, pose in summer pith helmets and detectives in street clothes on the steps of the old City Hall at 2nd and Locust, circa 1898. (Demolished for the old City Market in 1912)

*Des Moines Chief of Police
Sol Stutsman, 1890*

"The Des Moines Searchers and Advance Guard of the Fighting Prohibition Army"
County Constables: 1. Thomas Chapman 2. John Marlan 3. Frank Blyer 4. Joseph Mercer 5. Frank Pierce
6. O. C. West 7. George Hanson 8. George Hamilton 9. George Cleggett 10. G. W. Potts, 1889

COUNTY CONSTABLES: THE SEARCHERS

BY LINDA BANGER

Perhaps no group of men in the city was as despised and feared as the county constables, sometimes called "searchers."

Working under the direction of the county sheriff, they served arrest warrants and carried out search warrants. They often performed their duties with sadistic gusto, enjoying misusing the power of a badge. Although described as law enforcement officers, they were as likely to break the law pursuing their rough form of justice as enforce it.

Three of the more notorious were the team of Constables Hamilton, McGrew and G.W. Potts.

But one night in December, 1889, after a local gambler was brutally roughed up by Constable Hamilton, the men came very close to losing their lives.

The lawmen had just raided a gambling place near the Aborn Hotel at 4th and Court. While McGrew and Potts collared the gamblers and departed, Hamilton returned to the gambling room to gather evidence from the tables for the trial. He found one John Ring, who somehow had been missed in the raid.

Ring argued with Hamilton about seizing the gambling tables and was arrested by the constable, who roughly marched him up the street to be arraigned at the office of Justice of the Peace Johnson. When Ring began to resist,

An angry crowd chased the constables to 6th and Walnut.
Reprint: ***The DM Graphic***, December, 1889

Hamilton hit him with his club several times. The further they walked, the angrier Hamilton became. By the time they reached Walnut Street, his repeated blows had drawn blood. Ring shouted for help to the nearby crowd that had been drawn by the sounds of the ruckus.

"Murder!" the crowd shouted at the despised lawman. "Kill him!" went up the cry. "Slug him!"

Although a brute, Hamilton was not stupid. Sensing he was in danger from the crowd, he blew his whistle and Constables McGrew and Potts soon arrived at the scene.

The three men pushed their way through the howling mob to Justice Johnson's office. Ring, by this time, had been dismissed and was having his wounds treated by a doctor who had arrived at the scene. The three constables, thinking the crowd surely had dispersed, left the judge's office and started for home.

But the crowd had not scattered, it was merely waiting around the corner. When they spotted Hamilton, the shout went out, "There he is! Hang him!" The crowd continued to grow. Many recognized the opportunity to vent long held-in resentment and even up old scores.

The three constables knew they were in grave danger and did the only thing they could when faced with such overwhelming numbers: they ran. Chased by the crowd, they ducked around corners and ran up alleys, until they finally came to the Utica Clothing Store at 6th and Walnut. They lunged into the building, locking the door behind them. To their dismay, they found the exit of the store was also blocked by the crowd. There was no escape, so they fled into the store's vault.

The police arrived and advised the constables to brave the crowd and seek safety at police headquarters at 2nd and Locust, five long blocks away. Hamilton went off with half a dozen policemen to protect him from the crowd, which was estimated at 1,500. His colleague, Potts, took advantage of the confusion and bolted, taking "leg bail" in the parlance of the day. He was never seen again. This left the unfortunate McGrew to go it alone.

Accompanied by cries of revenge and the call to "get a rope," the shaken Hamilton approached the safe haven of the city jail. He was nearly there when a large, tough fellow managed to reach through the cordon of police-men and grab Hamilton by the shoulders. Hamilton shrieked and nearly wilted while the police shoved the assailant away.

Finally he reached city hall, where he was hurried into the police department and the safety of a jail cell. There he begged the jailer to hurry and lock the door. To avoid any missiles or bullets which might come through the jail windows, Hamilton crawled under a bench much to the delight of prisoners in the other cells, many of whom may have suffered at his hands. It is uncertain exactly what became of McGrew.

Newspaper editorials were eloquent in denouncing the brutality of the constables and the beating of John Ring. One pledged:

"Our state laws being such that constables residing outside of the city have a legal right to transfer their field of operations from their own townships or precincts to wherever they may desire, and whereas the city of Des Moines has no protection against a set of unprincipled scoundrels from outside townships, we have therefore organized and taken an oath that Des Moines shall be rid of these leeches." ✪

Hamilton assaulting Ring outside Harbach Furniture Palace at 4th and Walnut.

Six police officers escort and protect Hamilton.

Reprint: *The DM Evening News*, March 11, 1892

IT SURPRISED THE PEOPLE

THE HORRORS OF THE OPIUM DENS OF THE CITY HAD NOT BEEN DREAMED OF

SOME MORE NOTES UPON THE SUBJECT
OPIUM DENS ARE CONDUCTED IN SEVERAL LOCALITIES AND UNDER VARIOUS DISGUISES

The article in yesterday's News regarding the opium joints in Des Moines has naturally provoked much comment and the people express great surprise that such places are allowed to exist in the city. The police are not able to break up these places owing to the absence of any law bearing on the subject. If the legislature now in session would take up the matter and pass the laws of some other states on the same matter public interests would be subserved. Even with the law on their side the officers might not be able to entirely eradicate the evil owing to the strength of the awful habit when once confirmed, but such places as were described by this paper's faithful newsgatherer could never exist if the law gave the police ample power to punish the keepers of opium joints.

The opium joints have always flourished in Des Moines. About two years ago there was a large and elegant institution conducted in a large fine brick residence on East Locust. It purported to be a bath and opium cure house. So far as the baths were concerned, they were to be had amid elegant surroundings. But the place was nothing less than a high-toned opium

Opium den in early Des Moines
Illustration by Frank Miller from ***Looking In Windows*** by George Mills

joint and was visited by scores of people, many of them otherwise respectable, who daily indulged in opium debauchery. It broke up suddenly one day. The man who was conducting it was a sharper of the keenest edge. But he overreached himself by allowing a number of young girls to visit the place. Some of the girls who went there with young men or as visitors to young men who were being "cured" were of good family and not by any means bad girls. A few were induced to evil conduct by the debauching surroundings and the police arranged a raid on the place. The night before they were to swoop down on the place the manager fled.

There is a club of opium fiends which has a place of meeting not far from the Masonic Temple, on Mulberry street. The entrance to it is obscure and could not be found by one not initiated in the secrets of the club. But that it is frequented, or has been reached by a number of high-toned people is unquestionable. Among others who were shown to the writer to have been in the vicinity of this high toned joint are an old man and his aged wife who spent many years in the ministry of a Christian church. These two old people also eat opium at their home. Indeed, the latter form of using the deadly drug appears to be by far the most common method of inducing stupor, and, while not specially delegated to look for opium eaters, the commissioner of the News found many of them.

The great danger of this fearful business is the young and careless people of both sexes and there is a crying necessity for a law that will give the police and peace authorities the necessary power to adequately punish any party who furnishes another opium, and especially those who conduct opium clubs or joints. ✪

Left to right: **Patrolmen Isaac Hector, Thomas H. Lewis (father of labor leader John L. Lewis) and Herman Reich, 1895**

31

Chief Jim Jones, the four members of Des Moines Police and Fire Commission and the men of the Des Moines Police Department, July 4, 1906. Photo taken at the old downtown ball park between 4th and 6th on Grand Avenue

SCORCHERS AND RED DEVILS

BY JOHN ZELLER

The Des Moines Police must have taken notice of Mr. William Morrison. Hard to ignore was this tall husky foreigner, sporting a mane of black hair as he scurried back and forth carrying boxes of mysterious chemicals to a secret laboratory within the shadow of police headquarters.

Morrison was known around town as an English eccentric and odd vegetarian, quiet and reserved yet mercurial, given to the occasionally arrogant fit. Born in Coventry, England, and educated in Scotland, Morrison was rumored to be a genius, yet misfortune plagued him. Poverty-stricken and soon to lose his wife and only child to illness, he labored hard to realize his dream—to perfect the electric storage battery.

By 1890 Des Moines itself was becoming a very "electric" place. Electric lights were competing with gas. The street car company was retiring their horses for overhead wires and electric motors, and the sound of the creaking old flour mill at the Center Street dam was being replaced by the efficient hum of a hydroelectric generating plant.

But nothing electrified Des Moines in 1890 like the sight of Morrison's new invention—the world's first automobile! Morrison's auto was part of his grand plan. To demonstrate the superior power and lightness of his batteries, Morrison constructed a small spring wagon, installed an electric motor from a street car, and powered the contraption with his new batteries. If this thing sped along as he hoped, it would leave his battery competitors in its dust.

This "Sherlock Holmes" type of genius needed a practical Dr. Watson, and this he found in Dr. Lou Armst. Young Armst (later an ophthalmologist) was then a watchmaker and skilled machinist, and he had the money Morrison needed to do experiments. Armst rewound the electric motor armature, made the mechanical linkages and steering machinery, and most importantly, "greased

Des Moines-built Morrison electric auto, 1890

the wheels" to the tune of $21,000.

The chassis for the first model was built at the Des Moines Carriage Co. When the auto was tested in secret the steering failed, so Morrison disassembled the first car. He reinstalled the motor and batteries in a small boat and as he slipped his silent water craft among the puffing oarsmen and steamboats of the Des Moines River, Morrison made

plans for a second car.

Rumors buzzed at the 1890 Iowa State Fair that an "electric buggy" would show up. The crowd was disappointed when Morrison, still fiddling with details, failed to appear. But a week later, on September 4, 1890, 75,000 Iowans were swarming the streets of Des Moines. They came to witness the second annual Seni-Om-Sed Festival ("Des Moines" spelled backwards).

The spectators were impressed by the lavish, incandescently-lit floats of the moving carnival, but it was Morrison's demure little three-seat surrey that astonished them. Rightly so, for Des Moines got a peek at the future, what citizens of Chicago and New York had never seen: a horseless carriage.

Fame instantly illuminated both Morrison and Des Moines, but burnt out like a meteor. The inventor received 16,000 inquiries about his horseless carriage, including self-addressed, stamped envelopes. But Morrison, who was only interested in proposals from battery makers, removed two bushel baskets of useable stamps from the return envelopes and threw the mountain of letters away.

Horses were spooked by the "red devils"

DeBeltrand Grocery Co. ad for auto giveaway, 1900

Within the year, Morrison sold the car and the rights to the battery to a Chicago company. In 1893 they displayed it to a delighted crowd at the Columbian Exposition, and gave President Grover Cleveland a spin around the grounds in it, (a presidential first).

Two years later, Morrison's little electric car won the gold medal in *The Chicago World Tribune* Race, the first auto race in the United States.

Meanwhile, things went back to normal in Des Moines. Police were in the humdrum business of running in drunks in a horse-propelled spring wagon.

The population in general was in the midst of the bicycle craze. The high-wheeled "Penny farthing" bicycle of the Rover Boys mystery days had given way to the same low built, chain driven "safety bicycle" that we ride today.

Everyone, including children and women in "bloomers," set off in search of fresh air away from the soft-coal soot of Des Moines. For a few years, the auto was gone but not forgotten.

As for Morrison, he made a fortune inventing chemistry for refining gold ore. He returned to Des Moines and lived the good life with young wife number two in the glamorous Victoria Hotel. He sported about town carrying thousands of dollars on his person, always traveling in his favorite vehicle—the electric street car. William Morrison had no use for automobiles.

Des Moiners were hearing more about cars in magazines and newspapers. Montgomery Ward gave rides in 1897 at the Iowa State Fair in an electric runabout. News of steam-powered "Locomobiles" in Dubuque and Davenport in 1899 made Des Moines feel left out.

When livery stable owner Jesse Wells went East that year to check them out, the town hoped he would bring back a few to rent out. When he came back empty-handed, the town was disappointed. The gloom was dispelled by newspaper advertisements in the summer of 1900 announcing a steam-powered

Locomobile would be given away at the State Fair by the DeBeltrand Grocery Store.

The idea of owning the first automobile in town was thrilling news. Crowds at the State Fair eagerly awaited its arrival as Mr. W.W. Sears, bicycle sales department manager of the W.P. Chase Sporting Goods Company, was making final preparations for its maiden voyage to the fairgrounds. Crowds of street urchins and a couple mechanical mishaps slowed its initial voyage to one hour, but Sears got there. However, the dreams of the ticket holders were burst when Mr. DeBeltrand closed the grocery and absconded with the lottery money. Furthermore, he failed to pay the W.P. Chase Co., so the Locomobile ended up in the hands of W.W. Sears.

In 1901, a gasoline-powered auto sputtered up the hill to the capitol building and out climbed its proud owner who was, after removing cap, goggles and scarf, Governor Shaw. *The Register* reported that "to say that

he is infatuated with it is putting it mildly." The business of governorship was forgotten as he took all curious onlookers for short jaunts, often stopping to point out the many particularities of its machinery.

In that year the Iowa Automobile Club was founded with Jesse Wells as president. The club fought for better roads and for legal rights of "motorists." In the Traveling Men's Association parade of that year, seven locally-owned automobiles zipped along with the floats.

By 1902, the town was really rolling. In February, 18 autos were reported in town. Two bicycle dealers announced plans that they would sell autos of every stripe: gasoline, electric or steam-powered. The Des Moines Auto Co. was formed and announced plans to manufacture automobiles right here in Des Moines. *The Register* listed 25 automobiles and their proud owners. Doctors led the way, abandoning the horse and buggy for making house calls in little "runabouts."

These runabouts were tame little models equipped with "putt-a-putt" one-cylinder motors that could just keep up with a lazy bicyclist. But by 1903, the rich owners of the Grand Avenue mansions were investing capital in big "touring cars" with 15-hp, four-cylinder engines that left bicyclists far behind.

Bicycle racers, speed demons that they were, did not like being left in the dust. The Delta Bicycle Club arranged for a Des Moines first at their Independence Day Races at the State Fairgrounds. At 5:15 after six bicycle races, a greased pole climb, wheelbarrow and jackass races, a greased pig, bucking bronco and before the evening balloon ascension, Ralph Oaks in his 1903 Rambler won Des Moines' first automobile race.

By September, even the august city fathers were aware of speeding cars. *The Register* reported, "Automobile Problem Reaches Des Moines," and that the aldermen intended to "stop the scorchers." The city council passed the first speed limits: eight-mph downtown and 12 in the suburbs. They also required a bell, whistle or horn, lights and a city-issued automobile license.

A bill submitted that year in the State Legislature to license automobiles was decried in *The Register* as "silly, as almost no one has ever seen an automobile and probably never will." Surprisingly, the next year even the legislators came to their senses, issuing the first state speed laws and auto licenses. State Legislator William Corden of Winfield Henry County, paid the $1 fee and received Iowa automobile license No. 1.

With warm weather in the spring of 1904, the "Red Devil Riders" of Grand Avenue came out of hibernation. "Men wearing leather caps and goggles use the fine stretch of smooth asphalt for the establishment of records and the constant peril for pedestrian is left out of consideration." Indignant citizens report to the police the numbers that they can read on the new homemade state license plates. While police are tracking down the drivers of autos No. 17, 278, and 265, they make their first traffic arrest. A citizen's report has it that a Charles S. Denman, direc-tor of the Des Moines Waterworks, has been in his $5,000 Peerless sedan descending Grand Avenue "lickitycut."

By the spring of 1905, the police decided that citizen action is not enough. They assign mounted Officer John Penn to patrol Grand Avenue and stop reckless "scorching." The first offender, Dr. Wilton McCarty, sped by Officer Penn, who spurred his steed to gallop off in pursuit. An Ingersoll Line streetcar blocked traffic at 19th Street and saved the honor of the police force. Officer Penn dismounted, ran to the car, vaulted into the passenger seat and instructed Dr. Wilton McCarty that he was under arrest and should proceed slowly to the police station. The traffic squad had nabbed its first speeder.

Things got hot for speeders after the city's spring election of 1906. War was declared by the newly-elected and formidable alderman from the First Ward, John L. Hamery. The young son of (future police superintendent) Hamery had come close to being run down by a car, and Hamery vowed the speeding would be "a thing of the past."

That summer, Officer Penn was back patrolling the avenue, but now as Des Moines' first and only motorcycle policeman. Riding a Belgian-made Fabrique National four-cylinder motorcycle capable of 60 mph, he could out run any car in town. *The Capital* reported that Penn was "delighted with his new possession...previously the best he could do was to stand on the corner and make a noise like a policeman."

At 10 o'clock Friday night, June 8, 1906, Grover Hubbell was preparing his car for a fast evening spin down the avenue. Hubbell was the treasurer of the Iowa Automobile Club and son of the richest man in the state, and was very familiar with his big machine. But none of this mattered when he sped by motorcycle cop No. 1, John Penn. Speeding after his man, Penn reportedly vowed "aldermen and special police cannot beat the regular men."

It took Penn one mile to overtake Grover, "You're under arrest—fast driving. . . you can't get away from me. This machine can go 40 mph without noticing it." In front of the police judge, Hubbell protested that he wasn't going so fast. But Traffic Officer Penn stood his ground, "I have both a cyclometer and a speed meter on my motorcycle." None of this was news to Hubbell, as he had loaned that fancy motorcycle to Officer Penn to patrol that avenue. Now he had become a victim of his own kindness. Not surprisingly, next week Officer Penn was back working the desk at the police station.

The police were worried that the day was

Officer John Penn and "his" [Grover Hubbell's] Belgian motorcycle

First fatal auto accident occurred on November 22, 1907 in front of Dr. Coffee's mansion at 42nd and Grand Avenue

coming when somebody would get killed in one of those newfangled horseless carriages. Even before automobiles, they had hauled plenty of traffic victims in the police ambulance. Dangers included runaway horses, streetcar accidents, train crossing collisions, out-of-control bicyclists and pedestrians dismembered under the wheels of iron locomotives.

Des Moines' first automobile accident occurred September 7, 1902, when John Killmer and C.M. McLean ran into a dog at 6th and Grand. All totaled, the damage included several broken ribs and one broken clavicle, a sprained elbow, a lacerated nose and forehead and several flesh wounds. The dog's condition: unknown.

Even city officials were not immune. A runaway buggy in 1904 hurled the 300-pound bulk of ex-mayor Jim Brenton into the air when the horse was spooked by a passing auto. It took a hour to revive Brenton from his "dazed condition," but afterward the ever-congenial Brenton blamed no one save the horse, which he had previously believed to be safely "unafraid of the red devils."

Sixth Avenue and High Street must have been a good place to smash your auto into a street car because it happened again, this time to Grenville Ryan, who escaped injury but only "miraculously."

Yet, miracles only last so long. The odds caught up with Des Moines on June 21, 1905. Mr. D.C. Hall, the 51-year-old proprietor of the Fix-It Shop near Drake University, was coasting down the steep 15th Street hill on his bicycle when an auto driven by a chauffeur of the Iowa Automobile Co. zipped through the intersection on fashionable Pleasant Street. Stop signs were not yet invented. They collided and Hall fractured his skull. He was lucky to be only two blocks from the new and thoroughly modern Iowa Methodist Hospital, but not lucky enough. He died, becoming Des Moines first auto fatality.

Soon after, news of the first motorist to die behind the wheel shocked the state. On September 29, 1905, attorney F.A. Harriman was ripping along at 30 mph (twice the legal speed limit) three miles south of Hampton, Iowa, when he clipped a bridge abutment.

The machine plunged into a culvert, crushing the attorney beneath it.

For two more years, Des Moines speed demons would flirt with death and win. But the grim reaper had set a trap on November 22, 1907. It was a cool, moonlit Friday night, and a slight haze set a gossamer net across the night skies. Four spirited young people from the local automobile companies had set off with two friends for a brisk autumn joyride.

Charles Morrison, an employee of the Nattinger Sears Auto Co., was driving the five others about in his own small car when it acted up. He coaxed it back to the shop, where the girls decided to return home on the street car. Orlo Nattinger, not wanting to call the night quits, insisted that he drive them in the company's big REO Speedwagon.

Instead of taking the girls home to the east side, Nattinger spun out west on the "Grand Avenue Speedway." Nattinger's friend, Frank Getchell, who was riding in back with the pretty Isle Denny perched on his knee, badgered Nattinger to "open it up." The car "careened and lunged" westerly up the avenue. They were fast approaching the mansions of Dr. Coffee and J.G. Olmsted at 42nd Street, but in the dark shadows along the curbside lay the indistinct form of a heavy black tool wagon belonging to the Des Moines Gas Company. Its black paint and lack of safety lamps rendered it an invisible snare, even to the giant automobile's acetylene lamps.

The clock in the Olmsted mansion was striking midnight when Orlo Nattinger smashed into the unlit wagon. Six bodies flew through the air. Nattinger landed on his head and died instantly. His friend Getchell lay mortally wounded. Dr. Coffee attended him vainly as the police horse-drawn ambulance plodded along for a half hour before arriving. The girl on Getchell's lap was a lucky one. She also landed on her head, but her thick, Gibson Girl hair cushioned her fall. The other three passengers were uninjured. Des Moines awoke the next morning to the grim news that two young lives were extinguished in the night's breezes, and the city's dreamy honeymoon with the horseless carriage was over. ✪

POLICE PADDY WAGONS AND "BLACK MARIAHS"
"RED WHEELS SPUN LIKE BALL OF FIRE"

BY JOHN ZELLER

First police wagon and horses, westside station, 1882

Second police wagon and horses, eastside station, 1883

Police covered wagon whose curtains closed over many tragedies, 1895

In 1882 the citizens of Des Moines watched with pride as the state gilded its new capitol dome. The future of Iowa's capital city itself looked golden. The town fathers were paving the streets of downtown and eagerly awaiting the move into their first real city hall at 2nd and Locust. The building would house a genuine police station, courtroom and, conveniently, a city jail. But Des Moines police officers were most excited that they were about to get their first set of wheels.

Up to this time, policemen had relied on being big and strong enough to "escort" on foot (often dragging) unwilling suspects to jail. If there was trouble, the only recourse was to use the billy club or blow the police whistle in hope that help was within earshot.

But that year Mayor Carey and Police Chief Adam Hafner visited Chicago, and were introduced to the "District Telegraph Alarm," also known as call boxes, and police paddy wagons. When they announced their plans to bring the same to Des Moines, *The Iowa State Register* laughed, "After the council buys a patrol wagon it ought to buy a bicycle for the mayor and an omnibus for the aldermen."

The Leader joined the Greek chorus,

"When that police-patrol wagon is fetched out Mayor Carey would have us believe that every burglar, gambler and highwayman will flee for his life. Seriously, of what use is a patrol wagon in a little city the size of Des Moines? The expense of it will be 12 times greater than hiring a convenient dray or express wagon when a drunk needs to be hauled into headquarters—and that is the only use that such a wagon could be put to."

But by November when the new wagon was about to be finished, *The Register* had changed its tune. An article entitled, "Virtues of a Vehicle," opined, "... there are many other features which commend the wagon to the favor of the tax-paying public too numerous to mention."

The Leader was reserving judgment. When

the wagon made its debut appearance on December 6, 1882, it reported, "The patrol wagon was out yesterday for the first time. The newspaper reporters demand rides in it before the mayor gets any taffy." But a week later *The Leader* was enthusiastic:

> *"The new police wagon aired today and attracted wide attention. The fine, high-spirited blacks ran like the wind and the red wheels spun like balls of fire. The team, wagon, harness and alarm bell cost the city $750."*

By January, 1883 morning runs were made by the wagon from the jail to the county courthouse which, according to *The Leader,* gave a regal bearing to its passengers, the previous evening's public intoxicants. "Four or five guzzlers were taken down in a bunch yesterday, and it made them feel so lofty that they turned up their flannel proboscises [red noses] at the gaping passers-by." The next year the monthly police report for April totaled up 424 miscreants carried a total of 182 miles.

When in 1883 the city built an east side city hall, replete with police station and jail cells, the department also procured a second team and wagon. With the addition of a covered paddy wagon in 1895, the police were firmly in the horse-drawn age.

By 1893 the public was calling for another "big city style" improvement: an ambulance. Mrs. E.B. Whitcomb had gone to Chicago to check out the latest models and returned to town ready to donate the $500 needed to bring one to Des Moines. With the money in hand, the city council sprang into action, soliciting bids, debating, arguing, tabling motions and generally dithering away all of that year and half of the next.

At last, in July 1894 the Shaver Carriage Company produced the new ambulance for $700 (a $200 cost overrun). The city's new baby was pronounced "a thing of beauty" by the press, and then ingloriously confined to the "old tool house" just west of city hall that

stored dusty bags of lime. It was ready at a moment's notice of any emergency—except when the paddy wagon was out with the police department's only team of horses.

This problem was "solved" by moving the wagon to other horses, at the Wells' Livery Stable. There the liverymen used the ambulance as a sleeping room and coated the interior with their tobacco spit. The city also declared the ambulance off limits to calls from Des Moines' private physicians.

The Seni-Om-Sed floral festival of 1898 saw the city ambulance bring up the rear of the display, when an unknown camera bug snapped our only surviving picture of it.

While Des Moines at the turn of the century was one of only a handful of cities maintaining free ambulance service, it was sorry service, indeed. Even though the ambulance was in a bad state of repairs, doctors were demanding it transport their patients for free, while hack drivers fought this loss of their livelihood. The Red Cross offered to take it off the city's hands,

fix it up and set the rules for its use.

The hospitals made their move. Mercy Hospital in 1904 hosted a eastside-versus-westside doctors' baseball game to fund their own vehicle. Iowa Methodist Hospital then followed suit, announcing that the Kratzer Carriage Co. had just finished " . . .by far the best ambulance ever used in Des Moines."

By 1906, the police department's horse-and-buggy days were obviously coming to an end. The other officers must have been envious of Officer Penn, who was zooming along Grand Avenue on a motorcycle borrowed from Grover Hubbell.

Ironically, the police department, with 24 years experience with wagons, then set out to build the ultimate in horse-drawn paddy wagons. It turned out indeed to be the ultimate—folly.

That year the covered wagon broke down, forcing the police to rely in the middle of winter on the "antiquated" 25-year-old open

wagon (the cold ride reportedly cured crime and decreased public "orneriness"). But Police Chief Jim Jones announced that a new $800 patrol wagon was in the works. It would have rubber tires, roller bearings and be much bigger than the earlier models. Jones proudly predicted it would soon be hauling 16 to 20 men per trip at great savings to the city.

The newspaper men became tired of waiting and began to question policemen as to when and where they would see the famous wagon. Chief Jones, angry with policemen for whispering to newspaper reporters, ordered a general police review at the downtown ball-park where any irate citizen could point out any bad cops to the chief.

The policemen arrived, all spit and polish. They lined up and had their group photo taken. In the photograph, one can catch a glimpse of the new wagon sitting in the out-field, displayed on its first day of duty. Jones had silenced the newspaper critics of his white elephant wagon.

Jones couldn't savor his victory for long, because two weeks later the wagon's axle split in two and its sides caved in, spilling police-men into the street. This delighted the news-papers, who declared the wagon "discarded." One police driver reportedly asked the chief, "Isn't it liable to break down once a week?"

In 1908, Frank Shercliff was a "notorious diamond robber and a convicted murderer" on the loose. He needed to be caught at all costs, even if it necessitated

Detectives in police buggy, 1906

Patrol drivers Wilson Skinner and Tom Cross with police horses Peaches and Cream and the ill-fated $800 paddy wagon.

renting an auto. One cold day, newly-appointed police commissioner John L. Hamery rounded up three cops armed with repeating rifles. Following a hot lead, they jumped in a rented car with the commis-sioner at the wheel. With reporters close behind, they raced off to Mitchellville. When Shercliff failed to show up at the ambush site, Hamery jumped on the interurban trol-ley and headed back to Des Moines, leaving his officers and the newspapermen to return in the freezing open-air automobiles.

Meanwhile, Police Chief A.G. Miller was begging Hamery for his own automobile, because the newspaper reporters were beating him to every crime scene. In the spring of 1909, Hamery visited the Marshalltown Police Department to inspect their new automobile patrol wagon. Two days later he bought a Buick touring car for "emergency use."

The Capitol reporter showed up to see patrol driver Skinner receiving driving les-sons from the chief, as the department's first "chauffeur." He observed a rather sad-look-ing Officer Skinner: "He has been around horses all his life and to be separated from 'Peaches and Cream' and 'Ben and Mack,' the patrol horses, will almost break his heart." When the car failed to arrive (the city council was late with the $1,050 check), Commissioner Hamery wailed, "What has become of my benzene wagon?"

When it finally rolled into Des Moines, the new auto patrol car was an immediate

sensation. According to *The Register*,

"Des Moines Police never answered patrol calls with such enthusiasm as they did since Hamery got a touring car for gathering up prisoners. When the gong rings for the patrol, the officers in the station fairly tear each other's hair to get to the automobile. It seems the greatest difficulty is finding room for the prisoners."

The press reported that John Snook, an old timer and "veteran drunkard," purposely "fell off the water wagon" to get a ride to the station in the shiny new auto. "He leaned back in the rear seat, took off his hat and let the spring breeze ripple through his flowing locks in sheer delight."

The policemen themselves always rode the trolley cars on duty.

Did the new auto revolutionize police work in Des Moines? Not exactly. By 1911 the car was unavailable; Police Commissioner Zell Roe was using it for his personal transportation. The 1911 *Pictorial Souvenir of the Department of Public Safety* printed a nice picture of the big car with the apt caption, "Superintendent Roe in his auto." The department went back to hauling prisoners in its broken-down, horse-drawn wagon. The policemen themselves always rode the trolley cars on duty. When the streetcar men went on strike, Superintendent Roe rented his officers taxicabs.

During this time, Roe was squirreling away money into a police equipment fund to buy a big, expensive ($4,500!) automotive paddy wagon built on a truck chassis. The city auditor blocked the purchase for two years. While the policemen waited, Roe bought himself a new car, replacing the "old" Buick with 45,000 miles on it with a new "Mariah" auto. He sold the covered wagon to a lumber company, so when the replacement auto was a month late in arriving, the department spent a cold November in the ancient open wagon.

The new auto patrol was given its first workout November 9, 1912. Two "alleged drunks," Jack Roach and Pat Eagan, got the honor to be the first to ride in the new "Black

Mariah," with Officer Frank Badgeley at the "steering mechanism" That day *The Capital* reported that "citizens rubbed their eyes and gasped, but it is here to stay and the niftiest piece of mechanism that was ever owned by the Department of Public Safety." (Maybe they just gasped over the purple paint job.)

The paddy wagon-ambulance was such a success that in 1913 the city decided to use it strictly as a patrol wagon, and bought a second White Company truck converted into a full-time ambulance for $3,750. This time, they painted it a subdued gray and charged doctors $2.50 to transport their patients (still half the rate of the hospitals' horse-drawn ambulances).

The new motor ambulance answered its first call on December 3, 1913, to the Family Theater at 5th and Locust, where 16-year-old movie projectionist Abe Cary was feared electrocuted during the showing of "American Born", a five-cent western. City Physician Dr. G.E. Clift declared that Cary had merely fainted and sent him home in the new ambulance. In 1913, the city also motorized the fire department. The combined city fleet had grown so large that maintenance alone cost $5,000.

Two views of the first motorized "Black Mariah," 1912

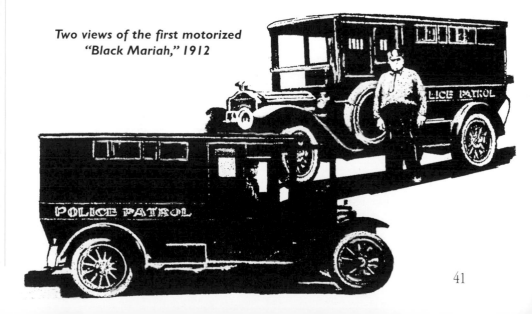

Superintendent Roe and "his auto," 1911

The police had been without a motorcycle since Grover Hubbell retrieved his fancy Belgian motorbike from the overzealous Officer Penn. Police Chief Miller and Commissioner Hamery even hatched a cracked plan to run down speeding cars with a bicycle patrol. Luckily, the next week Hamery visited Chicago and came back sold on police motorcycles.

The next year, the police rented a 1911 Harley-Davidson motorcycle to pursue a "chug wagon Chollie," who was terrorizing Des Moines by stealing fancy touring cars for joyrides. On May 27, 1911 he stole a car from outside the Hotel Savery and led policeman McMillen on a wild chase up Grand Avenue before he escaped down 42nd Street and thoughtfully returned the car to its original location. He was not apprehended.

Officer Harry McMillen was chosen to be the city's first official motorcycle cop. On May 25, 1911, after "many hours" learning to ride, he set out to patrol the Grand Avenue and Kingman Boulevard "speedways," where he arrested many prominent citizens. When a judge questioned his powers under the state's new but vague "Kulp automobile law," local pressure mounted to enact stronger municipal ordinances.

New Police Chief John Jenney bought two more motorcycles in 1912 to equip his now five-man motorcycle squad. City records list a purchase of two "seven-horsepower 'Indian' motorcycles with 'Prest-O-Lites,' speedometers and carriers, complete for the sum of $229.20 each from Jenkins & Co." The motorcycle patrol was a big success.

That June, "motorcycle man" Ed Weaver answered 225 calls and made 80 arrests. The fines received paid for two more motorcycles.

Assistant Chief C.C. Jackson was so excited he recommended dropping all walking beats in the suburbs to expand the motorcycle corps to 15 men. He extolled the work of night patrol officers Howard and McMillen, who tested the doors of 135 businesses every evening. Howard and McMillen became so popular that the residents along Grand raised $500 to pay their salaries and expenses in hopes of ending the intolerable "scorching" on the avenue. The advance publicity scared the speeders off and the officers did not write a single ticket, but the neighborhood declared it money well spent. Public relations for the flying squad's image rose even higher when John A. Brophy, star of the champion 1910 East High football team, joined the cycle squad.

The motorcycle soon proved to be a fair-weather friend. Even bundled up, Harry McMillen and Steve Howard still froze their ears and noses when they ventured out in January into the blustering winds skipping about on the unplowed icy and snow-drifted streets.

This led to wrecked motorcycles. The city paid out big money to fix them: June 1912 - $24; July - $64; and August - $80. Patching

Detectives riding in 1916 Maxwell

up the officers was yet another worry. Joe Newell crashed during his first riding lessons, smashing his face. Steve Howard was also cut and bruised when he collided with a grocery wagon. Thomas English was chasing two speeders when he ran into the 6th Avenue streetcar, which propelled him 50 feet in the air. He landed in nearby Mercy Hospital, the motorcycle demolished. Worst of all, the prized Brophy went airborne off a pile of sand Evel Knievel-style, fracturing his skull.

The expenses were certainly rising. In 1913, the motorcycle squad had jumped to six men with a payroll of $500 a month. Three new Harley-Davidson motorcycles cost an additional $850. But the biggest cost to the city was the embarrassment caused by the revelation that stalwart officers Howard and McMillen regularly employed their speedy machines to make unofficial calls to Mrs. Hast's "house of ill repute" at 602 East Walnut.

In 1914, Police Chief Jenney was replaced by Ed Crawford, who was not in love with motorcycles. The Denver police had already discarded motorcycles in favor of light automobiles. They had reasoned that a motorcycle cop had to call for a car to take the prisoner to jail, so why not send a car in the first place? Crawford announced that he would replace the bikes with autos as they wore out or were wrecked (at the rate they were being smashed it wouldn't take long). This worried the motorcycle men, who were too small and lightweight to be reassigned as regular policemen. By 1913, Des Moines had a total of a dozen motorcycles used by the police and smoke, health and fire inspectors. After three years of motorcycles marked by six major accidents that left two officers disfigured and one crippled, Chief Crawford began looking at automobiles.

In September 1914, the police inspectors traded in their little red Ford for a Chevrolet roadster. The next March, the police were authorized to sell three motorcycles along with five horses, two colts and the old White auto toward purchasing a new car. But even with the motorcycle corps payroll pared down to $250, there still wasn't enough money for the new car.

In 1916, the police sold one "Abbot-Detroit" auto and applied the $260 toward the purchase of two new Chevrolets at $790 each. The inspectors traded in two old Chevrolets and bought two new Maxwells. Even the motorcycle squad was kept alive by trading in two old Harley-Davidsons for two new and expensive ($570 each!) "Thor" model motorcycles.

Apparently, the police didn't favor the Chevrolets. They replaced them with two Dodges, which they traded for two new Buick D42 light sixes in 1918. The Buicks were replaced in 1919 with model "R" Hupmobiles. In the early days, the police never bought the same brand of cars twice.

The 1919 city report lists all the vehicles in the city garage:

White Co. auto patrol wagon	$1,000
White Co. ambulance	$1,000
2 new Hupmobiles	$2,900
Buick "Six"	$1,000
New Buick - health department	$1,500
Buick "Four" - electric dept.	$1,000
1919 Ford plumbing dept..	$ 900
Ford - detective dept..	$ 900
Indian Motorcycle w/ sidecar	$ 250
Harley-Davidson motorcycle	
electric department	$ 100
motorboat and engine	$ 150
row boat	$ 50

The police may have been fickle about cars, but for paddy wagons they were loyal to the White Motor Company. In 1918, they bought a new one-ton White Motor Company truck converted for police work for $3,636.75. These paddy wagons could even be popular with their passengers, as evidenced by this report in

Roy J. Chamberlain posed on the department's 1911 Harley Davidson, 1913

The Des Moines Tribune of February 23, 1916.

CALLS PATROL WAGON FOR HIS OWN ARREST
The telephone at police headquarters rang.
"Hello" answered James Cavender, secretary to the chief.
"Hello, police station?"
"Yes, what is it?"
"Send the patrol wagon out here."
"Where?"
"To 2006 East Grand avenue."
"What's the matter?"
"I want to go to jail."
"Who are you?
"J. Jamison. I live here."
"What do you want to go to jail for?"
"I can't get along with my relatives."
"Huh."
"Well, are you coming out after me?"
"I don't know; maybe you'll change your mind if we do send out."
"No, I won't. I want to stay in jail three days."
Cavender said he felt certain the man was not intoxicated from the way he talked.

It finally was decided not to send after the man as the police really did not want him.

Police automobiles were wrecked nearly as frequently as motorcycles. One crashed in 1916 while chasing bootleggers. In 1919

another car "turned turtle," flipping over and injuring officers Frank Harty and George Scarpino. At one point, the chief had only one running automobile and Police Commissioner Woolgar was using it as his personal car. This arrangement proved so convenient for Woolgar that he dispensed with his own auto, selling it to Officer William Straight. The

White Motor Co. ambulance, 1913

police department also had possession of a stolen car, but it was in the personal use of the police surgeon, Woolgar's son-in-law. In 1919, *The Des Moines Register* gleefully reported that after 37 years of experience with police vehicles in Des Moines, the chief of police of the capital city "now walks or borrows." ✪

SPIFFING UP THE POLICE IMAGE

BY LINDA BANGER

The new century was barely two years old when a new kind of reform began to blow through the Des Moines Police Department.

It all began when the Iowa Legislature passed a bill in the spring of 1902 placing both the Des Moines Police Department and the fire department under civil service regulations. Three commissioners were to form a

civil service commission to oversee the operations of the two departments. What changes this would bring few knew, although *The Register* editorialized that it was "an unnecessary fad" and that more power would be placed in the hands of the mayor and the commissioners. Nevertheless, police officers continued to be appointed by the mayor and discharged as he wished; the difference after the reform bill took effect was that politics could not be involved. No political patronage could be used or sought.

That spring, 14 new men were hired as policemen, pumping up the force from 40 to 54 officers. Pay raises were also forthcoming, bringing a beat cop a salary of $65 a month. The city they patrolled measured 54 square miles.

There was a considerable amount of anxiety among the ranks over the large number of changes planned for the department.

By the end of August, the new civil service commission had come up with over 100 regulations governing the police department.

Many of the new rules of the department addressed the behavior and appearance of members of the police force, as well as physical requirements: patrolmen must be at least 24 years of age and no less than five feet nine inches in height.

The chief of police was given full command of the department. He also had other specified, yet relatively inconsequential duties, such as keeping a list of all the bars, pawn shops and houses of "bad repute."

On October 1, 1902, the first civil service examination was held and 125 eager applicants lined up to take it. Those who passed would be required to take a second test within a year.

The questions on the civil service examination included simple arithmetic tests; reading a few lines from an eighth grade reader, a handwriting test, and listening to a statement as it was being read, and then rewriting the statement from memory. There were practical questions on the location of city streets and public buildings, such as the Union Depot (6th and Cherry) or the YMCA (4th and Grand). More questions of knowledge of the city were later added including: name five railroads coming into the city, locate by streets the state capitol, North High School, Mercy Hospital, the post office and the courthouse.

Literacy was important, but some of the force may not have been the best spellers, as was proved by a story told of an unnamed patrolman who had a report of a dead dog lying in the street at 28th and Brattleboro. The patrolman came to the police station to make out the report and asked a city detective if he would make it out for him. Reminded by the detective that he had passed a civil service test and could make out the report by himself, the patrolman sweated over the report for several minutes, stumped at trying to spell the word "Brattleboro." Abruptly he stood up, grabbed his coat and hat and started to leave the station. The detective

called out to the departing patrolman that he still had to make out the report. The answer came floating back, "Later—I'm going to move that damned dog down to Cottage Grove Avenue first!"

As the years passed, some of the regulations from the reform of 1902 were changed, amended or deleted. In 1912, physical standards were changed, requiring that a policeman could be no less than six feet tall, weigh from 175 to 235 pounds and be no more than 40 years old.

By 1914, following a new order from the Civil Service Commission, a variety of athletic tests had to be passed by every member of the police department from the assistant chief to the station janitor, to prove they were up to the physical exertions of enforcing the law. The police chief was exempt. He was not under civil service.

One bright October morning in 1914, the first group of 20 men met at the YMCA, filled with foreboding. They were ordered to be garbed in nothing more than their official dignity and a smile. To preserve their modesty and possibly prevent timidity, not to mention public ridicule, the tests were closed to the public. Doctors were on hand to examine the men following the physical tests of strength and endurance: climbing a rope ladder, a swimming race, a 100-yard dash and weight lifting. They were also sent racing up six flights of stairs, made to lift a 125 pound sack to their shoulders, and then sent for a quarter mile run around a small oval track.

Not surprisingly, considering that the men ranged in age from 35 to 60 years and a few of them weighed 250 pounds, some couldn't make it. Even though the tests and examinations had been ordered by the Civil Service Commission presumably to weed out physically weak persons, there was resentment at the police station following reports from colleagues who had endured the four-hour tests. "If they want to fire us," one cop exclaimed, "why don't they fire us and be done with it?" ✪

*Police Officer Ed Mellon using call box in front
of the Globe Department Store. He was then
the oldest policeman on the force, with a service
record of 23 years, 1919.*

JOHN L. HAMERY, FIRST DES MOINES POLICE COMMISSIONER
HIS WONDROUS EYES SCRUTINIZE

BY JOHN ZELLER

Des Moines of 1906 had never seen the likes of John L. Hamery. The newly-elected alderman was both politically unknown and unaffiliated with the political establishment, where other aspiring leaders quickly found their place in the machine politics of the day.

But the political machinery at city hall that had ground down lesser men snapped a cog on the flinty John L. Hamery. By 1908, when he became Des Moines' first police commissioner under the new "Des Moines Plan" of government, the town realized Hamery was more than just a man—he was a self-appointed crime-fighting, corruption-busting dynamo.

Greatness had been thrust upon Hamery at a young age. Thirty years earlier, in 1876, five-year-old Hamery was playing in the streets of Northfield, Minnesota, on a nice September day—the day the James Gang and Younger brothers robbed the First National Bank. One Swedish farmer lay dead in the street and John heard stories of how the bank teller's throat was cut. The boy watched as his Norwegian father and other farmers grabbed their guns and rushed out to hunt down the James brothers. These Minnesotans scorned the romantic Missouri legend that the James boys were "gentlemen bandits." To them, they were just evil, and evil had to be hunted down and brought to justice—a lesson Hamery learned young.

In 1880s the family took on a homestead in the Dakotas, where both his parents died young. Orphaned at age 11, Hamery drove the family cattle to market in St. Paul and walked the remaining 40 miles back to his grandparent's home in Northfield.

Young Hamery arrived eager for schooling. He spoke Norwegian and a smattering of German, but no English. By the time he moved to Des Moines and finished at Highland Park College, he had mastered Greek and Latin, and held a degree in classical literature. He then went on to Drake University for a law degree and to Still College of Osteopathic Medicine for yet another diploma. His spent his free time getting married, raising a family, buying real estate and fixing up old houses. For all his university training, Hamery was equally proud of his trade skills; the year he was elected to city government, the city directory listed him simply as "painter."

Aldermen Hamery and Eugene Waterbury were elected in 1906 as part of the independent

Poem in newspaper:

There is a man in our town, and he has wondrous eyes.
It is his job the conduct of this town to scrutinize,
He does indeed with great determination,
And starts, each time he turns around, a new investigation.

He investigates most everything you ever heard about.
He spied the wicked slot machines and promptly threw them out.
He caught the scorching autoists and hauled them into court.
In fact, investigation is really this man's forte.

He looked at Mayor Mathis once, and Mathis got uneasy.
And went and wrote out quite a check which he alleged were fees he,
Collected as police judge but clean forgot to docket.
(It's queer the way one will forget a thousand in one's pocket!)

Perhaps there may be some few things of which he's not yet thought-
Places where investigation might perhaps be brought.
And if perchance he's done things wrong, in your own estimation,
Just mention it to Hamery. He'll start investigation.

And when at last he's made us all good brethren and sisters,
Maybe he'll find a little time to amputate those whiskers.

Reprint: The DM Evening Tribune, January 25, 1909

Commissioner Hamery on the job

"scratcher ticket." Voters were encouraged to scratch off the names of the corrupt Republican officeholders and write in these honest newcomers, while not being asked to abandon their Republican loyalties. When the votes were tallied, the newspapers made big news of Mayor Mattern's narrow re-election but ignored Hamery's victory. John L. Hamery did not remain unknown for long.

In reward for his city council victory, Hamery was quickly expelled from the Socialist Party, to which he responded that he would try to bear up under the "crushing news." By his first day in office he had shaved off his trademark beard, not wanting to look like an "anarchist."

As soon as he was sworn into office, Hamery was off and running, immediately starting a campaign against reckless automobilists. The mayor swore him in as a special policemen to chase down speeders. When Mayor Mattern pinned the new policeman's star on Hamery's lapel next to his alderman's badge, *The Capitol* reported that "the array is imposing to say the least." Just three days later, the first speeder was nabbed — a horse and buggy being driven by one William Rhodes. The horse, a pacer named "Nancy," got off with a warning. The Dusenberg brothers of the Mason Car Company and subsequent fame at the Indianapolis 500 also received the attention of special officer Hamery, who ticketed them for making Grand Avenue into a speedway.

In his first year in office, Hamery collared unlicensed peddlers, snatched saloon whiskey from the lips of a policeman ("Medicinal!" the cop protested), and broke up gamblers by charging into one dive brandishing twin revolvers (both unloaded).

He also went after the corrupt political machine. As they sat on Hamery's bathroom floor, he accepted a bribe from George Hippee's henchmen of the street car company, while vice detectives and aldermen eavesdropped through the iron heating grate.

It was Des Moines' first sting operation.

Hamery was much loved and much hated. Political foe W.H. Brereton complained that Hamery had a "chip on his shoulder" and, surprisingly from a fellow politician, "a desire to get his name in print."

In 1907, Hamery began skulking around town in disguise with a note pad and Kodak camera, spying on the public works department. Counting the paving bricks at street projects, he tabulated discrepancies and discovered the missing bricks in the backyards of city workmen.

Des Moines' old ward politics, *à là* Chicago and Philadelphia, were supposed to come to an end with the municipal reform plan voted in in 1907. Under the new "Des

Moines Plan," the old three-member police and fire commission was abolished, to be replaced with a public safety commissioner appointed by the city council. The next spring election would pick the civic-minded councilmen who would implement the new plan of honest government. Paradoxically, the voters threw out all the reformers, except for Hamery. The old city hall gang of corrupt officeholders returned with the charge to implement civic reform.

They eagerly appointed Hamery Des Moines' first police commissioner, while leaving the lucrative supervision of public works and its fat contracts for themselves. While Hamery searched for a veteran police officer to be his new chief of police, the city hall gang went behind his back and chose a political crony, the East Side liveryman, W.P. Hume, for the job. Hamery was incensed at having Hume, Mayor Mattern's pal and alderman Wesley Ash's campaign manager, foisted on him.

But the Hume problem had to wait when Hamery declared war against the politically-powerful cigar store men who had bought off politicians with the proceeds of their illegal slot machines. As Hamery was rushing into cigar stores all over town, smashing slot machines, the cigar men and Police Chief Hume hatched a plan to be rid of Hamery for good. They circulated a recall petition in the taverns accusing Hamery of incompetence. Then they declared that if slot machines were an illegal amusement, so was all Sunday entertainment and filed suit to close Ingersoll Park, theaters, nickelodeons (movie theaters) and Sunday baseball. They hoped that the outcry would force Hamery from office; instead, they were vilified by the press, the public, and, of course, Hamery. The slot machines were removed and Police Chief Hume had to humble himself before Hamery to save his job for one more year, dogged at his every step by Hamery.

Hamery was described as "a lanky, loose-jointed individual with a voice that wouldn't frighten a field mouse," but that didn't stop him from taking complete control of the police department. He hired U.S. Army captain Frank E. Lyman, a veteran of the Spanish American War, to instill military discipline with spit and polish into his men. Lyman made standard issue the .38 caliber handgun and required regular target practice. The department also began formal classroom instruction on legal ordinances and report writing. But most important was a policeman's appearance:

"Neatly polished shoes, clean clothes and well-brushed and tightly buttoned

J. L. HAMERY of SPOTLESS TOWN

Reprint: **The DM Register and Leader**, February 16, 1910

"Our jailer's job is to sweep cobwebs from the cells."

"The Yegs all go to church now."

"When I closed the saloon on Saturday they thought it was my birthday."

"When I ran 'em out they all came to Chicago."

How Hamery looks to Chicago Cartoonist

uniforms will mark the appearance of the Des Moines Police Department from this time forward—John L. Hamery, Commissioner of Public Safety."

Hamery was honest and courageous, but he was from the old pragmatic school of politics. He was determined to do right in accordance with the wishes of the people, not to

reform the citizenry. On the issues of prostitution and drink, Hamery held the prevailing opinion that controlling vice through segregated red light districts and liquor licenses was the best one could hope for. Hamery was, himself, fond of boxing and wrestling, and believed that lust and overindulgence were the natural state of affairs for men.

However, the police commissioner was quickly swept up by the flood tide of Progressive Era reform. Women were calling for suffrage, temperance, city beautification, playgrounds and the eradication of "the social evil," i.e. red light districts. So when, in 1908, a meeting of a thousand reform-minded women and clergy called Hamery forth and expounded upon their displeasure, he quickly got religion. Earlier, Hamery had been reluctant to do the work of the Women's Christian Temperance Union and the churches, but now Hamery swore that, together, they would "do the impossible." Like his father chasing the James gang, Hamery got increasingly caught up in the pursuit of evil and declared war on the "social-evil combine" of the pimps, land-lords and bondsmen who profited from the flesh trade on East Court Avenue.

Since the big, wicked cities of Chicago and New York would be looking on, Hamery was determined that this new crusade of civic reform and moral cleansing would not fail. After the Des Moines plan of 1907, the city began to think of itself as a model for the nation. In fact, the next year Hamery spoke in Chicago before the Illinois Vigilance Committee, billing himself as "the man who cleaned up Des Moines."

And what of those natural urges? Now, Hamery was publicly espousing the purgative theories of Dr. Kellogg of the Battle Creek Sanitarium (brother of the Corn Flakes king), that sex was "unhealthy."

Other reforming celebrities wanted

Hamery's place in the public eye. He did manage to give Carry Nation the slip when she came to town in 1909, but he could not avoid local crusader John Brown Hammond, who publicly pilloried him over booze, cigarettes and the Evils-of-Apartment-Living. During one of Hammond's diatribes, Hamery seized his arm and "escorted" him from his office. Hammond sued over his alleged bruises, but lost the case. (Thirteen years later, Hammond got his own chance to be police commissioner.)

In his two-year tenure as police commissioner, Hamery introduced the Bertillon identification system to Des Moines (a system of identifying people through body measurements, markings and coloring); clashed with lenient judges; brought the automobile to the police department and battled against high milk prices (9 cents a quart!).

While he was fighting evil on every front, Hamery ran the police department as a dictatorial tyrant. He ignored the civil service commission—officers were often fired for "insubordination" over minor differences of opinion with the commissioner.

By the city elections of 1910, Hamery had accumulated many enemies. He had expressed a desire to retreat from public life, but re-entered the arena to fight the evil schemes of his foes. He told *The Register* that he would not match the hypocritical manner of his arch rival, John MacVicar. "I will not campaign with a Bible in one hand and a whiskey bottle in another, or an immoral woman on one arm and a minister on another."

Hamery was proud to announce that he spent just 50 cents on his campaign, yet was astonished when he lost the election. In the following years he occasionally reappeared as a candidate for city hall, but never again won public office. During prohibition, his name shows up in the newspaper as a liquor agent for the sheriff's office. (Police Commissioner

Chief of Police Albert G. Miller, 1909

John B. Hammond would confiscate the booze that Hamery had seized and stored in his own basement for "safekeeping.") Later, Hamery became statehouse gardener and built homes in the Drake neighborhood using bricks he obtained through political connections in the streets department.

When John Hamery died at age 76 in 1947, his neighbors on Witmer Avenue knew him only as an eccentric who lived in his unfinished houses in the winter and a tent in the summer, who rode the street car to work and returned home with milk and canned food, discarding the cans in the back yard and hoarding the empty milk bottles in his basement.

Only when they read his obituary did they realize that this was the John L. Hamery who had held the center stage spotlight for four years as city alderman, original Des Moines Police Commissioner and Public Citizen No. 1. ✪

Chief of Police George Yeager, 1911

HONOR ROLL

FRANK DELMEGE
Appointed: 1 May 1905
Died: 20 September 1909

Detective Delmege was working on the night of 20 September, when a call came in from his own residence that a man, John Smeltzer, was running drunk through the neighborhood with a shotgun, threatening to kill another neighbor. Det. Delmege and Patrolman Ross were dispatched to the scene.

They approached the suspect's house and saw him emerge from inside. Delmege called to him. Smeltzer walked to the edge of the lawn seven feet above the sidewalk, threw the shotgun to his shoulder and fired point-blank at the detective. Patrolman Ross fired at Smeltzer, hitting him three times in the chest. Delmege died at the scene.

Smeltzer survived his gunshot wounds to stand trial for Detective Delmege's murder. He was found guilty and sentenced to life imprisonment at Ft. Madison. He died there in 1920, just two months short of his 33rd birthday.

Delmege's brother, Sherman, who was also with the DMPD, was Chief of Detectives when he retired in the early '30s. ✪

*Des Moines Police
(probably eastside squad), circa 1909*

Matron Mrs. L.L. Babcock, 1911

Matron Mrs. N.P. Collins, 1911

Roy Chamberlain, 1912

	MAYORS	POLICE CHIEFS
1900	J.J. Hartenbower	F.A. Mathis
1901	"	"
1902	Jim M. Brenton	F.A. Brackett
1903	"	"
1904	G.W. Mattern	Jim Jones
1905	"	"
1906	"	"
1907	"	"
1908	A.G. Mathis	W.P. Hume
1909	"	A.G. Miller
1910	J.R. Hanna	G. Teager
1911	"	"
1912	"	J.W. Jenney
1913	"	"
1914	"	Ed Crawford
1915	"	"
1916	John MacVicar	C.C. Jackson
1917	"	"
1918	T. Fairweather	"
1919	"	Ab Day

53

Group photo of officers in front of police headquarters, 1911

Patrolman
Jeremiah Courtney, 1909

Patrolman
Joshua Suits, 1909

U.S. HISTORY

1900 Hawaii becomes US territory

1901 McKinley shot; Teddy Roosevelt President

1902 US Army from blue to olive drab uniform

1903 Wright brothers first flight

1904 New York City Subway opened

1905 First Nickelodeons open in U.S.

1906 "Typhoid Mary" found after 8 year search

1907 Oklahoma enters Union as 46th state

1908 Henry Ford introduces the Model T

1909 NAACP formed

1910 Barney Oldfield drives auto 133 mph

1911 Amundson reaches the South Pole

1912 Titanic sinks

1913 Fed. income tax; Ford's moving production line

1914 WWI erupts in Europe

1915 First taxi cabs, "Jitneys" in US

1916 Rose Bowl begins

1917 US enters WWI

1918 FLu epidemic; Nov. 11 Armistice ends WWI

1919 Babe Ruth hits 587-foot home run

54

GEORGE MATTERN
Appointed: 16 May 1916
Died: 12 April 1918

On the evening of 8 August 1917, Officer Mattern was patrolling his regular beat downtown when he heard shots being fired. As he headed toward the noise, he met the bandit and a shootout occurred, with Officer Mattern being struck by a bullet in the abdomen. He was taken to Mercy Hospital to undergo surgery. He lingered until April 12.

The suspect, who was fleeing from another officer after holding up a bar, escaped without injury. He was described as a white male in his early 20s. Even after an extensive search and investigation, no suspect was ever apprehended. ✪

LOCAL HISTORY

1900 Des Moines Auditorium burns
1901 Rock Island Depot & Victorian Hotel built
1902 Des Moines River floods 1902 and 1903
1903 Teddy Roosevelt visits Des Moines
1904 Iowa State Capitol burns
1905 Methodist Hospital opens
1906 Polk County Courthouse finished
1907 Fleming Bldg. 1st steel skyscraper in Iowa
1908 "Des Moines Plan" of government begins
1909 President Taft in auto parade
1910 Big "Municipal Day" parade & celebration
1911 Brooker T. Washington visits Des Moines
1912 New Municipal Hall opens
1913 Shops Building opens
1914 B.F. Allen dies in California
1915 Riverview Park opens
1916 Camp Dodge expanded for Mexican excursion
1917 Merle Hay killed in WWI
1918 Police Chief C.C. Jackson shot dead
1919 Fort Des Moines and Savery Hotels open

**Patrolman
William Bailor, 1909**

**Patrolman
Frank Badgley, 1909**

APRIL FOOLS AND TRUE HEROES

BY JOHN ZELLER

C.C. Jackson was Des Moines' only police chief to find himself without a police force to lead. He was a real policeman's chief, rising up through the ranks for 16 years. So it must have been humiliating for Jackson to have to step aside at morning roll call on April 1, 1918, as Polk County Sheriff John Griffin marched up to address "his" men—the assembled patrolmen of the Des Moines Police Department.

What could cause the Des Moines police chief to be stripped of command without a trial and replaced by the sheriff? The answer—twice-elected Iowa Governor William Lloyd Harding of Sioux City and World War I.

Governor Harding made himself infamous by warring on Germany through the sup-

Gov. W.L. Harding
Reprint: *The DM Register*

pression of individual liberties here in Iowa. Today he is remembered for declaring all foreign languages *verboten* in schools, churches and public meetings, and even over the telephone. He also personally canceled an operatic concert by German-born Frieda Hempel at the Des Moines Coliseum.

After the war, Harding pursued other enemies. In 1919, it was "Bolsheviks," members of the labor union International Workers of the World, or "Wobblies." In January 1920, he helped the federal government arrest Des Moines' Lithuanian coal miners for deportation during the Palmer Raids of the "Red Scare."

Add to this recipe of one corrupt governor, the tensions of a town of 115,000 with an undersized police force, an army of 40,000 soldiers at Camp Dodge and the trainees of the Negro Officer Training School at Fort Des Moines. Mix in one politically ambitious sheriff and a dash of one foolish and overzealous crusader, and you have all the ingredients for what the national police magazine, *The Detective*, entitled "A Monumental Blunder."

Events were set in motion on New Year's Day 1918, when Lt. H.H. Antles of the Fosdick War Recreation Commission of the U.S. Sanitary Corps, stepped off the train in Des Moines. Antles was shocked to be accosted by eight separate women whom he concluded must be of "easy virtue." He returned to Iowa in March to give the governor his official report that Iowa's capital city was a moral sewer and that drastic action was necessary to protect the morals of the soldiers of Camp Dodge—Cantonment 13 of the 88th Division of the National Army.

The Iowa Legislature gave Harding emergency powers to create a statewide police force to supersede all law enforcement in Iowa. *The Detective* characterized this as a "peculiar, unique and grotesque law. . . allowing the governor to virtually oust a chief of police without trial and appoint a political henchman." The new "Police Chief of Iowa," Sheriff John Griffin, had far-reaching powers. At his disposal was every policeman, sheriff, deputy sheriff, constable, military policeman and railway detective in the state. He could deputize citizens on the street, even against their will, into Governor Harding's new "secret service police force." Ironically, Polk County Sheriff John Griffin, though lacking the trademark mustache, bore a great resemblance to our enemy, Kaiser Wilhelm II of Germany. *The Detective* characterized Griffin as "Iowa's police dictator."

On April 1, 1918 (April Fools' Day), Griffin's troops sprang into action. The police raided and closed the dance halls Owl, Moose and Circle, arresting 65 people, 30 of them for "investigation." They indiscriminately rounded up any woman walking about on a public street as *prima facio* evidence of "streetwalking." It became unsafe for women to walk to work or even alight from a

trolley car. These women were herded by the police into the city and county jails and into local hospitals where they were subjected to humiliating medical examinations by male doctors in search of social diseases. They slept on the floor in crowded cells and were denied bail or legal representation.

For one frantic week the campaign waged on. Each night the vice squads strove to beat the previous night's record of arrests—Monday: 65, Tuesday: 84 and Wednesday: 97. By Thursday, women were staying indoors and not going to work, so the posses moved on to hauling in bellhops, minors caught in pool halls and auto speeders in order to keep the numbers reported to the newspapers on the rise. Sheriff Griffin told the Des Moines policemen to report to him all "suspicious" places and citizens and vowed that any officer who turned in a light report would himself be investigated. Governor Harding was pressuring Griffin to "do the job" or be replaced—other men were hungry for the position and the power; even ex-mayor John MacVicar ran for sheriff in May. Griffin warned the assembled policemen that he was "not going to take the fall."

By the second week another problem arose. While arrest rates were impressively high, the number of convictions were not. In fact, there was no evidence of wrongdoing against most of the women languishing in jail. So Sheriff Griffin resorted to third-degree methods, putting the frightened girls into a "sweat box" of intense interrogations to extract false confessions, in exchange for the promise that once convicted, they would be granted pardons and released. *The Register* reported, "the girls under a relentless crossfire of questions break down and confess to anything in their desperation rather than to continue the ordeal." *The Detective* asserted "women were railroaded into confessing for pardons to boost conviction rates."

The campaign heated to a fever pitch. Patrolman I.W. Halley on April 15, intent on

"Kaiser Bill " of Germany

stopping a speeding taxicab, riddled the car with bullets, killing passenger Sgt. Wilbur F. Lane of the 349th Field Hospital Corps. Black soldiers also were being subjected to intimidation and black women rounded up. The town fathers who typically turned a blind eye to such abuses, worried that Des Moines might become "off limits," and that the big flow of money coming in from Camp Dodge would be turned off. The local chamber of commerce complained that conditions here were never really bad and even the military police had to agree. All the soldiers needed, they concluded, was some supervision.

So the city reopened three dance halls under municipal management. The rules were strict. No "dips and hugs," no "shaky shoulders" and no "Venus dip." The city, leaving nothing to chance, delayed the start of the festivities while a Des Moines building inspector checked the dance floor and officially declared it safe.

The "Municipal Dance Hall Committee" put its stamp of approval on these evening events which entertained 3,300 dancers during the first week, even though one committee member complained that the music had too much "trombone" in it. *The Tribune* interviewed one young dancer, "Inez," who complained about being subjected to an evening of slow, dull, municipally-approved dance tunes. "What's the rock-me-to-sleep music? Never thought I'd glide to that 'Just a Baby's Prayer at Twilight' stuff. What's the matter with 'Shake the Chimmy?'"

By May, public enthusiasm for the crusade was waning. Mayor Tom Fairweather declared that he had had enough and would not sign any more medical detentions without evidence.

At summer's end, Lt. Antles, who started this whole mess, mysteriously reappeared to pay a visit on superintendent of public safety Ben Woolgar. On his way out of town, Antles left behind his "Dudley Do-Right," subordinate Lt. F.W. Madden, who promptly declared

John Griffin, Polk County Sheriff and "Iowa's Police Chief," 1918-1919
(mustache added)

any woman arrested within a ten-mile radius of Fort Des Moines to be under federal jurisdiction and subject to a jail term of one year. He also wanted "dope users" confined indefinitely at the state asylum.

Madden demanded a big meeting of the governor, Sheriff Griffin, judges, the city council, and the chamber of commerce, where he planned to dictate terms on the renewed war on vice. What he got instead was a two-hour donnybrook in which he was finally ordered to "sit down and shut up."

On the eleventh hour of the eleventh day of the eleventh month the guns fell silent in France. Des Moines, like the rest of the coun-

try, went wild with parades and parties. But three days later, no less than the secretary of war in Washington telegrammed Mayor Fairweather ordering him to show no laxness in the pursuit of vice. The War Department was particularly eager to pursue the evil of social diseases. Meanwhile, so many soldiers at Camp Dodge where dying of the influenza epidemic of 1918 that Harbach's Funeral Home ran out of space and had to stack the coffins with frozen bodies under tarpaulins in the alley.

In 1919, Governor Harding went from infamy to ignominy, when he was impeached by the Iowa Legislature for selling a gubernatorial pardon to a recently-convicted rapist for $5,000. While the Republican majority in the statehouse was ripping itself apart in its failure to convict him, Harding hid at home, suffering from "nervous prostration."

In the end only Chief Jackson, stripped of his command and having no part of the witch-hunt, retained his dignity and honor. While the moral crusaders were chasing down innocent women, Police Chief C.C. Jackson had his own personal crusade: to apprehend a real criminal, the dangerous desperado "Dutch" Cross. On December 13, 1918, Chief Jackson died in a shoot-out with Cross.

Des Moines was busy that year renaming streets and parks for Iowa's fallen heroes of World War I: Private Merle Hay and Captains Fleur and McHenry. The citizens of the capital city also honored their fallen police chief by lining the route by the thousands as his funeral proceeded to Woodland Cemetery.

Just hours after Jackson's death, a telegram arrived at the Des Moines police station from New York City. Jesse Jackson, the chief's son, had just arrived from the war in France on a hospital ship. The cable read simply, "Merry Christmas and Happy New Year." ✪

CHIEF CHARLES JACKSON

BY PEGGY SCHLEUGER

Des Moines Police Chief Charles Jackson's death on December 16, 1918 was the result of what was probably the most desperate gunfight ever waged in Des Moines between peace officers and a criminal.

The gunfight involved Iowa's most notorious criminal at that time, William "Dutch" Cross. Dutch Cross was wanted in three states for crimes which included cattle stealing, bank robbery and murder.

On December 12, 1918 police were informed that Dutch was in Des Moines at an east side residence. Upon receiving this information, Chief Jackson immediately rounded up four detectives who accompanied him to the residence.

The officers were met at the door by Dutch's wife. Dutch, who had scented trouble, had fled into a bedroom.

Jackson and his four aides pushed open the bedroom door, guns drawn and ready for action. A door at the end of the room indicated Dutch's location.

"Come on out, Dutch, called Chief Jackson, "the jig's up."

Dutch kicked open the door and came out shooting. One of the first bullets struck Chief Jackson over his right vest pocket. As the chief sank to the floor, he fired his own automatic hitting Dutch in the abdomen.

The four detectives carried the chief into the yard and an ambulance and reinforcements were called. Dutch lay writhing in pain for half an hour, then suddenly in desperation he jumped to his feet, burst through the back door, and headed for the alley.

Officers surrounding the house fired into the darkness and the bandit went down.

The battle had begun at 10:00 pm. Dutch was taken to a local hospital where he lived until 3:00 the next morning.

Chief Jackson lasted another three days, dying on 16 December. ✪

Hearse carrying body of slain Police Chief Jackson to Woodland Cemetery

Chief Jackson's funeral procession crossing Court Avenue bridge, 1918

Reprint: *The Evening Tribune*, December 13, 1918

SHERIFF GRIFFIN SAYS CROSS MOST SOUGHT FOR CRIMINAL IN 3 STATES

William Cross, alias Texas St. Clair, alias Bill Ryan, alias Dutch Cross, who died at the Methodist hospital this morning from a shot fired by Detective J.J. Hollibaugh, has been the most sought after criminal in this and surrounding states for the past six years.

When first heard of, Dutch Cross and his brother, Frank, were serving a twenty-year sentence at the Illinois state prison at Joliet, under the name of the St. Clair brothers. The charge against then was for horse stealing. They were pardoned two years ago and started operations at Boone, Ia.

At this time Dutch Cross was working with William Carter, who is now serving time at Fort Madison. They were raiding box cars and bringing their loot to Des Moines to sell. They were captured in this city and gave bonds for their release.

Cross then went to Warsaw, Wi. and pulled a clever deal. He dropped a nickel in a music box in a bar room and then called the bartender because the coin jammed. As the two were working with the machine Cross' partner robbed the safe. Cross was arrested in a hotel later and gave bonds and was released.

He then came back to Iowa and used a farm near Colfax, Ia. to hide stolen cattle, auto tires, pigs and a quantity of wool. I [Griffin] arrested him but he was released on bonds.

He then went to St. Joe, Mo. and married Hazel Johnson in a little town in northern Missouri. He was married under the name of St. Clair and later they came to Iowa and were remarried, this time using the name of Cross.

In 1912 Cross and William Carter were indicted for the murder of Dressel, who was found dead at his home. Carter appeared several days later with the deed for his property.

Last April Cross stole a car from Grinnell and drove to Valeria and robbed the Savings bank in that town, in the middle of the afternoon.

He was then arrested on another charge and taken to Newton, Ia. where he sawed his way to liberty.

Cross then started to carry liquor from Missouri into this state and was arrested last summer at Leon when he was found drunk with a carload of booze. He gave bonds again and was not heard of until last night when Chief Jackson was tipped off that he was in town.

Cross was out on bonds for a dozen offenses and numerous rewards are offered for him. Jackson is entitled to the reward. ✪

CORNELIUS "CON" McCARTHY
Appointed: 5 January 1911
Died: 29 September 1919

Above: "Con" McCarthy's badge
Below: Officers Con McCarthy and Jesse Kimms inside a Des Moines lunchroom, 1918

DETECTIVE CORNELIUS McCARTHY

BY PAMELA SHAPIRO

On September 27, 1919, Detective Cornelius McCarthy became the fourth Des Moines police officer killed in the line of duty.

Detective McCarthy had been working undercover with Harry Miller, a deliveryman for Flynn Dairy, on a series of burglaries occurring in the early morning. Miller had reported "a suspicious Negro" lingering among the houses on his route, and possibly entering them as soon as he left so the occupants would attribute any noises to the milkman. McCarthy, dressed in overalls, was able to apprehend a suspect identified by Miller as the man he'd seen earlier. McCarthy placed him under arrest and took him to Flynn Dairy headquarters, where he called the patrol wagon. While waiting for it to arrive, the suspect asked permission to sit down. McCarthy said he might. He seated himself on the curb long enough to pull a .32 caliber handgun from his shoe and shoot McCarthy in the chest.

Miller flung himself on the pavement to avoid being hit, and McCarthy staggered about twenty feet before collapsing at last. The suspect escaped, but not before firing additional shots at the approaching wagon, narrowly missing its driver, John Latham. One of its occupants, Cpl. A.J. Suess of the military police force, fired several shots at the retreating figure, who returned fire and vanished, leaving the Des Moines Police Department with two jobs: burying a beloved comrade, and finding his anonymous killer.

Con McCarthy was born in Chicago in 1871. He entered law enforcement as a police officer for the Union stockyards in 1908, and came to Des Moines in 1909 as an officer with a packing house. He joined the Des Moines Police Department in 1910 and made detective the August before he died.

Newspaper accounts of his murder are filled with descriptions of an upstanding gentleman who would not tolerate swearing among his fellow officers and always gave suspects the benefit of his doubt. One reporter pointed out that he lost his life by performing

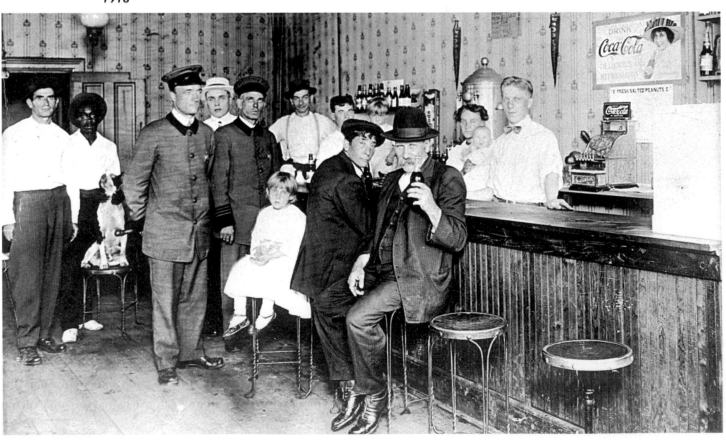

an act of kindness: allowing the suspect to rest for a few minutes on the curb.

The family he left behind, his wife, Katherine, and seven children aged 2 to 15, was the subject of subscription drives by all three city newspapers, one of which netted a contribution of $8.73 from the city newsboys, who viewed him as a "surrogate dad." *The Tribune* also established a trust fund for the children's education. Later, Mrs. McCarthy would join the police department herself, first as a telephone operator and later a matron. She remained with the department until her retirement in 1953.

The manhunt for McCarthy's killer began as he still lay on the sidewalk. The city was scoured by every officer on the force, with the assistance of many private citizens and the local chapter of the NAACP, acting on numerous tips that the unknown subject was hiding out somewhere in Des Moines. Men answering the description were brought to the station and questioned. Both Chief Day and Chief of Detectives James McDonald described in the papers their intention of keeping the suspect, once he was arrested, from being lynched. They planned to have him transported immediately to a nearby county jail for his own safety.

On October 9, 1919, police announced to the press that a man they'd had in custody since October 5, Brownie Browman, had been positively identified by Miller as the man who killed McCarthy. Police had arrested him after a young boy, Fred Seeburger, 14, found a .32 caliber revolver while playing with friends near a shack, and was approached by Browman. His trial for the murder of Det. McCarthy was waived to the grand jury, who found him guilty—an opinion reiterated after an appeal to the Iowa Supreme Court in May, 1921. Browman later died at Ft. Madison Penitentiary. ✪

Officer Con McCarthy walking his beat

Officer Con McCarthy

Reprint: *Souvenir Annual Ball Book,* 1921

RELIEF WORK OF THE POLICE BURIAL AND PROTECTIVE ASSOCIATION DURING 1919

The work of the Des Moines Police Burial and Protective Association during the last year has been among the greatest of any period since the founding of the organization.

With the launching of the 1920 program the association starts out with an even brighter outlook for service to its members and for enlargement in all lines of activity.

The main sums paid out during the last year were to the widow of Con McCarthy, amounting to $600 and to Mrs. George Staples and Mrs. August Hoffman to aid in the purchase of fuel and supplies.

The death benefit was recently raised to $1,000.

The association in these and countless other circumstances, has proved its tremendous value to its members and to the community as a whole. In safeguarding the lives and property of residents of Des Moines, members of the police department are required to face extreme danger almost daily. The association, through its benefits, assures to the men of the department protection for their families in case of accident or death. It meets a great need in the service and fills a service which could not be achieved in any other way. ✪

WHITE CHAPEL DISTRICT
SCARLET WOMEN AND OTHER RASCALS

BY LINDA BANGER

At the turn of the century, vice and sin reigned south of the Des Moines' business district. Indeed, the heart of the city's red light district lay only a few blocks from the police station, then at 2nd and Locust.

The area where the houses of ill fame, gambling dens and saloons were located extended from near 4th and Elm Streets to the Raccoon River, and was known as "White Chapel," named after the crime-ridden London slum made infamous worldwide by Jack the Ripper.

Ironically, it was at or near the location of the old Fort Des Moines, the frontier outpost of the Army dragoons in the 1840s. The red light district had sprung up where the city was born.

Silk-hatted dandies in fancy carriages and others in hacks flocked to the district as the sun went down. Every establishment had its own brand of beer furnished by a saloon that lent its financial aid to the place.

Following two lurid and sensational murders which included the stabbing of seamstress and prostitute Ella Barrett, and the lynching of Charles Howard, the public became so alarmed by the crime wave and apparent lawlessness that a call for a segregated, or separate, red-light district rang out. A "dead line" was established south of the railroad tracks on both the east and west sides of the river where there were no night patrols by the police. It was an unofficial and silent acknowledgement of a district in which anyone entering did so at their peril.

One of the more notorious establishments was Scribner's Row at 4th and Elm, and the queen of the "row" was a madam known as Jeanette Allen. She operated one of the fancier and more prosperous houses until she abruptly left town in 1898.

Her departure followed a year-and-a-half in the penitentiary, a sentence she was handed after she refused to name names regarding her involvement with state legislators. Upon her release from prison she fled to Skagway, Alaska, and Dawson, Yukon Territory. She returned to town in 1901 with a fortune reported at $80,000. Despite her profession, she was a woman of honor, and she used the money to repay debts left behind when she'd disappeared.

The years passed and the district became shabby. White Chapel became the hideout of every crook, petty thief and woman of low morals in the city.

Two men kept watch over the proceedings at White Chapel and made it their business to know what was going on and keep it under control. Patrolmen Clay Lewis, and his partner, Ira Miller, were considered the heroes of White Chapel. Once, Miller discovered safecrackers trying to open a safe in a saloon on the outskirts of the district. A gun battle followed in which Miller single-handedly shot it out with the bandits. His daring was the talk of the town for weeks.

White Chapel district tenement houses West 4th and Elm Street, (Pelton Avenue)

The days of White Chapel became numbered when the Burlington Railroad enlarged its switching yard. The company purchased property in the area and forced the tenants of the buildings to find homes elsewhere.

Vice then moved north to Cherry Street and across the river to East Walnut and Court Avenue, but even that was chased out around 1908 by Police Commissioner Hamery.

By the early years of the Great Depression, there were only two blocks of tenements remaining in the White Chapel district when the city condemned the buildings and ordered them demolished. With wrecking bars and sledgehammers the old buildings were torn down in early November, 1931.

The dust had hardly settled south of the city's business district when a new area of illicit enterprise opened up —this time it was practically in the shadow of the state capitol on the city's east side and just a couple blocks north of city hall.

Known as the Black and Tan District for both the black and the white streetwalkers

Two men kept watch over the proceedings at White Chapel and made it their business to know what was going on and keep it under control. Patrolmen Ira Miller, above left, and his partner, Clay Lewis, above right, were considered the heroes of White Chapel.

who plied their trade in the area, the establishments stretched along Des Moines Street from East 2nd to East 5th Street. The houses were mostly homely-looking, two-story, unpainted dwellings formerly occupied by the early residents of the growing city; people who worked hard, moved up in the world and away from their old neighborhoods.

Customers for the businesses could be found among the workers and passengers of the nearby North Western Railroad, which at that time had a depot at East 4th and Locust Streets; the tracks ran north past the district. The Swift Packing Company egg processing plant was also nearby.

To entice customers into their establishments, the women openly solicited business from the brothels' front porches and sidewalks. In fact, the district became an entertainment venue for Des Moines residents who drove their out-of-town visitors through the neighborhood to see the goings-on. Rural residents would often drive in from the country to cruise past the houses and gawk at the sin and mischief.

As early as 1929, the police had tried to get court orders to close the houses and penalize the occupants and property owners. The women were taken to the county hospital, then on 4th Street north of downtown, for medical checkups against venereal disease. This was in accordance with a national campaign against the disease, which was rampant at the time.

With White Chapel demolished and the Black and Tan District suffocated with court documents, vice in Des Moines was stamped out.

That is, until it popped up some place else. ✪

MAP BY STEVE PEGLOW

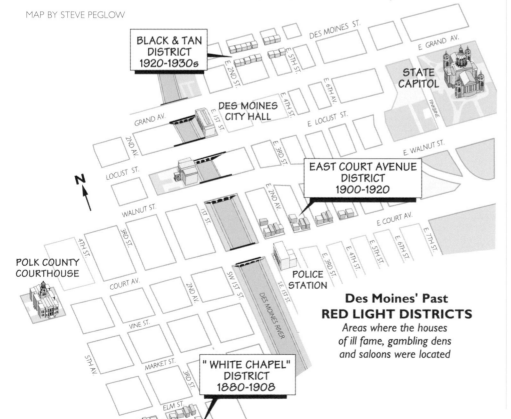

BLACK & TAN DISTRICT 1920-1930s

STATE CAPITOL

DES MOINES CITY HALL

EAST COURT AVENUE DISTRICT 1900-1920

POLICE STATION

POLK COUNTY COURTHOUSE

Des Moines' Past RED LIGHT DISTRICTS
Areas where the houses of ill fame, gambling dens and saloons were located

"WHITE CHAPEL" DISTRICT 1880-1908

Looking south downtown on 6th Avenue, circa 1930

Tommy gun rumored to have been used during shoot-out with Barrow gang in Dexter, Iowa, 1933

Des Moines Police Department Baseball Team, 1928
Standing, left to right: **Carl Vonn, Jack Ellis, Nels Pastel, Colonel Hill, "Jap" Crowe, Mose Clayman, Jack Lazarus**
Sitting, left to right: **Mott Hammond, Bert Powell, Johnny Rhoades, Tony Blacksmith, Earl Badgley, Frank Badgley**

OPENING THE DES MOINES POLICE STATION
WOLLGAR'S MIDNIGHT WALTZ

BY JOHN ZELLER

In the year 2000, the Des Moines Police station will be 80 years old, probably the oldest police station in the state of Iowa. The police headquarters has undergone a lot of changes over the years; now only a small fraction of the building is used as it was intended when it was finished in 1920 during Woodrow Wilson's presidency. Today, the building is crowded, outmoded and barely adequate for the needs of a modern city. But in 1920 it was called, "the finest police station in the West."

Officially it was named the "Des Moines Municipal Court Building." Its construction was envisioned in 1912 by Judge Hubert Utterback as a home for a modern municipal justice court system. He hoped to replace the pioneer Justice of the Peace courts that meted out uneven, slow and often corrupt justice. The municipal court justices, unlike the justices of the peace, would be trained lawyers, and juries were to be impaneled from a list of potential jurors, not merely men pulled off the street at random by a constable.

In 1915, the Bremmer-Parker Bill passed the Iowa Legislature, allowing Des Moines and other cities the right to abolish the old system. Des Moines started holding municipal court sessions on the fifth floor of the Observatory Building at 4th and Locust. By 1916, the clerk of court was weary from

working in the cramped conditions. He had a four-by-four foot room, one toilet and no place to hold prisoners.

Mayor John MacVicar and 83 affiliates of the Federation of Women's Clubs combined to champion a new court building, which would include a new home for the Des Moines Police Department. Both 1916 and 1917 went by as lawyers argued about the city's indebtedness. But Des Moines' citizens, even with World War I bond drives going on, supported a separate bond issue to finance building a massive beaux arts limestone police station on the river front.

A bid of $350,000 was accepted in 1918 from the A. N. Neumann Co. Their original bid of $416,000 was revised downward, leaving the third floor hospital unfinished; terrazzo reserved to the first floor; "Extra Fine Bedford Limestone" replaced with a generic "Indiana" variety; and excess ornamentation left out, all in order to bring the new building in under the low bid.

Construction began in May 1918. By November and the end of the World War I, the building was under roof. Arthur Neumann announced that they would have it completed by June 1919. As the structure loomed up on the river front, the builders were boasting of the sturdy reinforced concrete, entirely fireproof edifice. The four

courtrooms on the second floor were of particular pride. Their inspiration was Italian, the designs derived from the civil courts of Naples, Italy. Their walls were to be finished with Moran brocade, a silk fabric that even at 1920 prices cost $10 a yard.

Unfortunately, the United States after the war was gripped by severe inflation, particularly in building materials. As the 100 workmen were steadily finishing the building, the city was even more quickly running out of money. The plans for silk-covered walls were changed to cheap cork. The city added another $100,000, then later asked for an additional bond issue of $43,000. Nearing a cost of $650,000, the temple of justice was becoming a civic white elephant and political embarrassment. Pressures mounted to move into the building, finished or not (a move that would be regretted later).

On March 5, 1920, the "Muny" court moved its records into the new building. William T. Vinton, the first defendant in the new building, was convicted of "carrying a

Site of present-day police station, 1914

Des Moines Municipal Court and Public Safety Building, East 1st and Court Avenue

concealed weapon and assault to rob." The trial opened with these words by presiding Judge Mershon:

"That as the people come to this commodious and beautiful building to seek justice may it be the idea of this court that fair and equal justice will ever be given to high and low, rich and poor, of whatever faith, color or condition of life, to the end that in the operations and deliberations of this court no harm shall ever come to anyone."

Police Commissioner Ben Woolgar was impatient for his men in blue to move into the new building. His reign as police commissioner would end April 5, 1920, and he was determined to be the one to inaugurate the new station.

On Monday, March 22, 1920, Police Chief Ab Day lined up the patrolmen of the Des Moines Police Department and at 6:30 in the evening left the old station at 2nd and Locust, home to the Des Moines Police for 27

years and two months, for the very last time. After a short march down 2nd Street, then across the handsome new Court Avenue Bridge, they reassembled in the new building for the 8:00 evening roll call, thus inaugurating the modern era of the Des Moines Police Department.

They carried with them the department records and left behind the battered, rustic furniture of the old structure. Trailing along also were Jimmy Scott, Bill Smith, Bill Cox, Scotty Bruce, and Wayne Howard, the five prisoners convicted that morning who were to be honored as the city's first guests in the new calaboose.

On Friday the 26th at the end of the first week of business, the long first-floor hallway was transformed into a banquet room, as 300 police and family entertained themselves at a big housewarming for the building. After the meal the tables were cleared out, and Commissioner Ben Wollgar led the dances, waltzing happily across the terrazzo floor

until midnight.

Wollgar pushed hard to finish the building before April 5, so that he might preside over the official formal dedication of the building before leaving office. Wollgar's dream was never realized, and within two years the congratulatory handshakes of that night had given way to finger-pointing accusations of incompetence and calls for resignations over jail breaks and the unfinished condition of the big building.

Today we can imagine what a panoramic photograph of the ceremony would have looked like: the policemen at rigid attention, flags and bunting fluttering from the windows and the mayor atop the stairs, accepting the building for the citizens of the City of Des Moines. Unfortunately the scene never happened. Today, the devoted men and women of the Des Moines police report every day to a station that the city finally dedicated on May 14,1999. ✪

"Just Give 'Em a Chance"

BY JOHN ZELLER

It was Jailer Tom Cross's motto, but he didn't mean "a chance to escape." The year was 1921 and already a couple prisoners had snuck out of the new jail, but now Jailer Cross thought he had the kinks worked out. Old Tom put in long hours: he showed up at seven in the morning and worked 16 hours until 11:00 at night—eight hours off to sleep then back on the job. In the wee hours the police captain was to send a man around to look in on the prisoners.

State law made it a serious offense to break out. If caught, it meant a year in jail. Since most prisoners held by the city tended to be drunks and vagrants locked up for only a few days, escaping was really a stupid move. But in 1921, the city and Polk County were fighting a war over paying the county sheriff to house dangerous city prisoners. The city cried that the county was overcharging them. So municipal Judge W.G. Bonner ordered all prisoners, even ones with a reason to escape, held in the city jail which was conveniently located where he held court.

On Tuesday, December 13, 1921, when Jailer Cross left as usual at 11:00 pm, the prisoners were all sleeping on the first floor "bull pen." The jail cells on the second floor of the new building were still unfinished.

Down the hall on the south side of the building was a small bathroom where two prisoners had busied themselves for three nights with a hacksaw on the window bars. By 1:00 am Wednesday, they had sawed through one bar and bent it out of the way. A 12-inch gap and a 14-foot drop to the ground were all that separated them from freedom. Seven men slipped out, slid down a knotted blanket and scurried into the darkness over the Rock Island railway bridge.

Since the captain did not count noses during the night, the escape wasn't discovered until morning by poor Tom Cross. The alarm went out over the telegraph and telephones to neighboring towns that seven dangerous men held for crimes ranging from robbery with a dangerous weapon to breaking and entering, were on the loose. The police knew that the escapees had a big head start.

The prisoners who stayed behind said they had given them a send-off after midnight. Dewey Raney, the most dangerous of the men, bid the others adieu with a cheery "Goodbye, I hate to leave you but I am on my way to old Mexico." The police figured that they had split town that night by riding the rails.

The next evening, alarming news from

> **"The alarm went out over the telegraph and telephones to neighboring towns that seven dangerous men ... were on the loose."**

Jailer Tom Cross, 1921

Jail escapee "Legless Jack" O'Donnell

Sac City indicated that five of the bunch had arrived there on the Milwaukee train and stole a 1917 touring car and some warm winter coats, their current whereabouts unknown. The train from Des Moines had left town at 4:00 in the afternoon, which meant that for nine hours while the police were sending statewide bulletins, the desperadoes were out at the train station!

The Des Moines Register headlined, "THE JAIL IS A JOKE." Mayor Barton declared, "The jail was never accepted by the city." The architects (Keffer & Jones, Kraetsch & Kraetsch, Sawyer & Watrous, and Norman T. Vorse) countered that they had indeed received the last payment. Judge Bonner blamed the police, the police blamed Judge Bonner, and the city council blamed Police Chief Roscoe Saunders.

On December 19, the city council fired Chief Saunders and appointed 15-year police veteran Sherman Delmege as the new chief. Delmege rushed over to city hall to inform the council that he wouldn't think of leaving the security of civil service for the uncertain future of being police chief. The next day finds the city council and mayor reconvened in a stormy private session. One newspaperman

outside the door reported, ". . . at times all five seemed to be talking at one time." When they reappeared, Saunders had his job back.

That day, Ulis Redman, the only negro escapee, gave himself up. He never left town, but spent every day hiding from the police in darkened movie houses. He regretted that he had been too scared to sit through an entire film and now wished he'd seen some of the endings. In general he said he had had a good time, but added, "This is a good old jail and I am glad to be back." The others must not have agreed with Redman because none of them were ever seen again.

Life around the jail got back to normal for Christmas and New Year's. Then on January 16, 1922, the police arrested "legless Jack" O'Donnell, a likeable Irish pencil vendor who scooted around downtown on a roller cart. That night, a Mrs. Palmer called police to

report that O'Donnell, an old tenant of hers, was on her porch with a gun trying to break in. When the police arrived, O'Donnell was trying to wheel off in the snow, no gun in sight.

The officers felt sorry for amputee O'Donnell, who had lost his legs at the railway yards, and put him up in the more comfortable third floor "flophouse" instead of the second floor jail. O'Donnell feigned sleep, then took "French leave," scooting down the hall, three flights of stairs and out the front door. Happy-go-lucky O'Donnell was free again and looking for adventure.

After five days of fun on the run, he had had enough. Patrolmen Ogilvie and Lathan were dispatched in the patrol wagon to the corner of 6th and Hartford, where they found a drunken Jack O'Donnell waiting for them, reportedly "in a hilarious mood." ✪

NOBODY SEEMS TO BE DOING ANYTHING ABOUT IT

Ding Darling cartoon reprint: *The DM Register,* 1926

	MAYORS	POLICE CHIEFS
1920	Tom Fairweather	Ab Day
1921	Hardy H. Barton	M.J. Donoghue
1922	"	Roscoe Saunders
1923	Carl M. Garver	J.B. Hammond
1924	"	"
1925	"	James Cavender
1926	"	"
1927	Fred H. Hunter	"
1928	"	Roy J. Chamberlain
1929	John MacVicar	Henry A. Alber
1930	E.H. Mulack	"
1931	Parker L. Crouch	"
1932	"	"
1933	Dwight N. Lewis	"
1934	"	"
1935	"	"
1936	"	"
1937	Joseph A. Allen	"
1938	"	"
1939	Mark L. Conkling	"

HAVING A BALL

BY PAMELA SHAPIRO

For several decades in the middle of the 20th century, the Annual Police Ball was the social event of the year. Everyone from children to the governor could be expected to attend, and over the years this event raised thousands of dollars for the Police Burial Fund and several local children's charities.

It all started innocently enough, with a vaudeville entertainment scheduled for the evenings of 19-20 December, 1902. Ticket sales (at 50¢ a head for adults) exceeded expectations, and a nightful of "headliners" specially imported from Chicago thrilled the attendees. According to the newspapers next morning, "If Des Moines has the reputation of being cold, the audience last night did not maintain the critical standard." In 1902 the Burial Association did not yet exist. The beneficiaries of this performance were the officers currently walking the beat: they needed new overcoats.

In March 1913, the first Policeman's Ball was held at the Masonic Temple. The following year, 2500 people attended, and officers who usually deported themselves "with a stately stride were seen dancing the tango, fish walk, chicken flit and the hesitation waltz." The mayor and several councilmen were also observed cutting the rug.

February 1920 broke all records: over 7000 people attended the festivities, held by then at the Coliseum. Two orchestras playing on the first and third floors of that august structure helped to raise $6000 for the "Policemen's Burial and Protective Association."

In 1922 Chief of Police Saunders, with the support of several police surgeons and court bailiffs, walked the streets so the patrolmen might enjoy the evening at the dance.

Through the '20s, '30s, the War Years of the '40s and the economic boom of the '50s, the ball continued to be a drawing card year after year. But with the dawn of the '60s, the Burial Association had to acknowledge that the times were a-changin'. People wanted to stay home and watch Ed Sullivan, rather than set out into the snow to "hop with the cops." Attendance dwindled, and by the time the last get-together was held in the mid '90s, it had become a potluck dinner attended by officers and their families, and maybe a few folks from "outside" who cared enough to stop in and say hi.

Although the dance is no more, one memento remains. The *Annual Ball Book*, a yearbook of employee photos and advertisements from local businesses first published in 1910, continues to roll off the presses every year, and has proven invaluable to the members of the history book committee. ✪

Giving the public a glimpse of the first thousand tickets to the 1938 Annual Policeman's Ball are left to right. Officers Mose Clayman, Tom Watson, Ernie Carlson, Henry Van Grud, Bob Burns and Bill Taylor.

Above: **Officer W.L. (Bill) Kelly is practicing up on a few steps of the Charleston, which is expected to be all the rage at the 1926 Annual Policeman's Ball.**

	Des Moines Population	Des Moines Police Force
1933	142,599	147
1934	-	147
1935	-	147
1936	-	151
1937	-	151
1938	-	151
1939	-	151

*Swinging out to jitterbug music performed by the police band at the 1944 Annual Policeman's Ball held at the Moose auditorium are left to right: **Mrs. Barbara Fiori, her brother Patrolman Wendell Nichols; and Patrolman and Mrs. Max Cleveland.***

71

Auto Theft Bureau

BY PEGGY SCHLEUGER

In the spring of 1921, the diversion of stealing motor cars was becoming only slightly less popular locally than the national game of baseball.

From January to August 1921, the light-fingered gents of the motor world drove away 357 cars and forgot to return them. Detective squads managed to recover 125 of these vehicles, which as a record was not very good. Each month the list of missing cars was growing larger. City officials were determined to stop the rise in auto thefts, and as a result, the Auto Theft Bureau was formed on July 31, 1921.

The bureau originally consisted of four officers under the supervision of Assistant Chief Joe Newell. The first officers assigned to the Auto Theft Bureau were Patrolmen Fred Gagen and Hank Alber, and Detectives Meyers and Chamberlain. These officers soon earned the nickname of "The Big Four" raiding squad.

During the bureau's first month, August 1921, they slightly stemmed the tide of auto thefts. In that month 75 cars were stolen and 55 recovered. In September, 59 cars were stolen and 54 recovered. October was better still; during that month 68 cars were stolen and 75 recovered! The recovery statistics of the bureau continued to rise, and auto theft in Des Moines began to decline as the proficiency of these officers became known.

Professional thieves caused the Auto Theft Bureau the most trouble, but several rings of thieves operating in Des Moines and other cities were broken up through the efforts of Newell and his squad. Some of them had elaborate camouflaging plants to alter the appearance of the cars, making them unrecognizable even to the owners. Some had special die stamps for changing the identification numbers on the cars' engine blocks.

In addition to recovering stolen cars, the Bureau apprehended dozens of car thieves.

In response to its great success, the Auto Theft Bureau was expanded in 1924 to include six officers and a secretary.

Today, the Auto Theft Bureau is combined with the Fraud/Forgery office as the Special Assignment Section. This section consists of a lieutenant, seven police officers, and an investigative assistant. In 1998, Des Moines officers had a remarkable 88% recovery rate. ✪

The Sawed-off Shotgun Squad marching across the Locust Street bridge on May 5, 1923 at the annual review of the police and fire departments. "The shotgun squad is counted upon to be a discourager of automobile thieves, bootlegging caravans, yeggmen [safe crackers] and the like."

Reprint: *The DM Register*, May 27, 1923

THE BIG CHIEF

BY RICHARD CROOK

John Brown Hammond was born on August 27, 1855, and like his second cousin John Brown (as in "John Brown's Body Lies A-Moldering In The Grave") was a hard-headed, bull-in-a-china-shop moralist and reformer, a stubby little fellow with chubby cheeks, narrow mustache and round wire-rimmed glasses.

But in spite of (or perhaps because of) his outward appearance, Hammond was a tiger. He came to Iowa as a miner in the coalfields around Centerville in 1885, but by 1900 he'd found another calling: reform. He was a disciple of Carry Nation, leading the fight for the prohibition of booze in all its forms in Iowa, California and elsewhere in the country from the turn of the century to the late '30s.

From 1908 when he moved to Des Moines, to 1918, John Brown Hammond involved himself in crusading on all sorts of social-reform issues like the World Purity Federation against prostitution. That was a difficult platform; it was the general feeling in most towns throughout the country that red light districts were good for business, and running the prostitutes out of town was bad for business. He also worked for women's suffrage on behalf of the Women's Christian Temperance Union; for the Iowa Attorney General's office tracking down and prosecuting liquor law violators; and for the Anti-Saloon League and the Bone Dry League.

In 1919, a dream came true for John B. when the 18th Amendment to the U.S. Constitution (Prohibition) was finally ratified by the legislatures of 36 states. Those ratifying votes provided the necessary 75% of states that were needed to pass the amendment, and on January 20, 1920, the "Great Experiment" became a fact of life in the United States that would last for 13 years.

Hammond's first job during prohibition was to travel Iowa as an agent of the state attorney general's office, searching for anyone selling booze disguised as patent medicine or cosmetics (bay rum seems to have

John B. Hammond, 1925

been one of his favorite targets). Meanwhile, he continued his duties as a state agent and as deputy Polk County sheriff until 1922 (Sheriff W.E. Robb, himself a staunch prohibitionist and moral reformer, had deputized Hammond while John was still working for the state). In April 1922, however, John B. abandoned all his other duties when he was named Des Moines' Chief of Police.

After the elections of March, 1922, a whole new council had been voted into office. The voters in those days elected a mayor and five at-large city councilmen. It was left up to the council to determine who would be appointed to the commissions.

In a meeting at the Hotel Fort Des Moines on March 20, the newly-elected council members developed a plan for dividing up the commission posts among themselves. At that meeting the councilmen selected John MacVicar to be the new commissioner of public safety. The selection was made over his objection—he actually wanted to be the streets commissioner.

MacVicar agreed to serve as head of the police and fire departments only if he would have the council's full support in his choice of a replacement for then-chief Roscoe Saunders. The commissioners-elect agreed to his terms and he announced the name of his

candidate for the job: John B. Hammond, the well-known reformer, prohibitionist and, according to some people, certified lunatic.

If a person listens closely, he might still hear the echoes of the collective groans that must have gone up around town when MacVicar dropped that bombshell. One can imagine half the men in town dashing madly to their bootleggers to stock up, anticipating the hard times to come when Hammond took office and the winking at prohibition laws was over.

The gist of Hammond's plan for the capital city and its police department was to enforce to the letter all the "blue laws" that were still on the books. He wanted, he said, to provide safe and sane enforcement of the law. Such enforcement was to include stopping all noise that might disturb the "observers of the Sabbath," including Sunday movies, baseball games, speeders, and the operation of drug stores and shoe shine parlors. The citizens of Des Moines were entitled to some decent, effective law enforcement for a change, whether they wanted it or not. The town was getting entirely too rowdy to suit John B.

Hammond's very first order to his department was to pitch the drunks into jail. No more helping the sots home after they've been at the bootleggers. No more holding a drunk for four hours then letting him go home. "The home is no place for a drunken man," he announced. "He has no business with his wife and family. Chances are he'll beat them up." Clearly John B. was not only death on drunks, but on possible wife-beaters as well. "No bail until they sober up."

Hammond declared a few days after his "no bail for drunks" announcement that he was forming a "morals squad". Officers would go after prostitutes, bootleggers, gamblers, and anyone else involved in the spread of vice. The second part of his program was to take gun permits away from as many of the city's permit holders as possible. It was

73

estimated that 20% of the male residents of Des Moines at that time held gun permits and John B. didn't like that statistic one bit. There were 55 special policemen running on the streets (sort of early day rent-a-cops) and John B. wanted their badges pulled. He also opened a police substation at the state fairgrounds on the far east side of the city.

By mid-April, Hammond's plan was well under way. Over the Easter weekend, police arrested 101 men and women. Half were drunks, one a wife beater, two traffic violators and the rest gamblers and prostitutes. Chief Hammond's "no bail" rule was now expanded to include all sorts of desperadoes; police had a hard time finding places in which to house their overnight guests. Three weeks later, Hammond ordered his troops to go through the same program once again. This time they nabbed 94 malfeasants.

Not long after his appointment, John B. moved himself and his family into the police headquarters building. They had the third floor converted into living quarters. He believed in staying as close to his troops as possible at all times. One night in the summer of 1922, he tiptoed out of the headquarters building and went down to the Court Avenue bridge. A few minutes later the boys at the station heard someone yelling for help. They ran out of the station to find John B. in his night shirt and bedroom slippers. Just trying to keep the night shift on its toes, he said.

In July John B. changed directions, announcing that he and his troops would support striking railroad workers. Early that month the railroad shop workers had gone out on strike all over the country. Since there were five or six railroads operating in central Iowa at the time, the strike would have a major impact in Des Moines, especially if it

were prolonged by the railroad companies' use of strikebreakers. When he came out on the side of the union, Hammond announced that strikebreakers would not be welcome in Des Moines. His edict to any stranger in town who came to work in the shops during the strike was "out of town or in jail". The result was a relatively peaceful strike in the capital city. The railroad strike finally ended nationwide early in September 1922, after the federal government threatened to take over and run the railroads.

Later in July, John B.'s son, William, made the news. William had gone to a lunchroom on the east side one afternoon. When he sat down, he noticed that another customer had what looked like a pistol under his shirt. Hammond Jr. jumped up from his seat and announced that he was placing the man, William Ryan, under arrest. The younger Hammond was a short, slender fellow with a bit of a big mouth, and this time he'd tried to take someone bigger and tougher than he.

After Ryan tossed Hammond around for a few minutes, it became obvious to the smaller man that he wasn't going to get the job done by himself. Failing to get any help from onlookers, he tried to pull his gun. Ryan was an ex-army man who'd been in the government sanatorium in Colfax. He might have been a little on the loony side but he wasn't stupid. When no one came to aid young Hammond, he took the gun away from the boy, handed it to the owner of the diner, and ran out the front door. Two patrolmen who were in the neighborhood ran him down and toted him off to the police station. William Hammond was taken to Mercy Hospital for examination. Ryan must have given the younger Hammond at least one good crack: both the boy's eyes were swollen shut by the time he got to the hospital.

John B. needed someone to blame for the whole mess other than an ex-army man, and since nobody had stepped up to help his son during the scuffle, the lunchroom spectators

were a likely bunch. No one seemed to know who those folks were, so he decided on the next best thing and arrested the owner of the lunchroom, Peter Kotchweis.

At that time Des Moines had a fairly size-

John MacVicar, 1922

able Greek community, of which Kotchweis was a member in good standing. When Kotchweis' Greek friends went to police headquarters to bail him out of jail, Hammond met them near the front door. They tried to tell the chief that Kotchweis was a respectable businessman and should be allowed out on bail. Hammond's response was that he had "never met a respectable Greek." He tried later to play down the incident by claiming he'd never met any Greek before joining the police department, and that the only ones that he'd met since that time had been under arrest, and so on. (John B. spent a lot of his time explaining away his public gaffes.)

By October everyone in town had an opinion about how well or how poorly Hammond was doing on the job. His only real support on the city council was from John MacVicar—which stood to reason since it was MacVicar who had hired him in the first place. The other council members were trying their best to stay out of the controversies that the chief continually talked himself into. The city's churches, of course, supported him and organized labor, or at least organized labor's spokesmen, also came out in his favor. His support of labor during the past summer's strike had paid off.

Nearly everyone else was either completely anti-Hammond or at least disappointed in the job that he'd been doing. In mid-October the editor of *The Des Moines Tribune* charged him in court with incompetence and misconduct. That case made it as far as the city council chambers. In November, the councilmen passed a resolution to replace John B. A day or two later they rescinded that resolution and placed Hammond on probation for 90 days. He kept his mouth shut and his nose clean for those three months and the probation was lifted on February 4, 1923.

Three weeks later the editor of a local magazine charged Hammond with being a member of the Ku Klux Klan. The charge wasn't as far-fetched as one might think; in 1924 the Klan was at the height of its power and influence in the U.S. They had nearly four million members throughout the country, many of whom held elective positions at all levels of government. The order had a fair amount of influence in Iowa, as it had anywhere else in the United States, but sometimes those members who held public office chose to keep their affiliation under wraps.

Chief Hammond made a brief response in which he did not deny Klan membership, but stated that he'd never received any literature or attended any of their speeches. It was never shown positively that Hammond was a member of the Klan, but over the next several months he received Klan backing and support.

John B. announced in late fall that he intended to run for the city council seat that was being vacated by John MacVicar. Klan spokesmen came out in favor of Hammond for the commissioner's council seat, as did a number of the city's church leaders.

In March 1924, the partnership between Hammond and MacVicar that had been so strong in the past suddenly fell completely apart. In mid-month Hammond ordered a liquor raid on the Star Dress Club, an ostentatiously private social club, that was located at 421 3rd Street, about where the Civic Center Court apartments are today.

The raiders were four members of the liquor squad known around town as the "Big Four," led by Detective Steve Howard. They first asked for permission to enter the club, but when owner C.A. Godwin refused, they broke the glass out of the front door and went in anyway. The police report's description of the place left no doubt that it was a speakeasy. The single room had three tables, a few chairs and an icebox along with a bunch of booze. Tables, chairs and ice boxes weren't illegal but booze was.

Several days after the raid, Godwin filed assault and battery charges against Howard. He claimed Howard had hit him over the head with his fist. MacVicar entered the resulting political fracas when he called Hammond in and demanded the chief fire Howard for using unnecessary violence.

Hammond refused, and in a huff turned in a letter of resignation to the city council. In a blatant attempt to grab votes in the coming election he leveled a blast at MacVicar, accusing the commissioner of caving in to a mysterious "whiskey ring." Within a day, Hammond had a change of heart about the resignation and withdrew it. The city council had taken no action on it anyway.

In the meantime, voters had re-elected Carl Garver as mayor and had elected John Jenney to the council. Jenney was slated to become the new Commissioner of Public Safety. All this meant that both MacVicar and Hammond would be unemployed come April 1, about three weeks away.

The whole brouhaha eventually turned out to be an exercise in futility. MacVicar had filed misconduct charges against Howard before

the election, but the detective's civil service hearing wasn't scheduled until March 27, nearly two weeks after the election. Pending the hearing, Howard was suspended from the police force. By the time the hearing date rolled around, MacVicar apparently had lost interest. Since he would be out of city government in just a few days, MacVicar probably thought the hearing was a waste of his time. He never showed up and Howard was reinstated by the Civil Service Commission.

Upon taking office, the new public safety commissioner John Jenney suggested

John Jenney, 1928

that his choice as a replacement for Hammond would be the current chief of detectives, Sherman Delmege, a long-time member of the police force. Jenney's announcement drew an immediate blast from the mayor and the rest of the city council, since Delmege was rumored to be a member of the KKK. Jenney was told in no uncertain terms that he was not to appoint any man with ties of any sort to the Klan. The Klan responded by circulating recall election petitions against Garver and the other council members who were standing in opposition to Jenney. Nothing came of the Klan's efforts and, having lost his political backing, Jenney caved in to the rest of the council and named James Cavender as the new chief on April 7, 1924.

John B. lost his quarters at the police station. He moved his family to an acreage out on Hickman Avenue and vowed that he wanted nothing more than to work in his garden. He was out of politics, he said, but still intended to be active in the reform movement. Beginning in December 1924, that activity consisted of going after druggists in the Waterloo area for selling booze. He was acting in the capacity of "private dry raider," since no law enforcement agency had recruited him after his term as Des Moines' police chief.

By October 1925, he'd found a new cause. The World Purity Federation had again hired him to undertake another campaign against prostitution. Hammond directed his fire against apartment living, since apartment houses were the greatest menace to the morals of any community in those days, according to John B.

John B.'s railings on the evils of apartment houses bore little fruit. Within two months, he was back at work for the "dry" cause as a special investigator for the Des Moines police and the Polk County Sheriff's Office. Before Christmas 1925 he led an epic raid on the Kresge and Woolworth dime stores in downtown Des Moines. While completely surrounded by hordes of Christmas shoppers, the raiders valiantly seized several cases of bay rum.

The police chief, James Cavender, called the whole episode "bunk" and ordered the shaving lotion returned. John B. accused Cavender of being in cahoots with the bootleggers and called for his ouster. Cavender then had John B. arrested and tossed into jail for criminal slander, but he was quickly released.

In the late fall of 1926, Hammond decided to take his show on the road. He'd been named superintendent of law enforcement for the New York Civic League, a prohibition enforcement agency that had previously been active in the licensing and control of horse racing and moving pictures in New York state. John B. was going to dry up the Empire State, an ambitious undertaking for any 71-year-old. He lasted until June 1927.

By the election of 1932, the tide had turned against reformers and reform movements. Prohibition would last only a few more months. The national change-of-heart did not faze Hammond, though. Back in Iowa after his short-lived stay in New York, he con-

GERALD PICKETT
Appointed: 19 March 1923
Died: 24 September 1925

Patrolman Pickett, a motorcycle officer, was headed north on East 30th Street on the afternoon of 24 September. As he approached the intersection of East 30th and Maury, a sand truck driven by G. Cavender that was southbound on East 30th turned directly in front of his motorcycle. Officer Pickett was thrown against the truck, suffering internal and severe head injuries. He was rushed to the hospital, where doctors worked for three hours to try and save his life. He died that evening.

Mr. Cavender, an "old and trusted employee" of the sand company, reported to the station promptly as requested by detectives. He was not charged in the crash. ✪

JAMES STAGGS
Appointed: 26 March 1923
Died: 20 April 1928

Officers Staggs and Fred Davis were headed back to the station in their patrol car with a prisoner they had arrested for intoxication. They observed a sedan ahead of them zigzagging back and forth. Assuming the driver of the sedan was drunk, Staggs proceeded to draw up next to the car in an attempt to pull it over. The sedan suddenly swung toward the patrol car, forcing it to veer sharply to the left. At that moment a 6th Avenue streetcar was about to pass the two autos and Staggs turned his car directly into its path.

Officer Staggs' head was crushed and he lived only a few minutes. Officer Davis received a head wound and a skull fracture, and their prisoner had cuts and a skull fracture. ✪

tinued his campaigns against a host of evils: near beer, ginger ale, bay rum (again), apartment houses (again as well), prize fighting and horse racing. He was able to secure the Prohibitionist Party's nomination for governor in 1932 but lost to Clyde Herring. He polled only 1,415 votes statewide.

Old John B. died in June of 1940 at Lutheran Hospital in Des Moines. By the end of his life, he had taken the idea of moral reform to a whole new level of ridiculousness. He was 84 years old but still as active in the cause as ever. Just before his death, he

tried to organize the 18th Amendment Rescue Association, a futile attempt by a few die-hard, old time "dries" to bring Prohibition back. He'd outlived his old boss and political enemy, John MacVicar, by more than ten years.

As described by local writer Rider Richmond, "Des Moines never before, and probably never again will have another police chief quite like John B. Hammond." ✪

"A Unique Ability to Get Himself Into No End of Trouble"
Patrolman Charles A. Bryant

BY PEGGY SCHLEUGER AND W.L. JOHNSON

On June 6th, 1918, Charles A. Bryant was appointed to the Des Moines Police Department. There is little personal information that survives; he had been a mechanical shop foreman and school teacher, he hailed from Trenton, Nebraska and was married to Elizabeth Greenwood Bryant. He resided at 2004 22nd in the city.

A group photograph in the 1921 "Ball Book" shows Bryant as an average-looking policeman of unremarkable appearance, middle-aged, stoop-shouldered with a slight pot belly and a direct gaze. Officer Bryant would prove remarkable in only one respect: a unique ability to get himself and others into no end of trouble.

Bryant's first few years as a police officer passed without incident, but beginning in 1921 Charles A. Bryant dedicated himself to making life miserable for Chief of Police John B. Hammond.

It began innocuously enough. The first recorded complaint about Officer Bryant occurred on November 6th, 1921 while Bryant was attending a funeral. When the flag passed by, Bryant neglected to remove his hat. When a nearby overseas soldier remarked on the oversight, Bryant told him to mind his own business. The soldier subsequently complained to R.C. Saunders, the chief of police.

On April 17th, 1922, a complaint was received from Vernon C. Koons, a lawyer, who alleged that Bryant had failed to pay two notes at the Citizens Bank of Lorimar, Iowa, dating from 1920. This type of complaint was not at all unusual in those difficult financial times. Creditors often used police administration as leverage to get careless officers to meet obligations, and somewhat understandably, a police chief would try to avoid being utilized as a collection agency.

Chief Hammond responded that the notes were not incurred during his tenure as chief and that his department would not function as a collection agency, advising Mr. Koons to adopt some other means of making collection. Hammond's troubles with Bryant were just beginning.

Bryant was assigned in the traffic department as a beat officer, but soon ran afoul of Chief Hammond again with excessive absences from work. When Hammond's eyebrows began to raise, Bryant pleaded a foot problem which would necessitate an immediate transfer to less taxing duty. Hammond sent Bryant to doctors who promptly reported nothing wrong with the officer. On July 21, 1922, Chief Hammond advised Bryant of the doctors' findings noting that Bryant hadn't suffered so much as sunstroke and refused the transfer.

Bryant was returned to his walking beat of six blocks in the west loop, from Walnut to Chestnut, 4th to 6th Avenue.

A November 15, 1922 letter from John MacVicar, Superintendent, Department of Public Safety, to John B. Hammond related reliable information alleging that Bryant had unduly interfered with commerce in the Wilkins Bros. Store, when he was called to mediate a dispute between an unhappy customer and Mrs. Catherine Kennedy, manager of the hair goods department at Wilkins.

In a sworn affidavit, Mrs. Kennedy related that a lady customer purchased "some hair" but returned the next day and demanded the return of her money. Mrs. Kennedy declined to refund the money, citing laws which forbid the return of merchandise such as hair for "sanitary reasons."

The customer became indignant and left but soon returned with Officer Bryant who "refused to listen to the facts of the case" and threatened to arrest Mrs. Kennedy if she did not refund the purchase price. Mrs. Kennedy did so but later complained to the safety commissioner.

While Chief Hammond was reassigning Bryant from traffic officer to night patrolman, Bryant's wife, Elizabeth, divorced her husband on the grounds of cruel and inhuman treatment. Bryant took up residence as a single man at the Manhattan Hotel, which probably did nothing to improve his disposition but did set him up for his next indiscretion.

Several forgers who hit town from Minneapolis lodged at the Manhattan Hotel and quickly defrauded a number of local merchants including the Frankels, Younkers and Wilkins Brothers stores and the Fort Des Moines Hotel.

The party consisted of two men and two women who were posing as married couples and apparently were befriended by Officer Bryant.

Meanwhile, when the Frankels

Charles A. Bryant

store discovered the worthless checks and reported them to the police, one of the women was arrested and jailed. The next morning the officer and one of the forgers made the rounds to each store, took up all the forged checks and compromised each case. The band could not now be prosecuted as they had "voluntarily" returned to offer cash settlements.

Bryant then called up his superiors in the detective division and told them what he had done. An outraged chief of detectives ordered Bryant to bring his companion to the station, where the man was thrown in jail for a short time anyway. The case was hopelessly damaged however, and within a few days the forgers left town.

Meanwhile, the formidable John B. Hammond, Chief of Police, received yet another complaint involving Mr. Bryant.

One Robert Hughes of the Riley Apartments called to complain that an officer using "a clumsy story of protection" appeared at his apartment during Mr. Hughes absence and told Hughes' wife that he was "acting under the instructions of Assistant Chief of Police J.A. Newell and that he was calling to warn Mrs. Hughes that she was to be attacked by some unknown men." Mrs. Hughes became suspicious and told her husband, who reported it to the police chief. Police investigators produced a photograph of Bryant which was duly identified by Mrs. Hughes. Assistant Chief Newell repudiated any connection with Bryant and flatly denied having given the officer any such instructions regarding Mrs. Hughes.

That was more than enough for Chief Hammond, and on February 5, 1923 he fired Bryant. "I have the honor to notify you herewith that I have this day discharged from police service Officer Charles Bryant, for conduct unbecoming a member of the Police Department," Hammond wrote to MacVicar.

Bryant, however, was not to be disposed of so easily. He filed an appeal with the Civil Service Commission, continued working and eventually succeeded in regaining his job.

The night of February 7, 1923, was the Annual Policeman's Ball held at the Coliseum at 2nd and Grand Avenues. Bryant, as well as many other policemen attended, as did many notables of city society, as well as average citizens.

One such citizen was Guy "Speedy" Lane, a barber by trade and a resident of the Palm Hotel. According to Lane, he had known Bryant from a year and a half before when Lane had been "protecting two girls from a drunk man who was threatening them with a knife because they would not accompany him." Lane punched the drunk just before Officer Bryant showed up, indicated that the drunk was a friend of his, and tried to arrest Lane.

Lane explained the circumstances but Bryant still wanted to arrest him. Fortunately,

another officer came along and advised Bryant that he shouldn't arrest Lane without also arresting the other fellow. Bryant finally released them both.

But bad blood must have lingered when Bryant encountered Lane at the Policeman's Ball. They got into an argument on the dance floor, whereupon Bryant invited Lane into the men's toilet to "fight it out."

To the lavatory they went, where Bryant swung at Lane two or three times but missed. Lane retaliated by striking Bryant twice before Bryant jerked out his star and said that he would "show Lane who he was."

At this point a man named G.M. Perham, entered the toilet and rushed between Bryant and Lane to stop the fight. Perham was soon assisted in stopping the fight by two other men, John Kennard and Charles Connors.

Kennard advised the combatants to leave the men's room and everyone returned to the dance floor but Bryant, who could not find his star, which had disappeared during the melee.

Traffic Officer Wilson Skinner on horseback in downtown Des Moines, 1921

Later that evening while still on the dance floor, Bryant had another officer arrest Speedy Lane and Perham, the man who intervened in the fight, along with Kennard for good measure. The men were hauled to the pokey where they remained overnight. They were released the next morning after Chief Hammond had investigated. Although they spent a night in jail, they were never charged, arraigned, or fined. By February 13, they and several witnesses were signing affidavits against Officer Bryant. John B. Hammond once again asked Bryant for his badge but Bryant had lost it in the men's room.

Shortly thereafter Charles Bryant was reassigned to traffic control on the 6th Avenue river bridge, which was undergoing repairs. Less than two months later, on April 4, 1923, Bryant was working this assignment at the north end of the bridge when a vehicle driven by F.R. Porter with passenger Charles Dallemand approached southbound and was stopped at the bridge by Bryant.

Bryant directed them to cross over on the other side of the street in order to get by a parked ice wagon and then to drive down onto Birdland Drive. Whether Porter misunderstood Bryant's instructions or took exception to the officer's manner is unclear. He went around the ice wagon and then proceeded south over the bridge. He had gone about 100 feet when two shots rang out, causing him to stop his auto post haste.

Bryant rushed up to the car and in a "very excited manner" informed Porter that his was the third car which had tried to disobey his orders by crossing the bridge and that "he was going to see that there were no more such tactics pulled on him." Porter was temporarily cowed and quickly backed up his vehicle and went down Birdland Drive according to Bryant's instructions. Three days later, however, both Porter and his passenger were signing affidavits in the office of a livid John B. Hammond, Chief of Police. If Charles Bryant hadn't found his star, he had

discovered his gun.

Hammond sent an investigator to the bridge in an effort to document the incident, who soon cornered Mr. P. Shaffer, who was employed at the bridge as a trackman for the Des Moines City Railway. Shaffer confirmed Porter's story, saying he saw Bryant pull his pistol and fire two shots in the air before giving foot chase to Porter's vehicle.

Moreover, Shaffer was eager to talk of other things and said that he had known Officer Charles Bryant for some time, "ever since he ran for city councilman," and for the past, three weeks they had shared the trackmans shanty with him at the north end of the bridge. Shaffer further related that about a week earlier, during a snow flurry, he and Bryant were sitting in the shanty when Bryant suddenly pulled his gun from his holster and deliberately fired a shot through the side of the shanty. The direction of the bullet was "eastward toward the gun club and past the sidewalk which ran parallel with the

Des Moines Detectives,
left to right: **John McGrath,**
F.E. "Biddie" Timmons,
Inspector Carl Vonn and
Byron Johnson with slot
machine confiscated in a
gambling raid, 1928

shanty, about four feet off the ground as evidenced by the hole in the wall."

Shaffer continued: "A few days later, while I was outside the shanty, I heard a shot and as I went into the shanty. Bryant had his gun in his hand and there was a hole in the roof of the shanty. The next morning or two later, Bryant was again in the shanty with me, shooting toward the ground into a keg which is used for a seat."

He seemed to derive some pleasure out of these actions and kidded me about shooting the cigarette I was smoking out of my mouth."

Shaffer began spending most of his time on the south side of the bridge, and being cautious about presenting his profile with a cigarette dangling from his lip. With or without his star, Bryant was a thoroughly dangerous man.

When Bryant used his gun to stop the motorist on 6th Avenue Bridge on the morning of April 4, John Hammond gnashed his teeth. By that very afternoon, however, Hammond probably had no teeth left to gnash, because Charles Bryant was farther south on 6th Avenue giving yet another demonstration of his unique ability to deal with people.

Enter John L. Thompson, a local black attorney and Boy Scout Leader, who happened to be driving his Dodge touring car with his wife from their home at 1306 20th to his office.

At 6th and School, Thompson turned south and was following traffic at about 15 mph when he noticed a small Ford Speedster pull up beside him. Thompson noticed that the single seater speedster was packed with two children and a woman in addition to the driver. He pulled to the curb to let the speedster pass but it did not.

One block farther at 6th and Crocker, the little Ford racer suddenly shot up past Thompson's Dodge and whipped in front, forcing Thompson to the curb and tearing off the left front of Thompson's bumper.

According to Thompson's affidavit, filed several days later, the driver of the speedster jumped out and approached him. "I noticed on his approach that he wore the uniform of our local police force," wrote Thompson, "and a closer scrutiny showed his badge number as 24." (Charles Bryant had apparently recovered his star or received another.)

Thompson continued his narrative:

"Without any scruples for the presence of my wife he began cursing and swearing and abused us with his language. I asked him what I had done. He did not answer but grabbed the bumper which had already been damaged and tore it completely off, throwing it against the corner of the curb and remarking that he wished he had damaged the car worse."

Some of the witnesses to the incident took Bryant to task for his actions and placed the blame on him. Bryant commanded them to "shut up" and threatened that he would arrest them if they did not.

Thompson and the on-lookers concluded that the police officer was either drunk or crazy, but Bryant was determined to enforce the fledgling traffic laws. He arrested Thompson and took him to the Traffic Bureau where he was booked.

When Chief John B. Hammond discovered the unfortunate lawyer he promptly released him, tearing up the booking slip.

As soon as Charles Bryant heard about that, he went out and re-arrested Thompson on the same charge (operating a motor vehicle in a careless and imprudent manner) and hauled him in front of the Honorable Herman Zeuch, Judge of Municipal Court.

Surprisingly, on April 16, Judge Zeuch found Thompson guilty and fined him $10 even though Chief Hammond had once again fired Bryant five days earlier. Bryant appealed to the Civil Service Commission on April 12.

The next day the long-suffering police chief received another complaint against Bryant, this one from Dick Greco, a grocer at 7th and University. Greco alleged that Bryant bought $15.82 worth of groceries and cigars on credit, obtaining wholesale prices by showing his badge.

Bryant then filed a statement with the city council arguing it oust Chief Hammond for his release of John Thompson. Bryant alleged that Hammonds' act was illegal, citing Thompson's subsequent conviction in front of Judge Zeuch, and accused Hammond of abusing and exceeding his authority. For good measure he called the police chief "unfit and incompetent," and urged the city council to replace him with a man fitted for work, who would be "competent, fearless, impartial, unprejudiced and who will encourage the present members of the police department to perform their sworn duty without fear or favor."

Hammond answered in a fiery letter that he had known the lawyer for years to be reliable and truthful man, and would accept Thompson's statements over Officer Bryant's. Hammond also had a number of affidavits from witnesses that supported Thompson.

"Mr. Bryant has been a continual annoyance to this office on account of the great number of complaints that come to me about his conduct," wrote Hammond, "and it does not appear to me that his work is very reliable."

He noted further that the court case in which Mr. Thompson was found guilty was "very poorly presented" and important evidence on behalf of Thompson was not even introduced.

"I have no apologies to make to Mr. Bryant or anybody else" declared Hammond. He gathered up his ammunition and marched to the Civil Service hearing on the matter of the firing of Charles A. Bryant.

The city council backed the police chief and at long last, so did the Civil Service Commission. On June 9, 1923 a letter was sent to Bryant at the Manhattan Hotel that ordered him to turn in his star. The letter came back unclaimed—Charles A. Bryant had checked out. ✪

Supt. John Jenney and Staff, 1925
Top row, left to right: **Capt. M.J. Donoghue, Sgt. E.L. Lee, C.A. Nichols, Albert Wieland, Albert Foley, T.J. Hubbard**
Middle row, left to right: **Walter Griggs, Wilson Skinner, Edward Ward, Tom Cross, Frank Pierce, Victor Smith, Pete Welsh**
Front row, left to right: **Lloyd Brown, L.L. Eklund, Supt. John W. Jenney, Chief James Cavender, Roy Chamberlain, Carl Vonn**

Police Chief Roy Chamberlain driving Supt. John Jenney, circa 1927

Des Moines Police Shotgun Squad, left to right: **Ben Ward, unidentified, Henry Van Grud, Tony Blacksmith, 1928**

Motor equipment of the Des Moines Police Department, 1930

Police Ambulance, 1936

*Des Moines Police Department Radio Broadcasting Room
Telephone Operator Jennie Thomas and Radio Operator Jack Wills, 1930s*

Radio Control Panel, 1930s

Reprint: *The DM Register*, July 26, 1929

DES MOINES HASN'T ANY SPEED LIMIT FOR AUTOMOBILES, CITY SOLICITOR FINDS
SO MOTORCYCLE COPS CANNOT ARREST YOU—BUT THEY WILL

BY RICHARD L WILSON

The theory is that a motorist can drive down University avenue at a cruising speed of eighty-six miles an hour, wave blithely at a traffic policeman and go scot free.

The announcement Thursday by City Solicitor F.T. Van Liew that Des Moines technically is without a speed limit, and discussion prior to that in the municipal court, has given birth to many strange ideas.

OLD LAW IS INVALID
The facts are these, according to the city solicitor:

Until a new traffic ordinance is passed and residence, school and suburban districts are plainly set out, there is no speed limit in Des Moines, because

1. The old city ordinance is no longer valid since the state law specifically describes the manner in which the various speed districts within the city shall be determined.

2. The state law cannot go into effect on the clauses wherein it applies to cities because the districts have not been described or marked plainly as is specified by the statute.

THERE IS A STATE LAW.
The city solicitor made these declarations after a conference with Chief of Police Alber and Traffic Inspector Clark. Technically, he said, persons cannot be arrested in this city on a charge of speeding until a new ordinance which complies with the new state law is drafted and passed. Meantime there is a clause in the old ordinance which complies with the statute and levies a $100 fine for careless and imprudent driving. Speeding can be construed as careless and imprudent driving.

The new state law, as it applies to speeding in cities, provides for the description and marking of a residence district with a speed limit of twenty-five miles an hour, a business district with a speed limit of fifteen miles an hour and school district with a speed limit of fifteen miles an hour and a suburban district with no speed limit at all. So far these districts have not been described.

THIS STATE LAW PROVIDES:
The provisions in the state law are that a business district is a territory contiguous to a highway when 50 per cent, or more, of its frontage for a distance of 300 feet or more is occupied by buildings in use for business; a school district is a territory contiguous to the highway for a distance of 200 feet in either direction from a school house; a residence district is a territory contiguous to a highway not comprising a business district or a school district where 40 per cent or more of the frontage on such a highway for a distance of 300 feet or more is occupied by dwellings or buildings in use for business; a suburban district is all the rest of the town.

Now it rests upon the police department to count the houses and describe the districts in order that an ordinance may be passed. Van Liew announced he would write a letter to the chief of police requesting this service. The state, according to the law, will place signs on all state highways leading into the city, but it is only required to place these signs at the city limits.

NOW, DON'T SPEED
It is calculated that the new law will move the limits of the suburban district on main traveled roads in toward the heart of the city for a considerable distance. In this manner there will be no speed limit, even after the ordinance is passed, on the fringes of the city. The careless and imprudent driving clause will check speeders there.

But meantime don't let anyone tell you the police can't arrest you for driving too fast. Perhaps they can't, but they will. ✪

Chief of Police Roy Chamberlain, Sgt. E.L. Lee and T.J. Hubbard, 1927

Police Motorcycle Squad on Harley Davidsons, *front row:* **Edwin Lower, Elza Heaton, Sidney Pearce, Lawrence Mahaffey, Arthur Shores, Orris Gilbert, Charles Antrim, J.C. Heefner, Louis Hardenbrook, Sgt. Rupert Shepherd, E.L. Lee** *standing:* **Leslie Clark, T.J. Hubbard, Police Chief Roy Chamberlain, 1927**

A SHOOTOUT WITH BONNIE AND CLYDE
THE WAGES OF SIN

BY PAMELA SHAPIRO

Sure, you've seen the pictures. Clyde Barrow squinting into the sun, kneeling in front of a black Ford with guns hung on the grill; Bonnie Parker with a cigar in her mouth and a revolver on her hip. You've seen those pictures and heard a few vague stories of another time and place, and you think you know Bonnie and Clyde.

Bonnie Parker was no hardened gunslinger. Five feet tall and weighing less than 100 pounds, she didn't look very scary. Actually, the passably pretty strawberry blonde

Bonnie Parker

Clyde Barrow

had dreams of glory as an entertainer or poet, and liked being the center of attention.

Her boyfriend, Clyde Barrow, wasn't much more frightening. He was only seven inches taller than Bonnie, and when he died on a quiet Louisiana road at age 25, he still looked like somebody's kid brother.

The two of them, along with an ever-changing cast of companions, were responsible for a two-year trail of robberies, car thefts, kidnappings and murders that included the deaths of eight police officers and a jailer. Time and a few movies have turned them into pop icons, but they were actually just a couple of punks with itchy fingers. They were a product of their time, nothing more.

And when time caught up to Clyde's brother, Buck, in a Dexter, Iowa amusement park, Des Moines police officers were there.

HARD TIMES

The New York stock market crashed in October 1929, sending America into a depression only World War II would eventually pull

W.D. Jones

it out of. This calamity would have been enough of a disaster by itself, but it coincided with the worst drought of the twentieth century, resulting in the loss of thousands of farms across the heartland. Farmers who had borrowed from the banks found themselves unable to repay their loans, and the banks had no choice but to foreclose on their property. Add to that the failure of too many banks,

taking with them the meager savings of too many trusting citizens, and the country was quite willing to cheer on a group of bank robbers who gave Big Business what it deserved.

Clyde Barrow was first and foremost a car thief. He was a good driver and liked the power and speed a car gave him. He also liked nice clothes and the other things only money could get, and in 1930 he was sent to prison for the first time: 14 years for burglary. When Bonnie went to visit him in prison at Waco, Texas, he and his cellmate, William Turner, outlined a plan where she would go to Turner's parents' house, get his gun, and smuggle it into the jail. She did as they asked, and on March 9, 1930, they walked out of the prison. From that point on, Bonnie was in it as deep as Barrow.

They traveled the roads in a circle from their native Texas up through Oklahoma, Kansas, Missouri, Louisiana and back to Dallas to see their folks. Along the way they robbed banks, stores and gas stations, earning a reputation in the papers as almost super-

Des Moines Patrolman Sidney H. Pearce *(on right)* **helping to restrain Blanche Barrow at the site of the shootout in Dexter, Iowa, July 24, 1933**

Buck Barrow (on ground) **surrounded by posse after shootout in Dexter, Iowa**

human for their ability to shoot or drive their way out of every corner law enforcement managed to back them into. Bank robbers were not considered criminals by the public, as they felt the bank's money had all been stolen from its customers in the first place.

Then there was the thrill of a man and woman on the road, running from the law with nothing to protect them but each other and their Browning Automatics. Americans like that. The "Bloody Barrow Gang" was a source of excitement and romance to a newspaper-reading public desperate for anything to talk about other than the daily dire struggle to feed their children.

A CLOSE CALL

Clyde, Bonnie, Buck, Buck's wife Blanche and a teen-ager named W.D. Jones, stopped at the Red Crown Tourist Camp in Platt City, Missouri on the evening of July 18, 1933. They had spent the day holding up service stations in Kansas and they rented two cabins for the night. By the next morning, the desk clerk had gotten suspicious of the group and called the Missouri Highway Patrol.

At that point in its career, the Barrow gang (usually Clyde and Buck) had killed five cops and two citizens, and the entire Midwest law enforcement system was looking for them. The Platt City Police Department and

Platt County Sheriff's Office quickly gathered a posse and descended on the motel at 10:00 pm on Wednesday, July 19.

They parked an armored car in front of the attached garage containing the gang's only vehicle, and Sheriff Holt Coffey banged on the door and demanded to speak to the men inside. Blanche yelled back that they were sleeping in the other room, as the group snuck out the side door and into the car. W.D. told Clyde the door was blocked by an armored car, and Clyde responded by grabbing an automatic rifle and shooting through the garage door. Bullets hit the driver, Deputy George Highfill, and wounded him in the knees.

Buck was still in the cabin, and he opened fire on the lawmen standing outside. Their answering shots hit him twice in the head. Out in the garage, Clyde and W.D. were both firing their Browning automatics through the closed door; they wounded Sheriff Coffey. Blanche tried to get Buck out to the garage, but he was too heavy for her. Clyde dragged him into the car and jumped in the driver's seat. Telling W.D. to stand on the running board with his Browning, he hit the accelerator and burst through the closed garage door, W.D. spraying the officers with bullets. They fired back, shattering the windows.

Glass hit Blanche in the eyes. Clyde swerved around the patrol cars parked outside, and they got away.

Clyde drove out into the country and found an open field where he stopped to tend to Buck. His injuries were serious, but seeking help was out of the question. Clyde poured peroxide on the wounds and bundled everyone back in the car.

For the next two days, Clyde drove nearly without stopping. His band was in pretty sorry shape: Buck was certainly dying, and drifted only briefly into consciousness. Blanche still had shards of glass in her eyes and was in substantial pain. W.D. was wounded, and Bonnie had been badly burned in an accident some time before the Platt City shootout. They all needed rest.

At last, Clyde found a spot that looked promising: a quiet patch of woods about 25 miles west of Des Moines, in an area called Dexfield Park. The Middle Raccoon flowed nearby; fresh water and the cover afforded by the trees were exactly what Clyde was looking for.

Once they were settled, Clyde and W.D. drove into Perry to buy food and medicine, and to steal a second car. Upon returning, Clyde changed Buck and Bonnie's bandages, then he and Bonnie went for a drive to check the terrain. At a secluded spot away from the camp,

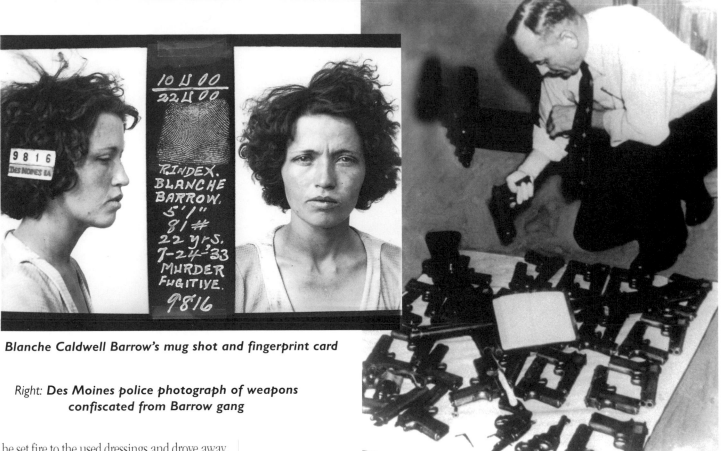

Blanche Caldwell Barrow's mug shot and fingerprint card

Right: **Des Moines police photograph of weapons confiscated from Barrow gang**

he set fire to the used dressings and drove away.

The Buck Stops Here

A few hours later, a local farmer named Homer Penn saw the partially burned bandages and recalled the radio broadcasts he had heard about the Barrow gang, who were suspected of being in the Dexter area. He called Sheriff Knee of the Dallas County Sheriff's Office. Knee immediately dispatched two deputies to locate the Barrows. They spotted them and telephoned Knee.

The sheriff worked through the night to assemble a posse that would eventually include members of the Iowa National Guard, the State Board of Investigation, Dallas County deputies, and Des Moines Patrolmen Odis Upchurch, Sidney Pearce, S.W. Seward, Ralph Brophy, Henry Van Grud, Omar Beardsley and Detectives Loren Miller and Lewis Hardenbrook.

Shortly before dawn on July 24, as the gang prepared to drive Buck home to Dallas, Bonnie spotted the approaching posse. She yelled to Clyde, who grabbed a Browning for himself and one for W.D. They opened fire on the lawmen, who began shooting back. Despite the barrage of bullets, all five gang members managed to get to the car, but as Clyde was driving away, a vigilante caught him in the arm with a shotgun blast. He lost control of

the car and it caught on a tree stump. He yelled for everyone to get in the second auto.

Clyde and W.D. continued to fire at the posse as Bonnie and Blanche tried to get Buck into the other vehicle. Bonnie was hit with buckshot; Buck was knocked to the ground twice by bullets; W.D. was hit by a bullet in the chest and pellets in the face. They still managed to reach the other car.

But before they could leave, the surrounding lawmen concentrated all their guns on that car. Bullets shattered the windows and punctured the gas tank. Clyde yelled for everyone to head for the trees, but Buck was hit yet again. This time it was too much, and he collapsed onto the ground. Blanche dropped down beside him, screaming for Clyde to help.

He tried, but was hit in the leg and shoulder; another bullet grazed the side of his head. As he staggered away after promising to return with another car, Blanche yelled to the lawmen to hold their fire. Bonnie, W.D. and Clyde disappeared into the bushes; at a nearby farm, they would soon steal a car from Valley Fellers and escape yet again.

For Buck, the trip was over. Blanche was

hysterical, yelling for a doctor, and as Des Moines Patrolman Pearce and Polk County Deputy L.E. Forbes pulled her away from her husband's side so his wounds could be checked, she fought their grasp. A *Des Moines Tribune* photographer, C.H. Schwartz, snapped a picture of her as she tried to twist away. It is a haunting photo of the rawest sort of news, a once-in-a-lifetime event at the moment it happened. Sixty-five years have in no way diminished its power.

Buck was taken to the hospital in Perry, where he died on July 29. Blanche stood trial in Missouri and served 15 years. Four surgeries were unable to save her right eye from the damage it sustained in Platt City. After she was released from prison, she retired to a legitimate life. She died in 1988, and is buried in Dallas.

On the day of her arrest, she was taken to the Des Moines Police Department to be processed by Identification Technician William Hammond. A brown folder with her mug shot and signed fingerprint card, labeled "Blanche Caldwell Barrow, Ident #9816," remains in the department's files. ✪

HONOR ROLL

HARRY OGILVIE
Appointed: 9 December 1919
Died: 12 July 1930

Officer Ogilvie was out riding with friends when he observed a car driving recklessly in the 2600 block of East Walnut. He got the car stopped, and as he approached it he was shot four times with a .45 caliber handgun. He died later that day.

His companions identified Russell G. Karlson as the gunman. He was arrested and charged with the murder of Officer Ogilvie. ✪

HONOR ROLL

RUPERT SHEPHERD
Appointed: 16 June 1923
Died: 1 August 1930

Sergeant Shepherd was critically injured as he rode his motorcycle across the streetcar tracks at 29th and University. Apparently, the tires of his motorcycle slid into the flangeway of the track, throwing him off balance. Trying to regain control, he swerved sharply, crashing into a steel trolley pole. He died as a result of a skull fracture suffered in the accident. ✪

HONOR ROLL

JAMES J. COWART
Appointed: 16 October 1922
Died: 7 December 1931

One day in 1926, Cowart had to use force when he arrested Arthur Thornton, a former county deputy. Five years later, there came a knock on Sgt. Cowart's front door. When he went out to answer it, a man standing in the yard fired a single shot through the glass-enclosed porch, striking Cowart in the stomach. Responding officers found Thornton fatally wounded in his automobile—the shotgun had apparently fired when he went to disassemble it. Cowart died the next day. ✪

Lawrence Mahaffey and 10 gallons of alcohol found in a Chevy coupe, 1930

F.E. "Biddie" Timmons, Lawrence Mahaffey and Roger C. West seized 64 gallons of alcohol at 2905 Hickman Avenue, 1928

INSPECTOR T.J. HUBBARD

BY PEGGY SCHLEUGER AND CAPT. W. L. JOHNSON

T. Jay Hubbard carried a lot of weight around Des Moines in the 1920s and early '30s, right up until the night he ate that double pork sandwich smothered with onions at the 7th and Grand Lunchroom.

Hubbard, a highly visible member of the Des Moines Police Department, had a gift for getting himself in the newspapers. As an inspector, a rank above captain which has since been abolished, and head of the department's Traffic Bureau, Hubbard was a public figure.

The darling of *The Des Moines Register,* he often appeared on those pages as a goodwill ambassador for downtown business interests, whether confessing that the *Register's* comic pages were responsible for his cheerful disposition, or inviting out-of-town motorists to ignore overtime parking restrictions to shop the loop. He was a portly man with a trademark smile who could still touch his toes (almost) for the photographers, even though he resembled a uniformed caricature of Al Capone.

He was head of the "Burial Society"* and his "big horn" was a favorite fixture at the Annual Policeman's Ball—a singular escape of those grim depression days, the event often sold more than 10,000 tickets. "He can turn down a supplicating over-parker with as broad a grin as ever graced an Irish face," read one babbling *Register* article.

Hubbard's rising star faded along with his famous grin on October 3, 1932, with another *Register* heading: "T.J. HUBBARD OUSTED FROM POLICE FORCE," followed by "Traffic Inspector Facing Charge by Girl, 20."

Alice Snook and her brother Kenneth had attended a dance in the loop the night before. After the dance Alice was to meet her brother and take the streetcar home. Kenneth had escorted another girl home and had not returned in time for the last streetcar. Alice couldn't find him.

She went to a cab stand at the Hotel Chamberlin and while she was engaging a cab to look for her brother, a man drove up beside them and ordered them to "move

T. Jay Hubbard

along." The taxi driver took Alice to look for her brother, explaining that the man who ordered him off the cab stand was Police Inspector T. Jay Hubbard. In those days cab stands were known contact points for prostitution and gambling, and a city ordinance prohibited cabs from lingering at hotel stands during early-morning hours.

The girl testified later that the man identified as Hubbard followed the cab to the east side and back downtown as she tried in vain to locate her brother. After she dismissed the cab, Hubbard allegedly drove up and ordered her into his car. She obeyed the order since she knew the man was a police officer. She expected him to take her home or to the police station. Instead, she charged, he drove to S.W. 28th and Park and attacked her. She eventually escaped from the car and ran screaming to a nearby house where she was taken in. She would later identify Hubbard as her assailant and describe an overpowering odor of onions on his breath.

Hubbard was arrested and fired from the police department, though he claimed it was

a case of mistaken identity. A sensational trial resulted. The state presented a chain of circumstantial evidence that included a report of the onion sandwich that witnesses testified Hubbard had eaten prior to the attack. Shoe impressions seemed to match those worn by Hubbard, and other evidence painted the jolly police inspector as the attacker. His wife testified that he had been at home.

On December 7, 1932, T. Jay Hubbard was found guilty. "Members of the crowd stood stupefied by the drama before them," the paper reported. A woman in the back of the courtroom fainted and Hubbard's wife collapsed and had to be helped to a couch. The case was prosecuted by a young attorney named Ray Harrison, later to become a long-time judge in the City's Municipal Court. Harrison was asking for life in prison.

He didn't get it. Hubbard was sentenced to 25 years at Fort Madison, but appealed the case to the Iowa Supreme Court. A new trial was granted and the case was back in a packed courtroom on December 3, 1934. Witnesses from the original trial were no longer available and memories had begun to fade. On December 12, 1934, Hubbard was acquitted. He had served a year and ten months in prison.

He never again played the big bass horn in the police band or graced the *Register* with his wide Irish smile. He lost his pension and faded from sight, his eventual fate unrecorded. The onions that smothered his double pork sandwich on that fateful night had also suffocated the splendid career of Police Inspector T. Jay Hubbard. ✪

*Today known as the Des Moines Police Burial Association.

HONOR ROLL

HARRY LINN BOOTON
Appointed: 26 September 1927
Died: 11 December 1932

Sergeant Booton and Det. George Cessna, two members of the "Booze Squad," observed a couple of suspicious men parked in front of a laundry and went to talk to them. Unbeknownst to them, the men were planning to rob the laundry, and as the officers exited their car, the suspects opened fire. Detective Cessna was grazed in the chest; Sgt. Booton suffered a severe bullet wound to the lower abdomen.

Investigating officers arrested three people and brought them to the hospital, where Sgt. Booton was able to identify one, Edward Farrant, 20, as the man who shot him. Booton died seven hours later.

Farrant was found guilty of murder and sentenced to life in prison. In December 1961, Governor Norman Erbe commuted his sentence to 90 years, making him eligible for parole. After serving 30 years for the murder of Sgt. Booton, Edward J. Farrant was released. ✪

NOT TALL ENOUGH
Patrolman Glen Barron who after more than a year's service on the force has again become the subject of a controversy [he] is said to be two inches shorter than regulations for a policeman. Barron is almost 5 feet 8 inches. The old regulations called for a height of 5 feet 9 inches but last June the Civil Service Commission changed the regulations to 5 feet 10 inches. The weight was also changed from 150 to 160 pounds. Barrons insists that his dismissal is for political reasons.

Reprint: *The DM Tribune,*
September 22, 1925

Hank Alber, 1929

LINE OF DUTY

BY RICHARD CROOK

For the past year, ever since March of 1935, Viola Moyer had been the cashier at the Belvedere Club. As jobs go it wasn't too bad. As a matter of fact, since Des Moines, along with most of the rest of the world, was wallowing in the depths of the Great Depression at the time, it was probably a pretty good job. Jobs of any sort were pretty hard to find in 1935.

Just about the time Viola started working at the Belvedere she met Steve Howard. Although sometimes their schedules didn't mesh very well, they had managed to stay together. Viola always went to work around five every evening and she didn't get off until about 2:30 the next morning. Steve worked days. He was a captain on the Des Moines Police Department and was usually off in the evenings.

He'd often go over to the Belvedere around 9:30 and have dinner with Viola, then go off someplace to fool around until she got off work. Sometimes he'd head off to some joint and sit around drinking with his cronies and sometimes he'd just go on back home and hang around there.

Steve joined the force in 1908 and had risen through the ranks more-or-less steadily over the following 27 years. He had one small setback in 1924 when he was suspended from duty after being charged with assault on the owner of a speakeasy on 3rd Street, the Star Dress Club. He wasn't suspended for very long, though. He was reinstated by the civil service commission after only a few weeks and had been in very little trouble since.

The evening of March 1, 1935 didn't seem to be much different than any other. Much of the winter snow had melted in the past week but there were still a few small patches here and there. Spring was still weeks away so it was cold after the sun set.

Howard showed up at the Belvedere as usual that night but he didn't stick around long. He told Viola that he was going to meet Oscar Hughes, an auto body and fender man at Hanifen's, at the Shrine for a couple of drinks and that he'd be back by the time she got off work, then he left.

Howard and Hughes hung around the Shrine for an hour or so then decided to go to Arvid Carlson's joint over on the east side. Carlson often invited friends to his place, the Unique Tavern at E. 18th and University, on Friday nights for a late oyster supper.

By the time the two friends got to the Unique most of the customers had already gone. Arvid Carlson was getting ready to take the day's receipts to the bank and he and his brother, Roy, were the only two people left inside the building. Carlson was relieved to see that it was Howard and Hughes coming through the front door and not a bunch of strangers. There had been a spate of robberies around the city during the past few weeks and Arvid was always a little nervous about carrying much money around.

A few minutes later Arvid walked out with the money leaving Steve Howard, Oscar Hughes and brother Roy in the tavern. The three men sat around until about 1:00 when Roy decided to close up for the night. None of the three men had anything else to do so they just sat drinking and b.s.-ing.

Just before 2:30 Howard got up to leave. He had to meet Viola at the Belvedere, he said, and needed to take off. That was all right with Oscar and Roy. They wanted to go home, too.

Roy snapped off the lights inside the building and held the door for his two friends. Steve Howard was the first to walk through. Just as he stepped down onto the concrete stoop in front of the tavern the other men heard a shot. Howard grunted and staggered back into the tavern. The gunman came in right behind him.

"Put up your hands", the man ordered. When a second robber walked into the tavern, they knew they'd better do what they were told. Howard was still conscious. He didn't seem to be hurt too badly and it appeared as though not too much harm had been done so far.

The two bandits ordered Carlson and Hughes to hand over all the money they had. It wasn't much. Hughes had a little over $50 on him and Carlson only had the little bit that had been left in the cash register after Arvid left. The gunmen directed the two to lie down on the floor near where Howard had fallen, then ran out the front door, slamming it shut, and disappeared.

Carlson called the police and asked for an ambulance for Howard who, although still on the floor, was conscious and talking. He was taken to Mercy Hospital for treatment. None of the three men who'd been victimized was able to identify either of the robbers. They thought the two men might have been around 5'9" and white. That was it.

In the meantime, Viola wasn't sure whether she should be a little miffed or not. Steve hadn't shown up at the Belvedere as he said he would. He was usually pretty good about that sort of thing. If he couldn't make it, he'd normally let her know.

When it became clear that he wasn't going to make it to the Belvedere that night Viola called a cab and left for her apartment. On the way she stopped at Brown's Drug Store at 15th and Grand for some cigarettes. Inside she ran into Officer John Dill, who told her that Howard had been shot. Stunned, she asked the cabby to drive her to the hospital.

Howard had been wounded more seriously than his two friends first thought. A .32- caliber bullet had been fired directly into his rib cage from only about a foot away, close enough to have left powder burns on his clothes and skin. It had missed all the large blood vessels in his chest but did manage to penetrate his right lung.

By the next evening, Howard seemed to be coming out of the woods. He'd lost a lot of blood and there was still the danger of infection but he was showing signs of improvement and by the next day he was able to talk with the investigators and reporters about the shooting. He continued to improve and by March 11 he was able to sit up in bed and eat his first substantial meal since being shot.

Appearances were deceiving back in those days, however. At around 6:30 that evening he suddenly slumped into a coma. His doctor was able to revive him but about an hour later he slipped into another coma, one from which he never recovered. Howard died at 7:40 on the evening of March 11, 1935 from a blood clot that developed near his heart.

Around 2:30 the following Friday morning Al Greenleaf was closing his restaurant, the Bonnie Café on E. 15th and Lyon, for the night. Just as he switched off the lights he noticed someone moving around on the sidewalk outside the building.

Greenleaf was taking no chances. Since the robbery over at the Unique, only about six blocks from his café, he'd begun carrying one of his pistols. Greenleaf was a member of the Des Moines Rifle Club and had owned a number of firearms over the years. He knew how to use every last one of them, too.

When he saw the shadow moving across his front window he drew his gun and stepped outside. Just as he stepped down to the sidewalk he heard the crack of a shot and felt the thunk of a bullet into the front wall of the café right next to him. Almost by reflex, he fired at the shadowy figure that he'd seen near the street. The man turned and ran away but Greenleaf stayed close behind.

Greenleaf followed the man for about a block and watched him go into a house at 1505 Lyon. When it became clear that the man wasn't going to come back outside, the café owner ran back to his restaurant and called the police. Responding officers found a man named Carroll "Chance" Barker lying in a bed in the home with a bullet hole in his stomach. Barker was whisked off to Broadlawns Hospital but by the time he got to the hospital he was in critical condition.

The DMPD learned that Barker had a lengthy arrest record. He'd just come back to Des Moines from Omaha where he'd been living since being released from the Nebraska State Penitentiary at Lincoln. He'd served five years there for shooting a man during the course of a holdup and prior to that he'd served a two-year stretch for burglary in the state prison in Oklahoma.

It isn't particularly easy to be a hard case when a man has a bullet hole in the belly but Barker did his best. When police questioned him after his surgery they could get nothing from him at all. He told them he'd been shot by someone somewhere down in the Southeast Bottoms but he wasn't entirely sure who it was. His name was the only information he divulged. Investigators found no weapons in the house with Barker.

As it happened, however, "Chance" Barker wasn't going to get off quite that easily. A man named William Milburn was raking leaves at a house near the Bonnie Café when he found a gun lying partially hidden in the winter-browned grass. It was a .32 automatic with a spent cartridge jammed in the extractor.

A police technician test fired the gun and compared the bullet with the one that had been taken from Steve Howard several days earlier. It was a match. They also located a man named Clyde Hayes who said he would testify that Barker had pawned that very same gun to him a month ago but had reclaimed it within the past couple of weeks.

Barker, of course, denied owning the gun or ever having been near either the Bonnie Café or the Unique Tavern when they were robbed. He claimed he'd been at a party at 1327 Stewart Street at the time Howard had been shot. Chance even gave police the names of a couple of people he claimed had seen him there but they didn't provide much of an alibi for him. One of the men told police that Barker had, in fact, been at the party that night but left with another person about midnight and didn't return until 3:00 am. The Stewart Street house was only a few blocks from the Unique Tavern so it appeared as though Barker had plenty of opportunity to do the crime. The police had almost enough to arrest him for Howard's killing.

The partygoer from the Stewart Street address gave the police another real interesting piece of information. He said that the person that Barker left the party with was a 16-year-old boy named Leroy Eubanks. Eubanks, the man said, lived in a shanty with a bunch of other people at 1401 E. 20th Street. A squad of policemen hit the E. 20th Street address shortly afterward and, sure enough, found Eubanks living there in a one room shanty with 10 other people.

The boy confessed to his part in the robbery immediately. He told investigators that he'd left the party with Barker and had gone to Barker's sister's home to drink beer. When they finished all the beer they had, they went over to the Unique to buy some more. When they saw that there were only a couple of people in the place Barker decided to rob it and was the one who'd shot Howard, Eubanks told them. That did it for the police. They charged both Eubanks and Barker with the robbery and with Howard's killing

Eubanks cooperated but Chance Barker sure didn't. Barker clammed up completely, claiming he knew he was going to die from his gunshot wound and could see no advantage to admitting to anything. He was right about one thing; he wasn't going to survive the gunshot. Chance Barker died of his wounds on April 2, 1935. Leroy Eubanks would be the only person tried for Howard's murder. The boy was sentenced to 20 years down at the Fort. ✪

Top step, left to right: **Inspectors Carl Vonn, Leslie Clark, Police Chief Hank Alber and A.H. Pedersen**
Third step, left to right: **Telephone operators Grace Mattern, Mildred Ofterdinger**
Second step, left to right: **Detective stenographers Irene Rinker, Mary Colavecchio**
First step, left to right: **Matrons Katherine McCarthy, Jennie Manbeck, Marie Brockmeier,**
circa 1929

MOBSTERS

BY RICHARD CROOK

In 1928, Prohibition was still the law of the land, but like everywhere else in the country, it was hard to convince many people in Iowa to obey something so obviously silly.

They wanted booze, they wanted to gamble, they liked having working girls on hand, and there were plenty of people around Des Moines ready and able to provide all three. The Capone crowd had taken charge of the distribution of alcohol throughout the Midwest early in the decade, and by 1928 owned or controlled most of the brothels, casinos and saloons in a number of states including Iowa.

Al Capone controlled most of the criminal activity in Iowa

In Des Moines after 1935, they owned and operated the Club Belvedere at 615 High Street and supposedly had an interest in Cy's Moonlight Inn at 73rd and University. The Moonlight was known as the place to go dancing or drinking (illegally before 1933 and the repeal of Prohibition). The Club Belvedere, the only place in town at that time that had big name entertainment, drinking and gambling, was operated for a while by an up-and-coming young Chicago mobster named Charlie "Cherry Nose" Gioe.

Charlie Gioe "Cherry Nose" kept a low profile overseeing Capone's liquor, gambling and prostitution interests in Des Moines from 1928 1936

Born in Sicily, he had grown up in an Italian neighborhood on the west side of Chicago and become a soldier in the Al Capone organization. He'd always been considered by the law enforcement community to be a lower-level mobster than his better-known friends, but within his own circle he was considered a reliable "company man," someone who could be trusted to carry out assignments, keep quiet, mind his own business and provide an honest count for his bosses.

Like many of the mobsters with whom he would become associated with over the years, Cherry Nose became involved in all sorts of criminal activity: extortion, gambling, bootlegging, prostitution—and even murder, some said. During his lifetime he'd met and worked with most of the big names in the organized crime business: Al Capone and Frank Nitti in Chicago; Lempke Buchalter, Frank Costello, Meyer Lansky and Lucky Luciano in New York; and Bugsy Siegel in Los Angeles.

Described as the fourth-highest man in the Chicago syndicate in the late '40s, Cherry Nose originally made his bones overseeing Al Capone's gambling and prostitution interests in Des Moines. He lived in the capital city from about 1928 through 1936, sometimes going by the names Charles Veltrie or Charlie Joye.

His nightclubs were the "in places" to go and be seen with Des Moines' smart set. Ronald Reagan, who in 1933 was the new, handsome sports reporter for WHO radio, became a regular; he would spin out west in his brown Nash convertible with the top down to make a dramatic arrival at the Moonlight. Reagan was in the business of being noticed, and Gioe was in the habit of noticing everything. Whether they were friends or just acquaintances, they knew each other.

Gioe tried to keep as low a profile as possible during the eight years he spent in Des Moines. Occasionally, though, there would be a gambling or liquor raid and Charlie would be named manager of the club for the occasion. His nemesis in Des Moines was Chief of Detectives Jack Brophy. Brophy ordered his men to toss Gioe into jail every time they saw him. Cherry Nose was told in no uncertain terms by the Des Moines Police Department that he was not welcome and to "get outta town." They were concerned that he might be trying to turn the capital city into a "little Chicago." Gioe didn't really care. He was bored to tears out here in the sticks and had bigger fish to swindle in Chicago anyway. By that time Al Capone was gone. The Chicago mob was now being run by Frank Nitti.

The mob brought Cherry Nose back to Chicago in 1936. He returned to the big city just in time to become involved in a brand new career: labor racketeering and extortion. With the repeal of Prohibition three years earlier, the mob had been forced to come up with other ways of making money and Frank Nitti hit on a dandy one.

In 1932, a low-level pimp and shylock named Willie Bioff teamed up with a man named George Browne, the business agent for the Motion Picture Operators Union, and began threatening theater operators around Chicagoland with a projectionists' strike. There would be only one way to avoid darkened movie houses and financial ruin—pay thousands of dollars to the union (read: Bioff's and Brown's trouser pockets).

Bioff's plan worked. The local theater owners began their payoffs and the two partners were on their way. It worked a little too well, though; when Nitti heard about all the money Bioff was making, he called the little fellow in for "consultations." It took absolutely no time at all for Bioff to see the wisdom in Nitti's arguments with the barrel of a revolver screwed into one of his ears.

Nitti's scheme was to run George Browne for president of the International Alliance of Theater and Stage Hands (IATSE). With control of the IATSE, they believed they could control the entire motion picture industry, and that is nearly what happened. By 1937, Bioff was firmly entrenched in Hollywood and negotiating directly with the movers and shakers of the industry.

Shortly after leaving Des Moines in 1936, Cherry Nose was sent out to California to over see Bioff and the new extortion racket, and over the course of the next four years the mobsters milked several hundred thousand dollars from motion picture moguls. The next year, Ronald Reagan showed up in Hollywood.

With Cherry Nose out in California, the Chicago bosses provided Des Moines with a replacement mob boss named Luigi Fratto. Fratto, now calling himself by his Irish boxing name, "Lew Farrell," soon made his presence felt in Des Moines. He was the operator of at least one legitimate business, a distributorship for Canadian Ace Beer. Farrell was also in partnership with a local gambler named Hymie Wiseman in a wire room called the Sports Arcade at 612 Grand. Local horse players could lay their bets at the Sports Arcade on races at tracks all over the country. It was said that a person could on occasion even lay a post-race bet at the Arcade if he were careful about it.

Another of Farrell's deals was a supposedly private casino called the Downtown Businessman's Club, next to the Savery Hotel. It was rumored that there were something in the neighborhood of eleven partners in the club. One of Lew's partners remarked several years later that it was the worst deal he had ever gotten involved in. It wasn't exactly clear whether the deal was bad because of a lack of profits, bad because of the heat downtown, or bad because of Farrell or some of the other partners—perhaps a little of all three. The Downtown Businessman's Club was finally shut down around 1950.

Little Lew eventually became interested in another local casino/night club named The Mainliner, on Fleur Drive. The Mainliner had one of the larger casinos in the area and the owners, Pete and Gladys Rand, regularly booked nationally-known entertainers for their floor shows. Lew was reportedly a regular, sometimes nightly, patron at the Mainliner for the better part of a year in the early '40s.

In 1942, Lewie decided the Rands needed another partner. It was rumored around town that Cherry Nose had piece of the Mainliner, but no one knew for sure. Farrell told the Rands that he wanted to cut himself in for a 25% share of the business. When they impolitely refused, it was obvious to the roly-poly little mobster that they needed some additional persuasion. He soon returned to the Mainliner waving a gun around and threatening to shoot up the joint if he didn't get his one-quarter partnership. It was likely that the Rands didn't take his threats very seriously, because all that Lewis managed to get that night was arrested.

A few years after the end of World War II, the city fathers in Des Moines decided that their town needed to project a brand-new image of itself to the public. In 1948, Polk County Attorney Carroll Switzer began a half-hearted clean-up campaign. The campaign intensified significantly in 1950 after Clyde Herring, Jr. was elected to the office, and

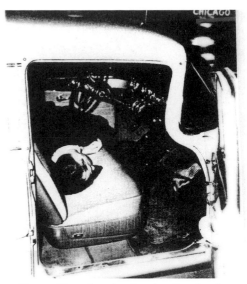

Cherry Nose lies dead in his Buick after being shot five times by two unknown gunmen, 1954

within a few years the open gambling and prostitution of the pre-war years was cleaned up to a certain extent.

Lew Farrell began to fade from the public limelight and was eventually involved as much in legitimate as illegitimate business.

Cherry Nose continued to be immersed in organized crime activities after his release from prison, until a night in 1954 when he was shot and killed in that brand-new Buick. He had just parked outside Angelos, his restaurant at Erie Street and Ogden Avenue on Chicago's Near West Side, when two gunmen walked up to the 1954 Buick with the Texas plates and cranked off 12 shots. Five of the shots hit Cherry Nose, killing him instantly, and several more blazed across the front seat of the car, out the passenger-side window past the passenger and into the side of the restaurant. The gunmen calmly appraised the passenger for a few seconds, then turned and strolled off into the Chicago night. No one was ever able to say for sure who they were.

The man in the passenger seat knew exactly what to do: he ran to the nearest phone and made a frantic call to Des Moines. He was told to get back to Iowa as fast as his little legs would carry him. It was left up to a passerby to report the shooting.

Hymie Wiseman, the passenger in the Buick with Charlie that night, was questioned by Chicago police a number of times

Hymie's Drive-In restaurant on Fleur Drive

about Gioe's shooting, but maintained that he'd never gotten a good look at the killers. After the excitement of the mob killings began to die down on the West Side (there had been seven in the past eight months) Wiseman returned to Iowa and went back into more or less legitimate business with Lew Farrell, co-owning a drive-in restaurant named, of all things, "Hymies."

By 1943, Frank Nitti's extortion scheme was starting to unravel. In 1941, Willie Bioff and George Browne were charged in federal court with extortion and labor racketeering. They were tried, found guilty and sentenced to ten years each in federal prison. Prison wasn't exactly what Willie had in mind when he got involved in the motion picture extortion industry, and he clearly wasn't real interested in having to spend ten years there. So, in order to reduce his sentence, ol' Willie rolled over on his partners from Chicago.

As soon as rumors of the indictments started to filter into Chicago in 1943, Frank Nitti got upset, and when he learned that his arrest was imminent he became really upset. Nitti was last seen alive stumbling around some railroad tracks in nearby Riverside, waving a whiskey bottle in one hand and cranking off pistol shots in the direction of a passerby who'd given him a hard time. By the time the police showed up, Nitti had shot himself in the head.

Bioff was the first federal witness ever to have been afforded a change of identity and relocation to another city, a forerunner of sorts to the Federal Witness Protection Program. But it wasn't enough to keep him out of the way of the boys from Chicago.

At around 11:00 one morning in November 1955, a short, round, balding man known to his neighbors as "William Nelson" kissed his wife goodbye in the kitchen of their home on Bethany Home Avenue in northeast Phoenix, Arizona. Just as he did every day, Bioff walked out to his garage, lifted the garage door and got into his 1951 Ford pickup. He had planned on going out to his

Des Moines police paddy wagon, Black Mariah

ranch to check on his cattle. Bioff pressed the truck's starter pedal, which closed an electrical circuit that connected the battery to the starter and an unusual automotive aftermarket device—several sticks of dynamite.

The truck was reduced to an unrecognizable pile of rubble only a foot high. Bioff's little round body, minus most of his clothing, one leg and much of his right arm, was

blown 20 feet out onto his driveway. Afterwards, neighbors said of "Mr. Nelson." "He was the nicest man you ever met. Didn't have an enemy in the world."

Lew Farrell and Hymie Wiseman both died of natural causes.

Ronald Reagan became head of the Screen Actors Guild and was last seen in California. ✪

*Patrolman Nick Bellizzi writes out one of 14
traffic summonses he issued in 35 minutes as
1:30 am to 9 am "No Parking" restrictions went
into effect, May 1939*

Des Moines Squad Car Ambulance crew, Patrolmen Tony Blacksmith and Walter Fisk, 1938

Left to right: **Theodore Strasburg, James Winters and Charles Welch, 1955**

Detective Ben Rich, left, shoots as world-renowned tap dancer, Bill "Bojangles" Robinson watches during pool match, 1940

FBI Instructor G. Cashmer Snell, center, shows Patrolmen Henry Jerome, left, and Carl Woxell the position taken to shoot from the hip when in close range of an asssailant's gun, 1944

Detective Scott Crowley destroys gambling devices confiscated by the police, 1957

THE WOMEN WHO HELPED TO KEEP THE PEACE

BY MARY BRUBAKER

While other kids bragged about their grandmother's chocolate chip cookies, I was able to say proudly that my grandmother, Carrie Cutler Goff, was a policewoman. I still feel a sense of admiration and awe that she was in some ways a pioneer in law enforcement. After her tenure in the '20s and '30s, the women who served the force steadily increased in numbers, diversity and professional skills, until one was named the first female captain in 1998. I am delighted to offer this tribute to the women who helped to keep the peace.

Policewoman Carrie Cutler Goff, 1927

Probably the first woman associated with the DMPD was the jailer's wife who lived in the log cabin jail in the mid-1800s and was said to have helped him lower prisoners by a rope into the cell through a hole in the floor.

In the 1911 *Pictorial Souvenir Book of the Department of Public Safety,* two middle-aged women, Mrs. L.L. Babcock and Mrs. N.P. Collins, are pictured and identified as matrons. A 1915 newspaper announcement of the wedding of Miss Ethy L. Fischer to S.L. Fiske, identified her as a "policewoman" who had been with Travelers' Aid services of the YWCA and the Woman's Home Missionary Society of the Methodist Church—groups interested in the "welfare of women brought into police and district courts." Chief Ed Crawford quoted as saying:

"I confess that when the department was established, I was a little afraid [policewomen] would be a police irritant . . .Fischer however has done her work as it should be done, has minded her own business and has pulled with the police just as she should."

Early records also show that a Mrs. Amos Fitzpatrick was appointed a matron in 1920, but died in 1923.

Carrie Cutler Goff and eight other women were featured in a *Des Moines Tribune* article by Ray Maxwell in August 1930 titled, "Nine Capable Women in Des Moines Hold Places in Police Department." The others were Policewoman Jennie Manbeck, telephone operators Mildred Ofterdinger, Jennie Thomas (widow of slain Police Officer Ollie D. Thomas killed on duty in 1925), and Grace Mattern. Mae Mitchell, Secretary to Chief of Police Henry A. Alber; Irene Rinker, Secretary to Inspector of Detectives Al Pedersen and Harriet Alber, clerk in the Detective Division comprised the clerical department. The article said, "A tenth woman on the force who is not yet under civil service and whose appointment is only temporary is Mrs. Willie Bailey, Negro matron."

The article features head shots of all nine and begins,

"When most persons think of the police department . . .they think of large men in blue uniforms with brass buttons or of keen-eyed sleuths moving noiselessly about in rubber-soled shoes. The average person seldom thinks of the nine women members of the force, who are civil service officers

Left to right: **Carrie Cutler Goff, Katherine McCarthy, Grace Mattern, Jennie Manback, unidentified, Harriet Aliber, Irene Rinker, Mary Colavecchio, Jennie Thomas, 1931**

106

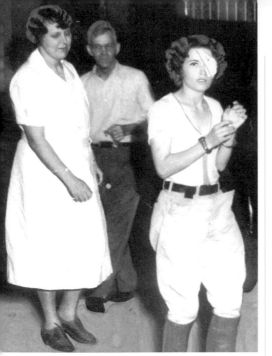

Matron Marie Brockmeier escorting Blanche Caldwell Barrow, 1933

with all the authority of a uniformed policeman who do their share in keeping the wheels of the law enforcement machinery in operation."

An earlier, undated article titled, "Women Now Answer Telephones of Des Moines' Police Station, Men Are All Put Out on Beats" pictured Ofterdinger, who had been chief operator at Northwestern Bell, sitting at the police switchboard. It said that her appointment, along with that of Mrs. Mattern, whose policeman husband had been killed in a gun battle, freed the men for active duty outside the station.

In the years prior to World War II, there was only one way to get in touch with anyone at the Police Department call the main number (243-4121) and talk to the switchboard operator. The operator routed all calls coming into the Police Department, including emergency calls. The person who called for police assistance would first have to tell their problem to the operator, who would ring the captain. The captain would hear the problem, then call the radio operator, who would dispatch a car. This process is a little more cumbersome than the one we have today where the police radio operator receives the call and dispatches a car immediately.

In the early 40s there were 10-12 beat officers, and 25 call boxes were still in existence. To insure their safety, the beat officers would report to the operator every hour by call box. They would also use the call boxes when they needed the wagon to pick up prisoners.

Another *Tribune* article of August 14, 1930 announces the appointment of Marie Brockmeier as a matron "to fill the vacancy left by the death of Mrs. Maude Wilkinson." In 1921, Wilkinson, was the first African-American matron appointed by the City, and she served until her death in 1930 at the age of 42.

Maude's sister-in-law Bernice Wilkinson, the wife of celebrated Police Officer William Wilkinson, served as a chaperone for local dances as required by law. An article by the *Challenger News Service* in l938 states, "While husband William was on the street routing out thugs, Bernice was routing smoking teenage girls out of restrooms." It seems that a city ordinance required that there be police supervision where dancing was allowed to ensure "decent behavior," such as keeping drunks and smokers and any man wearing a hat off of the dance floor. A *Des Moines Register* news article in 1951 named Lt. William Purdy as the supervisor, and pictured Hazel Allen as one of the chaperons. No doubt there were many other women over the years who "policed" the dances at public ballrooms like the Val Air and the Tromar.

Carrie Cutler Goff's colleague, Katherine McCarthy, was appointed a matron after the dramatic death of her detective husband, Con J. McCarthy, who was killed in the line of duty in September 1919. She was left with seven children and no savings.

Her grandson, William McCarthy, currently an assistant chief with the department, remembers that the matrons and policewomen were given full responsibility for women prisoners once they were brought to the station, and that they were highly respected by the male officers.

Long-time matron Jennie Manbeck said upon her retirement in April, 1947 that she hadn't felt "just right" since one of two girls trying to escape the previous October had struck her on the head with a fire extinguisher. She managed to get the girls back in their cells. Manbeck said that it was the first

Telephone operators, foreground: **Marye Dusenbery and Jennie Thomas, 1953**

time in 23 years on the force that she had been attacked. She was often given credit for turning around the lives of the female criminals she worked with because of her compassion and caring. Reminiscing about those years, she said she "tried to help people and any mistakes I've made have been of the head and not of the heart."

The early pictures of matrons show them in white uniforms similar to those of nurses,

Meter Maids, left to right: **Sheila Roemer, Wilma Johnson, Sheri Miller, Elizabeth Triggs and Officer Max Cleveland, 1965**

Des Moines Police Meter Maid patch

but an assertive and determined matron named Ellen L. Erickson, who joined the force in 1947, went to a tailor and had a navy blue skirt and a light blue blouse with blue epaulets created. She wore it with a black belt, tie and shoes. Her grandson John Woolsey, a retired officer, said that she wore the controversial uniform until called into the chief's office where he asked, "Ellen, what do you want?" She replied, "I'd like a purse and blue sweater." He then asked her "Why are you wearing blues?" She said, "Are you ordering me not to do so?" He said, "I can't do that," and from that day on, the matrons wore blue.

SWITCHBOARDS TO FIREARMS
Because early switchboard operators took all the incoming calls, their job required a great deal of finesse, judgement and a lot of patience, along with knowledge of the department. They often had to stifle some

snickers, like the time a caller was afraid that he would catch Dutch Elm Disease, or the woman who wanted her to "get on the ball and send some policemen to find her husband who had been out every night for a week." Another caller wondered "if it was legal to shoot dogs and children within the city limits."

In 1944, R. Dale Squires, who had been a police matron, was named the first woman juvenile investigator in the DMPD by Chief Victor Smith. Mrs. Katherine Powell, who had been a dance hall supervisor, was appointed "temporary matron" to fill Squires' position. That same month, Mrs. L.C. Johansen was appointed to the newly-created position of juvenile bureau secretary.

There was found no mention of firearms involving policewomen or matrons until an article in the *Des Moines Tribune* of November 7, 1951 headlined: "Policewomen To Take Up Firing Arms." Louise Crooks of Ottumwa, chairman of the women's meeting of the convention of the Iowa Association of Chiefs of Police and Peace Officers (IACP), asked the assembled women how many owned a revolver. One woman raised her hand and said "but I couldn't hit a barn with it." The women decided to seek instruction, but not to compete "with the men sharpshooters on the police force." Evidently the women took part in periodic marksmanship contests.

In April 1957, the Meter Checkers Squad was created. Called "meter maids" at first, they and their Cushman vehicles became a common target of bad tempers as they issued

tickets for traffic violations. Today's meter checkers are supplied with air-conditioned Ford Escorts, and they sometimes support officers at accidents and during severe weather.

" . . . THAT RIGHT TO BE AVERAGE"
The 1960s brought more responsibility, visibility and controversy to the women of the force. It is common knowledge that Chief Wendell Nichols was a high-profile leader who spoke his mind on almost everything, including his disapproval of women patrol officers. While he had no objection to women working as investigators, he felt the beat was no place for a woman. As long as he was the chief, women had a rather uphill climb. But the women's rights movement was gaining ground, and his prejudice was soon shown to be invalid, outdated and sometimes even illegal.

Long-time department secretary Donna Janson became a policewoman in 1963. One of Janson's first experiences in the field showed how resourceful women could be. She tells that when she knocked on the door of a crime suspect, it opened to reveal a man with a shotgun pointed at her. She quickly identified herself as the Avon lady and left the scene. "Don't tell me we don't have an edge sometimes," she was quoted as saying in a *Register* article in November 1981.

Janson was followed by Wanda Jones, who joined less than three years later, and by Joan Warne in 1968. Sergeant James Quick said of Warne when she became a detective, "I wish we had five more like her." Warne's husband, Ron, also a detective, said that they often solved crimes over dinner. Ironically, Warne was quoted in the above-mentioned Register article as approving of women in the detective bureau, but she adds,

I still don't believe in women in black and whites (patrol cars). We've had some, like Phylliss Henry, who have proved it can be done, but I'm still not convinced." Although there were no doubt others who agreed with Warne, it certainly wasn't the official leadership line. Assistant Chief Thomas Teale said in the same news story, "There's no difference between them and the male officer—except they wear different hats."

Henry was also quoted as saying the administration of Chief Billie B. Wallace was friendly to female officers: she points out the different styles of male and female officers, saying they all have strong points and weak ones,

"Unfortunately, the grading scale for women is still different. Maybe it's a subconscious grading scale. We've had average male officers for a long time. An average male officer is not considered a substandard officer, but an average female officer is more inclined to be considered substandard. I guess you could say we're still working on that right to be average."

There was nothing average about Henry. She was the only female patrol officer from 1972 until 1977. That year, Chief Nichols wanted to assign her to jail duty, but threat of a sex discrimination suit which could have lost the department federal funding kept her "out of jail" for awhile. Later, the feds said the women's jail should be staffed by women and there were not enough matrons, so Henry was assigned to the rotation. Her contention was that she should be treated like the other patrol officers who rotate in the jail, but because of their high numbers are only "in jail" for short periods.

When Henry joined the force she said that she wasn't a feminist, but because of the struggles she endured to advance in her career, she became one. When changes in

Sgt. Judy Bradshaw head of SCAT,
Back, left to right: **David Mulford, Chris Mahlstadt, William Breman, Joe Gonzalez, Michael Stueckrath, 1991**

civil rights legislation applying to public employees forced departments to hire women as patrol officers, not just policewomen, Henry, with the help of Assistant State Attorney Roxanne Conlin, overcame a series of barriers and finally was hired as a patrol officer.

One of the barriers she didn't face was the height and weight requirements which disqualified other hopefuls. Henry was instrumental in getting those requirements changed.

She became more and more visible to the public and was often sought out by the media because of her unique position. Her life has been documented in Louise Noun's book *More Strong-Minded Women,* and in

Henry's collection of papers in the Iowa Women's Archives at the University of Iowa. She left the force in 1982, and in 1994 was appointed United States Marshal for the Southern District of Iowa.

TODAY'S FEMALE OFFICER

As Officer Cindy Donahue drove me to the Police Academy one summer day in 1998, I asked her about the dangers faced by female officers and what had been her closest call. She said that she and her partner once tried to subdue a domestic abuser high on drugs who suddenly "went nuts" and became violent. When the man threatened them with a knife, they pulled their guns, and he kept yelling "shoot me . . .shoot me." A brawl ensued and after a call for help, it took four officers to subdue the perpetrator.

Cindy introduced me to the five young women being trained at the academy. They said they may lack some of the natural physical strength of the male recruits, but they make up for it with "heart" strength. One said, "heart takes us a long way because 90 per cent of the job is mental and only 10 per cent is physical." These thoughts were echoed by Academy Training Officer Dewey Roland, who added communication skills often are the most important part of any police encounter, and that women definitely have the edge there.

SCAT officers, *left to right:* **Larry Davey, Chris Mahlstadt, and Debra Richardson**
search suspects for drugs and weapons

POLICE VEHICLES

BY SPO CHARLES GUHL

Ambulance car, 1940

Des Moines police cars at the foot of the State Capitol, 1940s

An integral part of any police department in the country is its vehicles, and Des Moines has used a variety of makes, models and styles of motor vehicles throughout its history. In the early years of police vehicles, departments could order their police cars in any color scheme they wanted . . .as long as they were all black.

In the early 1940s the Des Moines Police Department began using a black and white patrol car. Our cars were painted in the traditional style—the doors and roof in white with the rest of the car black. Traffic Unit cars during this era were all white with the words "Police Traffic Division" on the front doors. In the late '40s, Traffic Unit vehicles were painted the usual black and white with the same wording on the doors.

In addition to the famous "paddy wagons," the police department also provided ambulance and cadaver transportation service for the city in the early 1900s and into the 1950s, with vehicles that came to be known as "Black Mariah."

By 1960, the department had 13 radio-equipped, three-wheel motorcycles, and 43 radio equipped automobiles.

Sometime during the late 1960s, the patrol division cars received their "new look"—a white car with a black hood and trunk. The police department door emblem that is still used today was put on the front doors of the vehicles at this time.

Manual transmissions were the standard until 1964, when the first patrol car with an automatic transmission was put into service. In 1969, air conditioning came on the scene.

Ford Motor Company has been the primary supplier of police vehicles for the department, however, there have also been Chevrolets, Plymouths, Pontiacs, American Motors (Ramblers) and Dodges. One Volkswagen Rabbit made an appearance in the fleet during the gas crisis in the late 1970s and early 1980s.

The patrol cars of the past are a far cry from the computerized, state-of-the art vehicles used now. Today's cars include power steering, power anti-lock brakes, power windows, traction control, dual air bags and, of course, the factory "police package" (heavy duty brakes, suspension, transmission, alternator and traction control disconnect device).

Above: **Police motorcycles retired to the garage for the winter, 1941**

Left: **Patrolmen Charles Rider and Omar Beardsley**

Motorcycles were also a vital means of patrolling the streets of Des Moines, especially in the early 1900s. The motorcycle of choice for police departments across the nation was the Harley Davidson and Des Moines was no exception, although this department has also used Moto-Guzzi motorcycles, Hondas and Kawasakis in its two-wheeler fleet. The Harley Davidson three-wheeled motorcycle was also used for a time, primarily for downtown loop traffic. There are currently seven Harley Davidson police motorcycles in the department's collection that are used by the officers assigned to the Tactical Unit. ✪

Above: **Patrolman Gus Groff leaving the police station, 1944**

Below, far right: **Traffic officer writing ticket at 6th Avenue and Walnut Street, 1946**

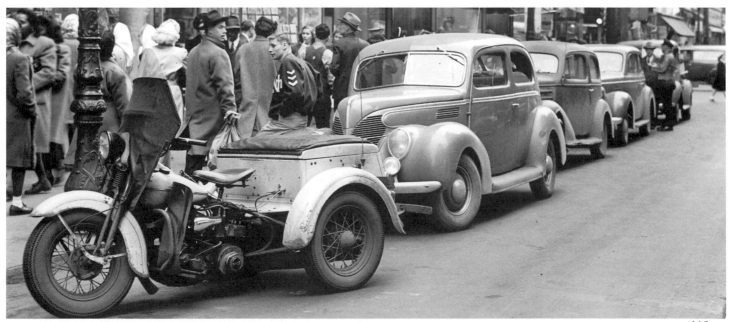

TRAFFIC UNIT

BY SPO CHARLES GUHL

One of the first so called "specialized squads" of the Des Moines Police Department, that dates back almost to the inception of this Department, was the Traffic Squad, or as it is called today, the Traffic Unit.

Historians and newspaper articles record the various types of "accidents" that occurred in this city during the early years. These turn of the century accidents involved the horse and buggy, bicycles, motorcycles, trains, street and trolley cars and, of course, automobiles.

The first official motorcycle officer was Harry McMillen who started on May 25, 1911.

Prior to Patrolman McMillen, another officer attempted to begin speed enforcement along the Grand Avenue hill west of the downtown area. This impromptu enforcement began in 1906 when Patrolman John Penn, patrolled on a Belgian made motorbike donated to the department by Grover Hubbell.

A minor accident between an automobile and a World War I soldier occurred on January 19, 1919.

This incident began when an automobile at the corner of 7th and Locust grazed Private Mike Rothats. Private Rothats became loud and abusive towards the driver of the car and Traffic Officer Charles Bryant stepped in to arrest the private. Another soldier intervened and both soldiers were arrested. When Officer Bryant went to the old Chamberlain Hotel corner to call the patrol wagon from a call box, more soldiers trying to free his prisoners attacked him. Officer Bryant blew his whistle to summon help but had it knocked from his hand. He then drew his pistol and fired three shots into the air. Several police officers heard the shots and came to his aid, however by this time the crowd had grown to an uncontrollable size. Officer Bryant turned in a riot call to the station and more patrolmen and military police came to his aid. When the crowd grew to an estimated size of 5000 people, a second riot call was turned in. A detachment of military police, which were stationed at the nearby Coliseum rushed to the scene, arrested the ringleaders and finally dispersed the crowd.

The first *Police Ball Book* that contains a picture of the Traffic Squad is dated 1921 and contains the pictures of 18 patrolmen. In 1927, the Traffic Squad became known as the Traffic Division, and was comprised of one inspector, one sergeant and 12 patrolmen. As 1930 came around, the traffic officers were divided into a Traffic Bureau with one lieutenant, one sergeant and six patrolmen; and a Motorcycle Division, with one lieutenant, one sergeant and eight patrolmen.

These early Motorcycle Division officers were proud of their machines and the distinctive uniforms that separated them from the regular patrol officers. The wheel and wings motorcycle patch was first worn on the dress blouse uniform wool coat beginning in 1913.

The Traffic Bureau continued to grow in size, mainly due to the increasing number of motor vehicles and accidents within the city, and by 1940 there were 22 officers in the bureau. A 1937 study of 137 cities across the country indicated that the normal traffic force should consist of four officers per 10,000 citizens, and if these figures were correct, Des Moines should have had three times as many officers in the Traffic Bureau.

It was 1940 was when the first two cars designated for accident investigation purposes were put into service.

With traffic accidents increasing at an alarming rate throughout the city, it became obvious that speeding was a factor that had to be dealt with by the Police Department. To combat this speeding, the Traffic Division obtained their first two "speed detectors" in 1954. These primitive radar units consisted of the radar detector box that was put on the trunk of the patrol car, and the inside electronic dial-graph unit. The traffic officer operating the radar would look at the needle on the graph to determine the speed of a vehicle and then radio ahead to the "stop car" and that officer would jump out and stop the violator.

Accident prevention and driver education was a top priority of the Traffic Division during the 1940s and 1950s. Officers would set up placards on downtown street corners that listed the number of fatal accidents in the

One of two white traffic investigation squad cars, 1940

Officer Kenneth Kline directing traffic in downtown Des Moines, 1952

city for that year. Along with these signs, a Traffic car with two giant loudspeakers on the roof would broadcast accident prevention messages as it traveled through the streets. Defensive driving courses were also given by traffic officers to citizens in the community during the 1950s and on into the 1960s.

In 1959, the first "white caps" appeared on the heads of officers in the Traffic Division. This distinctive cap color continued until 1969.

In the 1960s, traffic education was one of the top priorities of the Traffic Bureau. This

Chief of Police Howard Eide with first radar speed detector in squad car, 1952

Above, left to right: **Carol Peters and Michael Adams look over radar speed checking equipment installed in the front seat of police car, 1957**

115

education was based on the three "E's"-engineering, education and enforcement. Police officers from every division of the department participated by giving speeches at various luncheons, schools, civic organizations, and on the radio and television programs of the era.

The year 1960 also ushered in the introduction of the first meter maids for the Police Department who were assigned to the Traffic Division. Patrolman Tony Mihalovich supervised these first four women—Beverly Borlin, Hazel Martin, Betty Hassell and Anne Martin.

The personnel assigned to this Bureau during the late 1960s included 18 patrolmen for traffic enforcement and two detectives for hit and run investigation. There were three civilian radar operators who also assisted the three regular radar patrolmen. Around 1969, the Traffic Unit assigned officers to patrol the freeway that passed through Des Moines.

The Airport Security Squad began in 1971 as part of the Special Operations Section, under the jurisdiction of the Traffic Unit. Shortly thereafter, this Airport Squad became its own entity as part of the Special Operations Section.

In the three decades that have followed, the Traffic Unit has evolved along with modern technology and training. Officers of today's unit have specialized training in the use of laser radar, OWI processing, drug recognition, advanced accident investigation, technical investigation, accident reconstruction and a computerized mobile accident reporting system.

All of the specialized jobs within the unit such as radar enforcement, accident investigation, freeway patrols, hit and run investigation and the parking enforcement officers—formerly the meter maids of the 1960s, still exist today. ✪

Above: **Patrolman William Pierce** checks a motorist's license near Forest and Grand Avenues during a traffic check, 1952

AND THEY SHALL HAVE MUSIC

BY PAMELA SHAPIRO

Over the years, the Des Moines Police Department had a couple of baseball teams, a basketball team, an annual dance that for several decades was the social event of the year, a glee club, and not one, but four all-police bands.

The first band had a pretty short shelf life, and restricted itself to departmental functions. The second band, which would become much better-known, formed in 1942. Its eight members were Sgt. William Stevenson (banjo), Capt. A.C. Dunagan (tuba), Max Cleveland (sax), Arthur Beers (trumpet), Lt. Ted Strasburg (trombone), John Rider (piano), Charles Rider (vocalist) and Tony Mihalovich (drums). They were kept busy in Des Moines and throughout the state of Iowa, especially with the Goodwill Tour, which started in 1947 and sent them to as many as 12 towns in a day. They would play for the school children, parading through town in full uniform.

Max Cleveland tells a story about one night when they were up near Spencer, driving home late after a performance, when they came upon an accident on the deserted road. Being cops, they all piled out to help. Tony Mihalovich, a well-known fixture in

Des Moines Police Band
Left to right: **Bob Bradford, John Rider, Charles Rider, Tony Mihalovich, Max Cleveland, Harold Strasburg, Harold Cunningham, Ted Strasburg, 1957**

downtown Des Moines where he worked a dual role directing traffic and playing goodwill ambassador, proceeded to the center of the highway to do what he did best: assist oncoming cars with getting around the mess.

About a week later, Officer Cleveland was working downtown when he was approached by a gentleman. The citizen pointed at Officer Mihalovich, who was at his usual post waving vehicles through.

"Who is that guy?" he asked, obviously puzzled. "I was driving back from up north last Saturday night, and there he was in the middle of the road, directing traffic! Does he

patrol the entire state of Iowa?"

The third band enjoyed a brief life in the mid-fifties, with a lineup of several refugees from the second group. Like the first band, they pretty much confined themselves to playing at dances and events for department members.

The fourth band, "Legal Limit" didn't come along until 1994, and its instrumental lineup reflects the changing times: Mike Moody and Max Halverson on guitar, Larry Davey on bass, Ray Gallardo on drums, Rob Curtiss on keyboards and Pam Shapiro on vocals. While the original group played the swing music popular in the '40s, the current band delivers a mix of country, rock-and-roll and "oldies."

Their target audience is the same as in 1947, though. Legal Limit has performed at over sixty schools in central Iowa, playing for more than 10,000 elementary-school children during the 1997-98 school year alone. Their loud music gets the kids' attention, and in between songs they deliver the message that involvement with drugs and gangs will get you nothing but trouble. ✪

Des Moines Police Quartet
Left to right: **Patrolmen John Rider, Charles Rider, Inspector Roger West, William Pherrin and William Stevenson, 1940**

VOLUNTEER POLICE
RESERVE OFFICERS

BY SPO CHARLES GUHL

In 1950, a unique group of civilian volunteers was formed to assist the Des Moines Police Department with special events, traffic control and any disaster that might befall the community. This fledgling group was known as the Polk County Unit of the Civilian Defense Auxiliary Police, with many of them being hold-overs from the World War II Auxiliary Police.

The original group of auxiliary police consisted of approximately 35 men. The primary functions of this group of volunteers were to assist with traffic control in the downtown loop area and at various Christmas celebrations within the neighborhoods, during dignitary visits to the city and during spring floods. The motorcycle unit of the auxiliary police performed much of this traffic control.

The auxiliary officers held regular meetings that included training sessions in the various aspects of police work, along with Red Cross first aid training. One of the goals of the original group was to add 150 new members who would be able to provide first aid instruction to the community and to help with emergency first aid during emergencies. A yearly pistol shoot was also held for the benefit of the auxiliary officers. The auxiliary police received no compensation for their time and they had to purchase their own equipment and uniforms.

By 1955 this group had grown in size to 105 men and it was during this time that the auxiliary police started riding in patrol cars on weekends to supplement the regular police patrol officers.

In 1970, the name of the group changed to the Polk County-Des Moines Civilian Defense Auxiliary Police, and consisted of 75 men. Their on-the-job training continued to include riding along with regular officers on Friday and Saturday nights and on special occasions. Firearms and Red Cross first aid training were provided to these volunteers throughout the year.

In the mid-1970s the auxiliaries became known as the Des Moines Police and it was also during this time that the Iowa Law Enforcement Academy began requiring auxiliary officers throughout the state to complete a training program prior to being certified as reserve officers.

The Des Moines Police Reserves of today are required to complete 150 hours of law enforcement training within a four-year period before the State of Iowa can certify them.

Today's reserve force consists of ten officers who attend regular in-service training sessions in various aspects of police work.

The application process for a reserve officer includes a physical exam, background check, aptitude test and an interview. Today's reserves have all the powers of a certified police officer while they are working for the police department. These officers are required to ride with patrol officers at least 24 hours per month and they receive compensation in the amount of $1 per year in order to be eligible for workers' compensation coverage. The police department furnishes all of the equipment and uniforms for the reserves, with the exception of their duty weapon.

Reserve officers continue to provide a vital function for the police department by working with officers in the Patrol Services Division, Traffic Unit, Tactical Unit and the Vice/Narcotics Section.

In the age of community policing, these volunteer officers exemplify their devotion to the neighborhoods in which they live by providing these services. ✪

Des Moines Auxiliary Police
Left to right: **Capt. Harold Whitman, Capt. Harold Allen, Lt. Paul Scougal, Edwin Hillyard and Melvin Beaman** *far right:* **Auxiliary Chief Keith Surles**

Des Moines police original shoulder patch

Auxiliary police patch

	Des Moines Population	Des Moines Police Force
1940	142,599	151
1941	159,819	151
1942	-	151
1943	-	165
1944	-	165
1945	-	165
1946	-	165
1947	-	165
1948	-	165
1949	-	167
1950	176,954	179

Des Moines policemen dressed for the first time in their new winter uniforms. Capt. James Horsburgh briefs 12 traffic patrolmen wearing the blue blouse with new bright yellow and blue shoulder patch, new insignia of rank on the left sleeve and without the customary Sam Browne belt. The belt had been a part of the uniform since 1932. Motorcycle patrolmen were also required to wear the blouse instead of leather jackets. 1952

POLICE SHOULDER PATCH

BY SPO CHARLES GUHL

One of the most readily identifiable symbols of the Des Moines Police Department is the patch worn on the left shoulder of the police uniform. The same logo is also displayed on the front doors of all marked vehicles within the department's Patrol Services Division and Identification Section.

The concept for the design originated with the official seal of the City of Des Moines that was used in the 1950s. This seal consisted of a picture of the west side of city hall that was encircled by the words, "Seal of the City of Des Moines." Police Lt. William J. Wood, who was assigned to the Services Bureau, is credited with designing the first police shoulder patch in 1952. Lt. Wood used the original seal of the City, changing the wording to read, "Des Moines Police." This embroidered design was then surrounded with a yellow felt material that was rounded at the top and straight at the bottom, as illustrated in the picture. This original design was worn on the uniforms of Des Moines police officers from 1952 until 1956.

In 1956, the design of the patch was modified, with a more accurate depiction of the city hall building being embroidered on a yellow cloth material with a dark blue border, that was changed in shape to be straight at the top and rounded around the bottom. This design is still worn today, and is still used as the emblem on the patrol vehicles of the police department. ✪

THE WALL

BY RICHARD CROOK

The lady made her first appearance in Des Moines early in 1911, during an economic boom that the area was enjoying for a change. The local folks downtown had their first glimpse of her on the northeast corner of 7th and Grand. Prior to that, there was nothing on the east side of 7th between Grand and High streets but an empty lot and the George Fosdick home at 509 7th.

She'd been brought to town by Charles Cargill, a Chicago hotelier of some note, and she was a fancy sort of a lady, tall and sturdy-looking. It had taken him the better part of a year to get her up and running but finally, in 1911 they were all set. The Cargill Hotel was open and ready for business.

She was three stories high with 58 rooms, each $1 and up, hot and cold running water, some with baths. One dollar for a room wasn't exactly cheap hotel space in those days. Those were the days when a man with a good job could buy a brand new Buick for $1,500 or a house in the new subdivision near Drake University or by Union Park for less than $4,500. A working man could rent a house for $15 a month and go out to a roast beef dinner complete with dessert for $.25. However, the Cargill would be a strong competitor to the older hotels in town—the Savery, Kirkwood and Randolph—and would stay strong for another 20 years.

Lavonne Bevins came to Des Moines from Burlington in 1936. She'd been the manager of the Iowa Hotel there, and when she got to the capital city she went right back into the same business. By the early '40s, she'd married and taken over as the manager of the old Central Hotel on Grand. She also helped her husband, Joe, at the Theater Cigar Store business, across the street from the Paramount Theater. Lavonne was born in Forest City in 1911, the same year that the Cargill was completed. She was a slender, attractive woman with shoulder-length

In spite of being stark naked and on their way to jail, they must have been tremendously relieved to be out from behind that lousy wall with no ventilation.

brown hair, and was foxy enough to have caught Joe's eye as soon as she got into town.

Having a wife didn't slow Joe down very much though. He liked to play, and one afternoon he and one of his cronies decided to take the train to Minneapolis for a night or two on the town: a little gambling, a lot of drinking and a bit of accommodating companionship with some of the local talent. Lavonne was suspicious about the whole program and took a later train to the Twin Cities to check out Joe's story. She went to the hotel where she knew he would be staying, and caught him in bed with two girls. Lavonne dragged him back to Des Moines the next day. He later told a friend that it was the "worst goddamned train trip" he'd ever taken. The two were divorced a short time later, and by the time 1947 arrived Lavonne, on her own again, had negotiated for the purchase of the Cargill.

Lavonne had a few quirks of her own. On one hand she was apt to spend her money as fast as it came in. She kept the old hotel in good repair and replaced much of the old furniture with new things that she'd picked up from a southside furniture dealer. She had amazed the dealer by whipping out a fist-sized wad of bills from her purse and paying cash, several thousand dollars.

She'd been known to hand out money to strangers, too, just on the strength of a hard luck story. Once in 1950, a man and his wife and their two children came through town from Ohio looking for work and needed a place to stay. Lavonne put them up for free at the Cargill and paid for their meals until they could get back on their feet. She gave them a brand new $100 bill when they left.

On the other hand, she was as apt to walk off with something that she wanted while browsing through a store. Once, while visiting in Spencer, she went to a local grocery and decided to take a jar of peanut butter home with her. She was arrested for shoplifting and the local police found $800 in her

The girls began coming in shortly after they got Lavonne's call.

purse along with the purloined peanut butter.

It wasn't too long after Lavonne bought the Cargill that it became a focus of attention for the Des Moines Police Department. The rumor around town was that the hotel not only had a few prostitutes working her third floor, but was also harboring "out-of-town hoodlums." Indeed, occasionally during the late '40s, a purported bank robber from Omaha named Kenny Kitts was known to come to town and take advantage of her hospitality.

The rumors persisted, and finally in June and October, 1948, she was raided. The October raid netted 11 bad guys, six of whom were charged with various non-felonious indignities. Two were charged with "keeping a rowdy room" and fined $25. Four others were awarded 30 days in the county jail for vagrancy, sentences suspended on the condition that they vamoose, Dodge City-style. The others weren't charged but were sent to a local hospital for physical checkups before being released. Lavonne wasn't arrested in either of the 1948 raids, but the cops certainly knew who she was.

After the October raid, things settled down around 7th and Grand. The out-of-towners had been sent back out of town and, although in most ways it was business as usual, Lavonne tried to keep a low profile. In

1949 she even changed the name of her establishment from Cargill Hotel to Hotel Gillespie. The name change apparently didn't do much to alter the old gal's image around town, though. She was still known as a big-action house and she still drew thrillseekers from all over the country. Men came from Minneapolis, Kansas City and San Antonio for the fun, and women came for the money. Maybe the reason the name change didn't take, was that Lavonne had neglected to replace the big sign that stuck out over the sidewalk at the corner of 7th and Grand announcing "Cargill Hotel" in letters ten feet high. But by 1950, Lavonne changed her mind again and was back to calling the old gal Cargill again.

The county attorney at the time of the October, 1948 raid, Carroll Switzer, had allowed some gambling and prostitution to go on. At least it was allowed by default; vice was good for business downtown, and many downtown business interests were opposed in any crackdowns that might cut into profits. So the business and pleasure of vice was allowed to continue downtown as long as it wasn't accompanied by other, more serious crime, like robbery or murder. There were some gambling and brothel raids in Des Moines during the '40s, but these were usually conducted in response to specific complaints rather than being part of a larger reform scheme.

A stricter attitude toward vice took hold in the capital city after the municipal election of November, 1950. The Democratic candidate for Polk County Attorney, Clyde Herring, was elected by a sizable margin over his Republican opponent and former boss, Carroll Switzer. The son of ex-governor and ex-senator Clyde Herring, young Clyde had run on an anti-vice ticket. He'd claimed throughout the campaign that he was an experienced anti-gambling prosecutor, having taken part in two gambling raids in 1948 during his tenure as a prosecuting attorney.

In those days Iowa had no legal gambling, and beer-only taverns. One source of entertainment for the average person was to follow the antics of the Des Moines Police Department's liquor squad as they raided bar after tavern all over the city, attempting to stem the illegal sale of liquor-by-the-drink. The liquor squad had plenty of places to choose from—in 1950 there were 50 taverns in downtown Des Moines, all crammed into a west side downtown area that was only four blocks long by seven blocks wide.

Herring and the Des Moines Police really had little choice when it came to enforcing the liquor rules—it was state law! No whiskey could be sold by the drink in Iowa, and Des Moines was the capital city. What would folks from Grundy Center think if they found out their taverns couldn't sell booze, but Des Moines could? The State of Iowa insisted and the cities complied. No booze!

The girls were all back to work before midnight. Lavonne had managed to convince five of her out-of-town customers to hang around for awhile, and they were rarin' to go. They were ready to shell out their money just as soon as the girls could get up the elevator to the third floor.

THE RAID

The parking lot at Roosevelt High School started filling up with cars around mid-evening on Saturday, October 14. Casual observers might have wondered if a PTA meeting had been going on. Anyone taking a second look might have noticed a couple of odd details for a PTA meeting. All the people that were coming to Roosevelt that evening were men in the 25 to 45 year-old range. The weather was still nice, so most of the men were wearing only light jackets, not heavy enough to conceal the strange bulges at their belts or under their arms.

There were 82 people crammed in the Little Theatre classroom that night. Most knew each other and should have—they were all in the same business. The auditorium that night was packed with 36 city police officers lead by Chief Frank Mabee and the head of the vice squad, Lt. Arvene Nelson; 31 officers from the county sheriff's office; seven Bureau of Criminal Investigation agents lead by the Bureau Director, R.W. Nebergall; seven folks from the county attorney's office led by the man himself, Clyde Herring; one FBI agent and two reporters. Those 82 people knew they were going to end up participating in something big.

Herring broke the news: they were going to hit the Cargill and they were going to hit her hard. It was Herring's show and he had every detail of the action planned. Every cop would have specific responsibilities and everything was to be carefully timed.

The raid was to start at exactly 12:15 am, and the entire square block between 6th and 7th and between High and Grand was to be secured. There were officers assigned to the building owned by Ted McGreavy just to the north of the hotel; others would secure the Princess Apartments adjacent to the hotel on her east side. There would be officers on her roof as well as at her back entrances in the alley, and there would be officers in the street in front of the hotel to divert traffic away from the area. By 12:15, everyone was in his place and crouched to spring into action.

In spite of the tight security, someone let the cat out of the bag. Several times during the evening Lavonne got phone calls warning her that there was going to be a raid somewhere, but no one knew for sure exactly where. She was concerned enough to contact all her girls early in the evening and tell them not to show up that night until she called back.

Around 10:00, Lavonne started getting antsy. Customers were coming in and she had nothing to sell. She was losing money and the girls were too. They'd been calling in all evening wanting to know what was happening. Everyone was pestering Lavonne and she was getting tired of it. Even Joe, her ex-husband, had come down from his upstairs apartment, asking what was going on.

Around 10:30 pm Lavonne decided that they'd waited long enough, and told Joe and a Cargill employee she was bringing the girls in. Joe wanted her to wait until she was absolutely sure that the police weren't going to show up. After all, she'd been taking in $30,000-$40,000 every weekend, so what difference did the loss of one night's earnings make?

Easy for Joe to say, it wasn't his money. Lavonne had her mind made up though, and started calling the girls in; she would eventually round up eight. Those would be the most expensive phone calls that Lavonne ever made.

The girls began coming in shortly after they got Lavonne's call. Most lived downtown anyway, some in the Cargill and others scattered among the 15 downtown hotels that were in operation in those days. At the time of the raid there were only three Cargill women who maintained a permanent home in Des Moines, and lived in a real house with a real mailbox.

The girls were all back to work before midnight. Lavonne had managed to convince five of her out-of-town customers to hang around for awhile, and they were rarin' to go. They were ready to shell out their money just as soon as the girls could get up the elevator to the third floor. Everybody was happy again—temporarily.

At precisely 12:15 pm, two men dressed in work clothes came through the front door of the hotel and walked through the lobby—just two more fellas in from Baxter or Spring Hill or someplace else in the country, out for a night in the big city. One of the men went to the elevator and the other, a BCI agent named Dick Carmichael, walked up to the front desk.

"Got change for this ten-dollar bill,

buddy?" the big agent asked the clerk who was minding the front desk. The clerk stooped down to get change from under the counter, but before he was able to straighten up he was hit squarely on top on the head with something solid. "It about knocked me cuckoo" he said later. The BCI agent had sapped him.

Lavonne, standing near the front desk when the commotion started, knew exactly what was going on. She made a dash to the back of the counter, where months before she had installed a warning system for the third floor. She mashed the button before the BCI agent could stop her, and a buzzer sounded throughout the third floor. When the alarm went off all the girls knew the drill.

At the same time she had the alarm system installed, Lavonne had hired a carpenter to build a false wall in room 322. Behind that wall was a small hiding space, two feet deep by eight feet wide; just big enough for two or three medium-sized girls to hide in for

awhile without too much discomfort. The eight girls, all in their working clothes—that is to say, no clothes at all—rushed to room 322, slid open the secret panel and squeezed themselves inside.

Fortunately they were all medium-sized or smaller, but once inside they found that there wasn't room to sit down or even move around. They had to stand there, front to back, spoon-style, until Lavonne signaled the all-clear. They stood there like that for the next six hours.

In the meantime, things were heating up downstairs. The desk clerk was taken into custody and, after the buzzing cleared up in his head, was ordered to give the cops a guided tour of the hotel. At first there was little to see. The raiders detained all the men they found on the third floor, plus a second employee. They searched Joe's apartment and found a few interesting items but nothing they could charge him with. In another

employee's room they found a number of bottles of whiskey with out-of-town liquor stamps, but were unable to charge anyone with possession of the illegal booze.

When the police got to Lavonne's room, they found the most interesting evidence of all: money and lots of it. When they were finally done counting the loot, Herring and his fellow raiders found that they'd located over $40,000 in cash (Lavonne later swore that there was at least $60,000 in cash taken during the raid).

In spite of all the searching and rummaging around, and all the grilling of Lavonne and the others, the police had located no prostitutes. Was it possible to operate a bordello without prostitutes? Herring didn't think so.

The searchers figured that the girls were hidden in a secret room somewhere. One worn-out derelict that they rounded up told them about a carpenter who'd been brought in to build a wall upstairs somewhere, but the old

The Cargill Hotel Raid, 1951

sot wasn't sure exactly where. Finally, after several hours of talking to arrestees, tapping on walls and trudging up and down hallways, one observant young assistant county attorney noticed something strange. Although the hallway outside room 322 was exactly the same width as the rest of the hallway, the room itself seemed to be two or three feet narrower than the other rooms on the third floor. They hauled in the derelict again and he admitted to having done some painting on the third floor in a cubbyhole, but claimed he couldn't remember where it was for sure.

They knocked a hole in the wall and, sure enough, there were the girls huddled together in the tiny cell.

They knocked a hole in the wall and, sure enough, there were the girls huddled together in the tiny cell. In spite of being stark naked and on their way to jail, they must have been tremendously relieved to be out from behind that lousy wall with no ventilation. The temperature inside the space would have been at least 30 degrees hotter than outside; it felt like a steambox and stunk like a polecat den. The women must've been exhausted, as well; they'd gone behind the wall at just after midnight and didn't get out again until around 6:00 in the morning, and weren't a bunch that spent too much time on their feet.

The men were booked at around 5:00 am on Sunday and each was released on $100 bail about four hours later. They were all charged with frequenting a disorderly house. The Cargill girls were brought to the city jail about an hour later, charged with resorting to a house of ill fame and released on bonds of $500 each. Lavonne was released after providing a $1,000 bond. The women, Lavonne included, were all required to get physical checkups. Lavonne hired a limo for them and all nine showed up together, riding in style to a local hospital at 8:30 Monday morning.

Under normal circumstances everyone would have pled guilty, paid their fines and gone on about their business. Indeed, that's exactly what happened with the men. Lavonne and her girls were a different story, however. The girls and the hotel continued to hold the interest of the county attorney's office and the police. The department detailed a number of vice and liquor officers to do nothing except watch the hotel. Their perseverance paid off when several days after the raid, two of the officers who were staking out the Cargill saw one of the women leave the hotel with a man and get into a cab. The officers followed the cab to the Hotel Fort Des Moines a few blocks away, and watched the pair check into a room there. The woman and the man were arrested (the second time in less than a week for her) and charged with frequenting a disorderly room. The following day police even arrested the cab driver who'd taken the pair to the Fort Des Moines. He would lose his chauffeurs license.

By the end of the second week in November, it was all over for everyone but Lavonne. The men had paid their fines and gone home. The girls had also paid their fines and either gone on about their normal business—though not at the Cargill anymore—or left town for places less cranky. But Lavonne didn't get off quite that easily.

On December 7, she was fined $1,040.80 and sentenced to spend a few days in the Polk County jail. Then the IRS took over and she was treated to federal tax evasion charges. The IRS slapped a $500,000 tax lien against her assets and immediately took charge of the $40,000 taken in the raid. In 1952 she was found guilty in federal court, and sentenced to two and one-half years in the federal prison in Alderson, West Virginia. Furthermore, she was levied a $390,000 bill for back taxes and fines. She was released from prison in July, 1954, after serving 15 months of her sentence.

Lavonne soon moved to Hot Springs, Arkansas, where she got into the gambling and hotel business again for a short time. When things began to heat up in Hot Springs during one of that city's periodic vice crackdowns, she got out of the business entirely and moved back to Des Moines to live quietly in retirement until her death in the mid-1960s.

Things were pretty much over for the Cargill after the 1951 raid, too. Now over 40 years old, she had lost her popularity as an investment opportunity among downtown real estate interests. She was operated as the Earle Hotel for several years, then for a short time as the Curtis Hotel and finally as the Lux Hotel for several years during the late '60s and early '70s. Eventually she went on the tax sale lists and was picked up by Ted McGreavy, a used car and taxi cab man, for $55,000. She was torn down in 1973, an ignominious end for an old lady who'd started life amid such high hopes. There's now a city parking garage on the spot at 7th and Grand.

Clyde Herring hadn't been able to show that the Cargill operation was part of a nation-wide prostitution ring as he'd hoped, but he did help to accomplish a couple of things. For all intents and purposes, the 1951 raid ended large-scale prostitution operations downtown. Dissatisfaction with Iowa's antiquated liquor laws led to sanctioned "key clubs," ostensibly private clubs where a person could legally buy liquor-by-the-drink (from their own bottle). The good old days were gone for good after 1951. ✪

Above: **Patrolmen Martin Polley, unidentified girl, Lorin "Snus" Miller and Tony Mihalovich, 1950**

Above: **Radio dispatcher William Thornton**

Left: **Patrolman Vear Douglas is flipped by FBI agent Richard Kober during judo demonstration, 1946**

125

"I MUST HAVE MADE A MISTAKE"

BY RICHARD CROOK

One of the quickest solutions to a capital crime case in Des Moines came on November 30, 1953.

At about 8:30 that Sunday evening, police found the body of a woman under a billboard in a vacant lot at 10th and Crocker Streets. She'd been beaten, raped, bitten and mutilated, but was still alive when an ambulance arrived to take her to the county hospital about two miles north of where she was found. She died before the ambulance got her to the hospital; the cause of death was a crushed skull.

Earlier that evening, police had received a phone call from someone who had seen a man carrying an unconscious woman across that lot and dumping her near the billboard. The caller identified the man as James R. Byrd of 917 12th Street.

Two police officers, James Allen and Charles Swertfager, were dispatched to Byrd's home to bring him to police headquarters for questioning. When the officers got to the 12th Street address, Byrd was nowhere to be found. Around 10:00, Allen and Swertfager saw a car pull up to the front of the Byrd house. James R. was in it and the officers arrested their man before he had a chance to climb out.

Police determined that the dead woman was Mildred Hanson, the wife of a laborer at Iowa Power and Light Company (the predecessor of today's MidAmerican Energy). The Hansons lived about a half mile west of where Mildred had been killed, at 675 18th Street in one of the big, old, ornate homes in the Woodland/Pleasant area that had been converted to an apartment building years earlier. Their neighborhood was filled with block after block of this sort of building and was the rental area of choice for working people. Rent was cheap and the neighborhood was within walking distance or a short curbliner ride of the downtown business area.

A number of neighborhood taverns dotted the neighborhood—Tommie's, Mario Berti's and Schneberger's Tap, and there were a couple of small grocers, one or two inexpensive restaurants, a coin laundry and even two funeral homes. It was a fairly self-contained little section of the city. The steep hills and dense tree cover throughout the old neighborhood made it appear gloomier than it really was.

Mrs. Hanson was a bit of a party girl and had been arrested for public intoxication on a number of occasions during the year preceding her death. On the night she was killed, she and a friend, Alberta Gillespie, had been to a party at a house belonging to Mrs. Melrose Miller next to the lot where her body was later found. As it turned out, James R. had been to the party that evening as well, celebrating his early release from jail the day before.

On November 21, James Byrd had been sentenced to seven days in the county jail for disturbing the peace and an additional three days for public intoxication. The judge had specified that he had to serve his sentences consecutively rather than concurrently, with the intent that James would spend a full 10 days in jail. However, Thomas Reilly, Polk County Sheriff at the time, said that the commitment order had not specified that the sentences were

126

be served consecutively, and released James R. on Friday, November 28.

The incorrect commitment instruction to the sheriff meant that James was out on the street after serving only seven days. He was released on the morning of November 28, in time for the Saturday night party at Mrs. Miller's place. The deputy clerk of court who had made out Byrd's commitment order later stated, "I must have made a mistake."

Under questioning, a few days later Byrd admitted to having been at the Saturday night party and having seen Mildred Hanson there, but at first he denied having done anything to her. Then his story changed a bit. He said that he'd merely "slapped her once." He was trying to get her to give him some of her money. A little later he admitted to having "inflicted some of the wounds on her body" but still maintained that he hadn't killed her. "It was a guy from Kansas City who'd done it," he claimed. "I don't know who he was, though. The fella run off after he was finished with her."

The court wasn't buying any of Byrd's mumbo-jumbo, and Judge Howard Brooks ordered him held without bond on a charge of murder.

Byrd continued to insist that he was innocent of Mrs. Hanson's killing, but after several days of questioning he did admit to being part of a ring of armed robbers that specialized in holding up grocery stores in the city. Since the preceding August, the gang had hit five small grocers and a service station, all on the city's near north side, netting a total of about $3,000.

Police arrested Lester Jernigan and Henrietta Scott for the robberies. A third member of the gang, Freddie Donald, was already in custody; he'd been arrested six weeks earlier on an unrelated charge and

THE JUDGE COMMENTED THAT JAMES' STANDARD OF BEHAVIOR WASN'T QUITE UP TO THE SAME LEVEL AS THAT OF A NORMAL PERSON.

had been in the county jail ever since. He was there when he was hit with the robbery charges. Bonds ranging from $15,000 to $50,000 were set for the three, but none could raise the bail. They were kept in jail pending trial. The fourth member, James R., was, of course, not going anywhere either. He had much bigger problems to contend with than robbery charges—Iowa still hanged convicted murderers in those days.

James R. and the other three had to sit around in the county jail until their trials came up early in 1954. Henrietta, Freddie and Lester were tried first. On January 13, 1954 all three pled guilty to armed robbery charges and were sentenced to 25 years. Henrietta went to Rockwell City and the two men to Fort Madison. The men would have the opportunity to see James R. again later at the Fort. If they had a bone to pick, they could take it up with him there.

In March, 1954 in an apparent plea bargain agreement, the armed robbery charges against James were dismissed and he pled guilty to second-degree murder. He told the judge that the reason he'd killed Mildred Hanson was that she'd been rude and nasty to him at the party that Saturday night and he'd decided that he didn't have to put up with that sort of abuse. The judge commented that James' standard of behavior wasn't quite up

"I DON'T KNOW WHO HE WAS, THOUGH. THE FELLA RUN OFF AFTER HE WAS FINISHED WITH HER."

to the same level as that of a normal person and sentenced him to 50 years confinement at The Fort. He was whisked off to southern Iowa the very next day.

James spent 15 years at Fort Madison before being released in 1968. Apparently he was a bad boy again after his release, because he was returned to The Fort in February, 1969 and stayed there until his final release in March, 1972. He moved to Missouri and resumed his old hobby of armed robbery. He was sent to prison there for another 25 years in the mid-seventies.

His cronies Freddie and Lester stayed in Fort Madison until 1960. Lester either learned his lesson or moved out of the state because he didn't get into trouble again in Iowa. Freddie, however, committed another misdeed in mid-1966 and was shuffled back to prison until October, 1969. Henrietta was released from Rockwell City in January, 1959.

The irony of the whole thing was, if that deputy from the clerk's office had done what he was supposed to, Byrd would have stayed in jail until Tuesday, December 1. Mrs. Hanson would have gone to the party at the bootlegger joint on 10th Street that Saturday night, but with no James R. there she would have come away alive. But the deputy Clerk of Courts wasn't the only person to have made a mistake; James R. made plenty of them himself.

In any case, Des Moines police were able to identify their man in about a half hour and had him under arrest within a couple of hours. In less than a week they were able to solve a series of armed robberies, as well. It was one of the quickest closures to a murder case in the history of the department. ✪

BY PAMELA SHAPIRO

As you might expect, being a police officer is a complicated job. There are so many things to remember: state and federal laws, Miranda warnings, where all the stuff you have to carry goes on your uniform belt.... No one can be expected to remember it all, in addition to the myriad departmental regulations, so memory refreshers have always been provided by the printed word.

Departmental Rules and Regulations and Standard Operating Procedure (SOP) are two documents that set out, in substantial detail, the expectations, requirements and no-nos that all DMPD employees are to look out for. Covering everything from daily patrol duties to the permitted hairstyles for female officers, these two guides are militaristic in their thoroughness. They also tell the reader a great deal about what the department feels is important.

Many moons ago (1955, to be exact), these rules conveniently appeared in a Little Black Book which fit comfortably in a uniform or suit jacket pocket. Should an officer suffer a momentary memory lapse on the topic of handcuffing combative prisoners, help was just a page away. Now that we are firmly ensconced in the Information Age, said small book has morphed into something much more detailed and much more weighty. Literally. It has been replaced by a binder entitled *Rules and Regulations* and not one, but three *SOP* volumes: one for each division. A peek inside these publications reveals that while many things have changed, a few have remained comfortably the same.

In 1955, prisoners who would be in a cell over 24 hours were permitted tobacco and matches (in a non-metal container). They might have periodicals to read ("providing they are not of a lewd or salacious nature"), but not newspapers. Interestingly enough,

THE RULES

officers were permitted to read neither periodicals nor newspapers while on duty. Officers also were not permitted to smoke while in uniform "in such a manner as to attract public attention."

Now, of course, smoking is not permitted anywhere in the police station, as it is a government building.

The *Little Black Book* gives a sample of the business cards detectives were permitted to hand out in the performance of their investigations. One of the more peculiar items printed on those cards was the officer's home phone number. Guess there was no such thing as "off-duty" in those days.

Among the more substantial changes are the accepted circumstances under which an officer may fire his or her gun. In 1955 and today, there is little issue about discharging a service weapon when the officer or someone else is in immediate fear of their life. A bit more complicated are the circumstances described back then as, "to effect the capture of, or prevent the escape of or rescue of a person whom the officer has reasonable cause

to believe has committed a felony."

The 1994 version reads,

"when the employee reasonably believes that such force is necessary to effect the arrest of a person who, in the employee's mind, is known to have committed a felony if:

The person has used or threatened to use deadly force, and;

The employee has made a reasonable attempt to make known his official identity and intent to arrest, and;

That identity and intention, in the employee's mind, has been in fact transmitted to the person to be arrested, and;

All other methods of apprehension have been exhausted, and;

The employee reasonably believes that such discharge of firearms can be done without substantial risk of injury to innocent persons."

Obviously, being a police officer can require some pretty quick thinking.

Other changes over the years have involved less "legalese," but that doesn't necessarily mean they are easier to take. One of the most visible and substantial involves the equipment patrol officers carry with them all day, every day they are on the job.

In 1955, officers had to purchase their own uniforms, weapons, handcuffs ("if desired") and streetcar tokens. In a 1952 *Tribune* article about rookie officers, George Hibbs laid out for the camera the jackets, pants, shoes, flashlight, ties, holster and flashlight he purchased for $386.93 (this in a year when the starting salary was $275 a month!) They even had to buy their own bullets. Now, the officer must provide their service weapon and shoes. Detectives and

IN 1955, OFFICERS HAD TO PURCHASE THEIR OWN UNIFORMS, WEAPONS, HANDCUFFS ("IF DESIRED") AND STREETCAR TOKENS

other plainclothes officers must purchase their own holsters.

Patrol officers' wallets may complain a little less than those of their brothers in 1955, but their lower backs are probably complaining more. In 1955, an officer had hanging from his black 1 3/4" leather belt a holstered revolver, extra ammunition, handcuffs and key, flashlight, and sap. Today, an inner belt of velcro supports a black patent belt that carries all the above plus a case containing latex gloves, a portable radio, a can of mace, a PR-24 baton, and a cellular phone. All but a few officers now carry a .9mm rather than a revolver, and the extra clip takes up yet more space than the cylinders of old.

The current *Rules and Regulations* contain a passage on sexual harassment—a term no one had yet heard of in 1955. Changing laws and the ever-growing possibility of lawsuits have also added a lengthy section on complaint procedures and "how to conduct an interview" rules, along with the care and storage of all tapes of such interviews. Mention now gets made of the Miranda warning (also unknown in the '50s).

Of course, many things remain the same. Officers still cannot work in "taverns" and still cannot purchase liquor while in uniform—even if their tour of duty has ended for the day. They are still expected to treat the public with impartiality. They are still required to remain awake while on duty ("If unable to do so, they shall so report to their commanding officer who shall determine the proper course of action.").

And down in dispatch, civilian employees answering the telephone are still handling (as in 1955) "a large number of calls, some of which may be of an urgent nature and requiring ability to obtain essential information from excited persons." ✪

Senior Police Officers Mark Schleuger and Anthony Gomez

U.S. HISTORY	LOCAL HISTORY
1940 Nylon stockings sold in stores	**1940** Iowan Henry A. Wallace elected V.P. of U.S.
1941 Japan attacks Pearl Harbor	1941 Iowa Air National Guard created
1942 German army reaches Stalingrad	1942 19.8" of snow January 1st
1943 Rogers and Hammerstein produce "Oklahoma"	1943 WACS move into Fort Des Moines
1944 D-Day, Allied invasion of Europe	1944 Victor Smith 6th police chief in 4 years
1945 A-bombs on Hiroshima & Nagasaki, WWII ends	**1945** Sailors & Soldiers monument dedicated 48 years late
1946 U.S. grants Phillippine independence	1946 State of Iowa Centennial celebration
1947 First Polaroid camera; First supersonic flight	1947 First parking meters in Des Moines
1948 Ghandi assassinated in New Delhi	1948 Art Center built in Greenwood Park
1949 "Bikinis" introduced in U.S.	1949 City Manager/Council government enacted
1950 Korean War begins; first Peanuts comic strip	**1950** WOI is first local television station
1951 Julius and Ethel Rosenberg convicted as spies	1951 Cargill Hotel raid
1952 First Hydrogen bomb exploded, Elizabeth Queen	1952 First radar traffic units
1953 Playboy magazine; Yankees win 5th World Series	1953 Downtown Des Moines gets one-way streets
1954 Nautilus, first nuclear-powered sub launched	1954 WHO television goes on the air
1955 Kermit the Frog born	**1955** KRNT builds giant downtown TV tower
1956 Elvis Presley's "Heartbreak Hotel" hits Top Ten	1956 First televised Civil Defense alerts
1957 Russians launch Sputnik 1—first satellite	1957 Ray Soderquist terrorizes DM in airplane
1958 First Xerox machines	1958 First African-American Judge L.T. Glanton
1959 Alaska and Hawaii became states	1959 Merle Hay Mall (Plaza) opens

CHAPLAINS

BY ANNA KINGERY

While serving in the US Naval Reserve Unit in Des Moines with then Chief of Police Howard Eide, Rev. Charles Smith (Smitty) suggested to Chief Eide that he could be of

Rev. Charles Smith

some value to the department. He had served as a chaplain to Naval Shore Patrol during World War II, and he thought that experience would help him minister to Des Moines police officers. From that conversation came the Des Moines Police Chaplain Corps.

On June 30, 1959, Rev. Charles Smith was appointed as the first Des Moines Police Chaplain. Monsignor Father Edward

Monsignor Father Edward Pfeffer

Pfeffer came on board as the Catholic chaplain soon after.

Rabbi Steven Fink and Father James Holden (replacing Monsignor Father Pfeffer, who had died) volunteered to serve in the Des Moines Police Chaplain Corps beginning April 2, 1985.

Father John Ludwig replaced Father James Holden, who had become ill, as the Catholic chaplain in 1989. After many years of service to the Des Moines Police Department, Rev. Smith submitted his resignation in 1997.

In addition to teaching at the academy and assisting in department ceremonies, chaplains are available to assist individual needs. They are skilled in counseling individuals and families. In addition to marriage counseling, they are available to address problems of stress management, parenting skills, coping with divorce, family communications, family finances and spiritual concerns. All discussions between department members and chaplains are confidential ✪

Des Moines Assistant Police Chief Floyd Hartzer, *right,* **showed George McMickle some of the modern 1957 police weaponry. McMickle, 80, was a police officer here in the early 1900s.**

Left to right: **Anthony Andreano and Radioman Percy Parker, 1953**

BIG SHOT

BY PAMELA SHAPIRO

Of course, it started simply. Patrolmen Kenneth Kline and Ray Steiner were out on routine patrol in the early morning of February 26, 1958. As they drove down the street just a block from the station, East 2nd and Walnut—they noticed a car with a damaged front end parked along the curb. Sitting beside the car was a Ruan cab.

Kenneth Kline

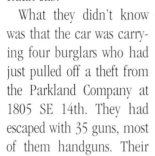

What they didn't know was that the car was carrying four burglars who had just pulled off a theft from the Parkland Company at 1805 SE 14th. They had escaped with 35 guns, most of them handguns. Their car had stalled, so they called for a cab and were in the process of transferring their loot between the two vehicles when the squad car showed up. Two of them, Larry Shelburg and Beth Ann Robson, were inside the cab. The other two, Gary Lee Wessling, 17, and Richard Craig, 19, were standing between the two cars.

Kline approached the disabled car and looked inside. He saw several of the guns immediately, lying on the seats inside. He also saw one in Wessling's hand. He yelled to Steiner, "He's got a gun!" and Wessling opened fire. Kline ran for cover behind a nearby utility pole, but was struck in the back and went down. Steiner fired through the window of his squad car, and Wessling fell.

Meanwhile, Craig ran to the lawn of the U.S. courthouse and began shooting at Steiner. Steiner returned fire until he emptied his pistol, then went back to the squad car for his shotgun. He said when he "got back into action," Wessling was lying on the ground beside the cab driver, later identified as John O'Keefe.

At this moment, R.L. Klein of the Division of Criminal Investigation happened by. He

spoke with Kline, who was still lying wounded on the ground. He immediately radioed for help, and disarmed Craig. He went to check on Wessling, and confiscated the gun lying beside him as well as three more pistols from his clothing.

Betty Kline was awakened at 3:00 am to find two Des Moines officers standing on her porch. As a police officer's wife, this was a moment she couldn't help thinking of—but to her relief and joy, the news was that her husband had been shot, but his injuries weren't serious. She rushed to the hospital, where one look at Ken told her "he would be all right."

The cab driver wasn't so fortunate. He died at the scene, the victim of six gunshot wounds to his chest. Shelburg's testimony named Wessling as the killer; he claimed he watched as Wessling "blasted away at the cab driver," and said that they had talked previously about having to kill O'Keefe because he would see the guns.

In those days there was no such thing as a medical examiner, and O'Keefe was buried without an autopsy. Later, his body was exhumed, the bullets extracted and sent in for ballistics tests which would eventually prove he was actually killed by a police shotgun, not the handguns the two thieves were using.

The details of the gunfight are confusing, and it is still unclear how O'Keefe could have been already on the ground when Steiner first got ahold of his shotgun—the only one used in the battle. However, witnesses and participants, especially in something as chaotic and terrible as a running gun battle, can become confused. Fortunately, forensic science is pretty reliable, and the murder charges against Wessling and Craig were dropped.

They still stood trial for the attempted murder of Patrolman Kline, though. Wessling's lawyer had argued that his client

didn't have complete use of his faculties on the night in question, as he had been drinking beer and ingesting seconal—a barbiturate referred to in the newspaper as "red devils." The jury wasn't interested in excuses and found Wessling guilty of assault with intent to commit murder. At Craig's trial, another jury convicted him of a lesser charge: assault with intent to commit manslaughter. Wessling received a sentence of 30 years; Craig 10.

Ray Steiner

Some would say Wessling didn't have a chance in this life. Less than three weeks before that burglary-gone-wrong, his father, Albert Wessling, was arrested along with William Quinn and George Coon. The three of them, with Quinn as their leader, were said by authorities to be part of a safe-robbing ring that had been looting Iowa stores for four years, and Albert had a record going back to 1934. While the younger Wessling lay in the hospital recovering from his injuries, Dad was brought to visit him. The paper showed a photo of Albert, handcuffed, bending over his son's bed while Polk County Sheriff Wilbur Hildreth and Deputy Bert Long watched.

But in his final interview before being taken to Anamosa, Wessling had some advice for his peers.

"I thought I was smart. I did things I shouldn't have done. I took things sometimes that didn't belong to me. I ran around loose and thought I was a big shot.

"I was a sucker."

He expressed the desire to become a barber some day. ✪

Standard police weapon,
.38 calibre revolver, 1960-1970

Traffic Officer Bill Reintz at
6th and Grand

Anthony Hoyla riding Des Moines
police three-wheeler

Paddy wagon officers take suspect away

THE HISTORY OF POLYGRAPHS

BY SPO MICHAEL McDERMOTT AND
JIM O'DONNELL

The Des Moines Police Department has been using the polygraph as an investigative tool since 1960. That year Don Knox became the department's first polygraph examiner. Since then, there have been eight other police employees who have served as polygraph examiners: Charles Heller, Gary Marker, Bill McCarthy, Mike Leeper, Jim O'Donnell, Jinny Garrison-Nickerson, Ralph Roth and Mike McDermott.

There have been many advancements in the polygraph field since then, and several changes in the instrument used by the department. The mechanical polygraphs of the 1960s were replaced by electronically enhanced instruments in the 1970s. Those machines recorded on a paper graph the physiological changes of the person being tested, and the graph was then analyzed by the polygraph examiner. Today the machine is computerized and uses a software program that automatically interprets the recorded charts with the assistance of the polygraph examiner.

Polygraph examination results are based on the scientific fact that when a person lies in response to relevant or pertinent questions, the fear of detection has an effect on the central nervous system. Certain uncontrollable physiological changes occur when a person lies. Those physiological changes are recorded on a graph for the polygraph examiner to interpret and diagnose.

The department's polygraph examiners are trained at the Keeler Polygraph Institute in Chicago, Illinois or Argenbright Polygraph Institute in Atlanta, Georgia. Initial training is a minimum of eight weeks at the polygraph school followed by extensive on-the-job training. Our polygraph examiners continually work to enhance professionalism in their field by attending seminars while maintaining membership in state and national polygraph associations.

The polygraph is used, and has been used, in virtually every type of criminal investigation including homicides, rapes, robberies, kidnappings, car thefts and burglaries. All

Keeler polygraph used in the 1950s

persons applying to the department as police officers must take a polygraph exam, which assists us in gathering information about them to help in the selection of the most desirable candidates for employment.

The polygraph has been used to clear the innocent person falsely accused of a crime, as well as to determine the guilty perpetrator of an offense. It is a partner to law enforcement because of its capabilities as a scientific diagnostic instrument in determining deception and truthfulness.

When administered by a competent and trained examiner, the polygraph is an invaluable investigative aid. The skilled examiner uses the polygraph in conjunction with the empirically-developed "polygraph technique" to diagnose truth, just as a doctor uses the x-ray as a scientific, diagnostic tool to determine a hairline fracture of the skull.

The Des Moines Police Department will continue to use the polygraph, as it has for the past 40 years, as a professional investigative aid to law enforcement. ✪

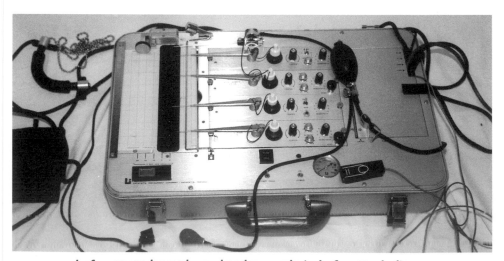

Lafayette polygraph used today, made in Lafayette, Indiana

134

Motorcycle Patrol, 1960
Left to right: **unidentified, unidentified, unidentified, Paul Thomas, Lou Kircher, Robert Webb, James Beardsley, Harold Grossnickle, Henry Jerome, Tony Mihalovich, J.C. Heefner**

Lt. Russell Lewis conducting the first weekly uniform and appearance inspection.
Left to right: **Patrolmen William Bonner, Edwin Kracht, Joseph Dunham, P.A. Jones, Guye DeFrancisco, Donald Hartline, Jasper Trout,** *far right,* **Wendell Nichols,** *1961*

A BRIGHT STAR FALLS

BY PAMELA SHAPIRO

Back in the '50s and '60s, there was a show on television called *Dragnet*, which dramatized true stories from the files of the Los Angeles Police Department. Its star was Jack Webb; he played a laconic cop named Joe Friday who was given to deadpan observations on the errors of man. In an episode where he is faced with a fellow officer gone bad, he wearily admits that such things will undoubtedly happen, "as long as we have to recruit from the human race."

M.B. Brightman, Jr.

Inevitable or not, police corruption is a heart-wrenching calamity—disastrous in that there are few circumstances under which the actions of a few can have such a devastating effect on so many. The people invest their police with an extraordinary responsibility: in order for them to do their job, we must trust them implicitly. If one officer damages that trust in any way, we will look at them all with suspicion and worry.

That reaction surfaced quickly when the news broke on September 13, 1960, that a confessed burglar named Richard Long had implicated three Des Moines police officers in a series of burglaries over the previous four to five months. Their names appeared on the front page of the *Des Moines Register* under a banner headline, "Chief Suspends 3 Policemen."

Martin Brightman, Jr., 25; Melvin Nicodemus, 35; and Richard Elwell, 27, were removed from duty by Chief Howard Eide in the course of a grand jury investigation that had begun on September 2. That morning, officers responding to the site of a burglary at Des Moines Drug Co., found Brightman's checkbook lying beside a loading door. Approximately $800 worth of watches were missing from inside the business.

Brightman was the son of one Des Moines detective and the nephew of another. Nicodemus had a brother on the force. Elwell worked a one-man car on First Watch (11:00 pm to 7:00 am), and Brightman worked a one-man on Third Watch (3:00 pm to 11:00 pm). Nicodemus was assigned to a two-man car on Third Watch, but for a time back in August the other man in the car had been Brightman.

In those days, officers worked the streets with no direct supervision. The entire watch was under the control of maybe two or three supervisors who spent the evening in the dispatch office. Trip logs were handwritten, not computerized for easy reference and cross-checking. This basically meant an officer working alone could disappear from the scope for hours and not be missed.

Brightman quickly emerged as the man with the most to fear. On November 15, a jury was selected to hear the state's case against him. The charge: grand larceny, stemming from the burglary of Royal Cleaners on April 8. Two suits disappeared from the business; one of them, valued at $102, would later be located by detectives in a closet at Brightman's home. In a startling turn, the defense declined to present a case on Brightman's behalf, and he was found guilty on November 17, 1960. He filed an appeal, but the judge pointed out that he'd had a chance to tell the jury about his innocence. The judge took his refusal to mean that he must have had nothing to tell them, and so denied the appeal.

In January 1961, Brightman's second trial got underway. Again the charge was grand larceny, this time for a box of tools valued at $2400 that had disappeared from Fortune Laboratories. This tool box turned up in the possession of a man named Paul Hurd, who told police Brightman had given it to him in exchange for some work he was doing on Brightman's racing car. Brightman took the stand this time and countered that Hurd was a liar and Long an admitted thief, and no one

should believe them. The jury did, though, and returned another count of guilty. On the two charges, Brightman was sentenced to 10 years in prison at Anamosa. Before he left, however, he was interviewed by investigators—an interview which resulted in a signed statement implicating "more than 20" other Des Moines officers.

City Manager Gunter Elder reacted swiftly. He announced that Chief Eide and Assistant City Attorney Terrence Hopkins would begin interviewing the officers involved immediately. These officers could not be accused based on Brightman's word alone; corroborating

Melvin Nicodemus

evidence would have to be uncovered. They hired the Keeler Institute of Chicago to administer polygraph tests to the men concerned. Chief of Police Eide was the first to submit, saying he wouldn't ask any of his men to do something he was unwilling to do himself.

Meanwhile, Nicodemus and Elwell had filed suit against the city for their sus-

Richard Elwell

pensions. Elder prepared for a hearing to investigate their conduct and the charges against them. They filed another suit to prevent the hearing from taking place, so he fired them immediately. When they learned that they, too, would be taking the lie-detector test if their appeals continued, they dropped them on February 6, 1961.

On February 15, former officer John Timmons, 27, was arrested and questioned with regard to Brightman's allegations. On February 20, the city council created a three-

136

member committee of civilians to look into the mess and try to "recommend a cure." They were also considering the formation of a public safety board, headed by someone who would be appointed by the city manager. This person, as well as the two-member "Bureau of Security, Inspection and Investigations," would not be a police officer—thus presumably assuring the public some measure of objectivity in departmental investigations.

On February 28, Edward Crozier, 31, was fired. As an officer implicated by Brightman, he was asked to take the lie detector test. This he was willing to do. What he was not willing to do was sign a waiver releasing the Keeler Institute from any liability with regard to what might happen to him as a result of the exam; he viewed this as a violation of his constitutional rights.

On March 1, the *Des Moines Tribune* shouted the news that Officers Richard Carlson and Marlin Long had been dismissed for the same reason. Their firing, as well as Crozier's was conditional, however: they had five days to reconsider and take the test. On March 3, Crozier did, after being told the waiver would not be necessary. Marlin and Long followed suit, and on March 7 the headlines announced their guilt. Their discharges were confirmed. Crozier was cleared and returned to work on Monday, March 6.

On Thursday, March 9, the stakes were raised drastically with the arrest of Assistant Chief Charles Andreano. The charges against him, made public on March 20, included that he failed to investigate a report made to him by an officer that other patrolmen had been seen taking merchandise from the premises of International Harvester in 1958; that he had accepted bribes from two officers to elicit a promise that he would try to get them promotions; and that he had accepted gifts from a citizen after promising to use his influence to get the citizen's brother hired on by the department.

On March 14 a story appeared announcing that James Dalton, former FBI agent, would accept command of the police and fire departments on April 1, in the newly-created position of "Administrative Assistant to City Manager for Public Safety."

Another blow fell on March 15, when Howard Eide was asked by the city council to resign as chief of police on the grounds that, ultimately, if these things were occurring under his command, it was his fault. He refused, so they demoted him to his previous rank of captain, and placed Assistant Chief Vear Douglas in his office on March 16, 1961.

At this point, rumblings began that it was time to make some changes in the civil service laws governing the position of chief. The chief was required at the time to be a man who had "risen through the ranks"; hiring someone from another agency was not possible. Many people felt this was wrong; that it restricted too greatly the pool from which a man might be chosen to lead the largest police department in Iowa. Vear Douglas was appointed interim chief until they could see about getting that law changed, but he would eventually make the job permanent and hold it until 1969. Eventually the rules were changed, but it wasn't until the appointment as chief in 1984 of William Moulder of the Kansas City Police Department, that they got their wish.

Mention the name Martin Brightman to a veteran Des Moines cop and you will likely get a grim nod. Mention the name to a rookie and you will probably get nothing. But whether they know it or not, Brightman is responsible for one of the most important relationships in their current worklife: shortly after this case came to light, the patrol division was completely restructured. No longer would the watch supervisors spend their eight hours in the radio room. Each watch was split into several squads, and each squad placed under the direct command of a sergeant who was sent out in a patrol car with his men—an arrangement that continues today. ✪

BEYOND THE CALL OF DUTY

Officer Kenneth Kline and a young boy he rescued from the Des Moines River are pulled by ropes to the surface of the Court Avenue bridge. Kline received the coveted Andrew Carnegie "Hero Award," a plaque, a medal and a $500 cash grant. 1960

THE GIRL FROM SOAP CREEK

RAMONA COX

She loved life, but the last sound she uttered was a chilling scream in the night. Her murder remains an unsolved mystery.

STAFF WRITER

Charlie Russell had just gotten off work about 10:00 one Sunday evening and, as usual, had gone over to see his girlfriend, Sharon. Charlie and Sharon had been going together for some time and they tried to spend as much time together as they could.

Sharon lived with a friend from Allied Mutual, Jackie Prosser, in a small apartment at 1530 Woodland. It was the girls' first experience with living on their own and it wasn't exactly like living at home. The Woodland/Pleasant neighborhood wasn't precisely the sort of area they'd have picked had they been given much of a choice. But, even though there were some pretty weird characters roaming the neighborhood sometimes, it was cheap and fairly safe as long as they kept their doors locked.

It was loud sometimes. They could often hear the noises from the two taverns in the area, Tommie's and the Woodland Tap. The traffic out on the street was noisy, too; cars seemed to race by at all hours of the day and night. But sometimes the loudest noises came from the front apartment of the small house next door. They didn't know the young woman who lived there, but they did know that she had visitors often and seemed to party a lot. Their apartment window looked right out on their neighbor's bedroom only a few feet away.

Things were fairly quiet at 1526 Woodland that Sunday evening. Charlie had parked his car right in front of the small house and he and Sharon and Jackie were standing talking on the sidewalk halfway between 1526 and 1530. All of a sudden the three teenagers heard a woman scream. The sound seemed to come from inside 1526 about where the bedroom was. Startled, the teens looked back and saw a light from one of the rooms in 1526 shining down into the space between the two houses and they could see a curtain wafting

in the breeze, out the open window. A few seconds later they heard what sounded like furniture being knocked around. The loud noises lasted a minute or so and then stopped and they saw a man's arm reach out the window and pull the curtain back inside. The blind was pulled down, sending the narrow space between the two buildings into darkness. Then there was nothing but silence.

The three teenagers weren't quite sure what to do. The racket could have been anything from a lover's spat to an ax murder. Charlie decided to drive down to the Loop—the local euphemism for the downtown

Ramona Cox a few months prior to her death.

area—to locate a police officer, but there were no police to be found on that quiet spring evening. On his way back, he met a friend and talked for several minutes before continuing on his way. It would be nearly a half hour before Charlie got back to Woodland Avenue.

Sharon and Jackie were standing at the curb when Charlie pulled up at about 11:30. They were still unsure about what to do about the whole business. After all, they'd heard no other noise coming from the apartment at 1526 since the big racket and things seemed pretty calm. Then another, different sound from 1526 caught their attention. It sounded as though someone inside the apartment were trying to open the front door. The teens just stood there on the sidewalk waiting to see what would happen next.

Suddenly the bedroom blind—the one the arm had pulled down earlier—snapped back open. As the teens peered back into the gloomy gap between the two buildings they saw a figure fall through the window and land on the ground on all fours. It was a man: five-foot-seven or eight, stocky, short dark hair, dark-complected and wearing a white shirt and dark pants. As soon as he hit the ground the man was up and running, south toward High Street a block behind the Woodland apartments.

Charlie and the girls were finally convinced: they needed to report all of this to someone. It turned out that what happened inside 1526 Woodland that night was a lot closer to an ax murder than a lovers' spat.

THE BEGINNING

Highway 5 stretches out of Missouri one hundred miles northward toward Des Moines, a narrow two-lane road winding its way through the rolling hills of southern Iowa. To someone who's not been through the area before it's a pretty drive across short, flat, mesa-like stretches of typical Iowa farmland, then dropping down into small wooded valleys.

For a young person living in southern Iowa in 1956, there wasn't much along Highway 5 to offer in the way of excitement or adventure. A good time for them meant a trip into Centerville on Saturday night for a movie or to a dance, and an occasional drive to Des Moines to look around or go to the State Fair in August. To stay in one of those small towns—Moravia, Attica, Hartford or Lovilia—meant that a new grad had to be resigned to a life in which nothing ever really happened. A girl just out of school sometimes felt as though she were being strangled to death; nothing to look forward to except getting married early, having kids and sitting there listening to the traffic on the highway going north.

As soon as they were old enough to understand what "going north" meant, many a girl in Moravia could talk of nothing else. Move to Des Moines. Get a good job and make some money. Get a car of her own. She could love her parents and extended family and the friends she made while growing up and still want to get away as fast as possible.

Rear door of Ramona's house

There was little opportunity in a town like Moravia for an ambitious girl and little chance for excitement if she stayed. Peace, quiet and routine are not the things that girls just out of high school long for.

Janet* and Marianne were like that. They could talk and think of nothing else. Even though she was only sixteen when she graduated from Moravia High School, Joyce felt she was ready to go right then and there. Their other friend, Mona, wasn't so sure. Mona was a year behind the other two in school and although she had always joined her friends in their plan-making and dreaming, she was going steady with Larry Brown and thinking about staying in Moravia.

Janet wasn't sticking around though, and neither was Marianne. They'd made up their minds—they were moving to Des Moines as soon as they graduated. There was no way they could tolerate the crushing sameness of their small home town anymore. They wanted to do something before they settled down to homes, husbands and children.

They found a place near where Janet's sister, Jane, was living on the west side of the city at about 31st and Grand, a nice area right on the bus line a few minutes' ride from downtown. They unloaded the car, packed away the things they'd brought along with them from home and settled in. They'd start looking for jobs first thing in the morning.

They thought it would be simple, but the city was gigantic compared to their little hometown. How did anyone ever find their way around? With all the businesses in a place that big, finding employment ought to be easy. There must be jobs everywhere. Maybe at Bankers Life Insurance or Equitable. If you didn't want to be stuck in an office all day maybe a job at Look or Meredith. They were hiring. They were hiring at the packing houses, too. Swift hired women to work in their plant as well as men, but yuk!, that smell. Besides, Swift was on the far southeast side of town, too hard to get to from 31st and Grand. The girls would concentrate on getting something closer.

It didn't look like Mona was going to make it to Des Moines, though. By the time 1956 rolled around she and Larry had started to get real serious and just before graduation he'd given her a diamond. She'd decided to forego the big adventure up north and stick around Moravia.

However, things don't always go quite as planned. By the summer of '56, Janet and Marianne had gone their separate ways. Janet was at Paramount Pictures; she would soon be promoted to a spot as booker, releasing films to movie houses around central Iowa. Things had changed for Mona, too. Larry's mother hadn't exactly approved of their relationship and by June the engagement was off. It was very hard on Mona; she really loved that boy and it hurt her that he'd gone along with his mother instead of sticking it out with her. She didn't think there was anything left for her in Moravia and decided

As soon as they were old enough to understand what "going north" meant, many a girl in Moravia could talk of nothing else. Move to Des Moines. Get a good job and make some money.

*Not her real name.

139

to go north after all. The timing was just about right; it looked as though there might be a place for her at Janet's.

With Janet's help Mona found her first job fairly quickly, as a stenographer at Commercial Credit Corp. on 10th and Locust, about two miles straight east of the apartment. The trip from 31st and Grand to the downtown area was a short, easy bus ride. The buses were packed with people every morning and with the very same folks every evening. Like Mona and Janet, many were young girls from out of town riding to and from work every weekday.

LIVING IN THE CITY

The girls lived at the apartment at 31st and Grand for about two years. In 1958, they decided to move to the Woodland/Pleasant neighborhood. Janet and Mona lived at the apartment house on Pleasant for about a year and a half before they decided to split up. Janet had gotten another promotion at Paramount and was now making enough money to afford a place of her own and a car. Mona had taken a job at Iowa Guarantee doing the same sorts of things that she'd done at Commercial Credit but at a little higher wage. Besides, she'd discovered the nightlife in Des Moines since she turned 21. She had met several interesting men and wanted to be on her own.

Mona moved about four blocks away from their old place at 18th and Pleasant to an apartment at 604 16th Street. Her place on 16th had a lot of things going for it. There was a small grocery and a laundromat only a block or two away on Woodland. There were also a couple of popular clubs—taverns, really—within easy walking distance. Tommie's was a small neighborhood bar at 17th and Woodland that was a popular hangout for young people, many of them from the immediate neighborhood.

The Woodland Tap was three blocks east at

The bathroom in Ramona's small apartment. Ramona fought with her killer in the bathroom. The condition of the bathroom indicated the ferocity of the struggle.

14th and Woodland and a different sort of place entirely. The Tap had been a well-known hangout for gamblers and hustlers of all sorts for years and would continue to be so for years to come. Pool sharks and pool shark wannabes from Texas, Minneapolis, Omaha, Chicago came to the Tap to try their luck and skill against the local boys, often without a whole lot of success. The place was usually packed, especially on weekends and when there was a big money game going on. Mona liked to go there sometimes just to watch the action, have a few drinks and soak up the atmosphere.

Mona was starting to fly a little higher by the time 1961 arrived. She moved over to the south side of town to an apartment at 630 Bancroft. At her Bancroft digs she was a little closer to one of her new favorite hangouts, L'il Joe's, a joint at the corner of SW 9th and Davis Streets, just south of a hilly, wooded oasis in the middle of the city named McRae Park. She'd also gotten tired of the rat race at Iowa Guarantee and had taken a job at Orville Lowe, a downtown automobile dealership.

Through her job at Orville Lowe and at a downtown Edsel dealership she'd met a lot of folks in the car business. She liked one man in particular, someone she'd met at Ralph

and Anthony Bumpilori's club, the Silver Dollar, over on 7th and Grand. The man was a car dealer himself, sort of. He and his brothers were in the business of auto wholesaling, buying cars in one part of the country and transporting them somewhere else for resale. He was fun and he had a lot of money and wasn't afraid to spend it. The fact that he was married didn't bother her too much. She got to go on business trips with him every once in awhile and once he loaned her a late model Cadillac convertible to drive home to Moravia for the weekend. Des Moines was starting to become everything she'd hoped it would be.

But the fun didn't last. By February, 1962, she'd broken off with the car dealer and moved back to the old neighborhood, this time only a block or two down the street from Tommie's. She'd also met another businessman, this time one who owned a real business with a real office in a real building. She'd gone to work at a new job at C.D. Wilcox Co., on Murphy Street, but money was tight now. Her new friend wasn't nearly as generous or quite as much fun as her old one, but he did let her use his new Lincoln once in awhile. She took a second job as a cashier in the evenings at Ardan's, a department store at 12th and Locust, and settled into her new apartment at 1526 Woodland.

THE MURDER SCENE

Officers arrived at Ramona's house at about 11:10 pm on the night of April 29, 1962. The door was locked, so two of them went in the window out of which Charlie had just seen the suspect jump. In the middle of the living room floor was Ramona's nude body, blood-smeared, with a bedspread wrapped around her head. One of the officers touched her—she was still warm. Thinking she could still be alive, they removed the bedspread but could detect no pulse.

A large pool of blood had gathered around

They followed the trail, and it led them to the bathroom where Ramona Cox had likely spent the last few moments of her life in a terrible struggle.

her, and they could see a trail of blood down the hallway where she had obviously been dragged into the living room from somewhere else. They followed the trail, and it led them to the bathroom where Ramona Cox had likely spent the last few moments of her life in a terrible struggle.

There was blood everywhere; on the walls, the floor, the bathtub. Blood splattered across the toilet and onto the cleaning supplies under the sink, which was ripped partway from the wall. Investigating officers surmised that Ramona had probably just finished taking a bath and was standing unclothed in front of her bathroom mirror putting her hair up in rollers. Her murderer came up behind her, reached around with a large knife and plunged it into her throat. It pierced her trachea and the main artery to its right, as well as the upper lobe of the right lung. Coroner Dr. Leo Luka stated in his report that the depth of the wound was five inches. Death would have come quickly.

The assailant dragged her lifeless body into the living room and raped her. He then spent the next half-hour or so trying to clean up some of the mess (the knife was left, washed clean, in the bathtub). He also tried, apparently, to mop up some of the blood on Ramona's body. Investigators assumed he had wrapped the bedclothes around her head to try and minimize the mess and keep from getting more blood on himself, but we know now that this is also a common psychological reaction by someone who is "ashamed" of what he has done and doesn't want the corpse to "see" him.

THE SUSPECTS

The police department launched into overdrive. Hundreds of people were stopped on the street, visited in their homes, and spoken to on the phone. Disgruntled divorcees phoned in anonymous tips about their ex-husbands. Ramona's large circle of friends pitched in their two-cents' worth. Her picture was shown to just about every bartender on the near north side. All leads were chased down, and in the end the cops were looking at two pretty strong suspects—two people who could hardly have been less alike.

Frederick Leon "Fritz" Jackson was a 25-year-old with an arrest history and a hatred of white people. The only tangible physical evidence left at the scene was a t-shirt with several hairs caught up in it that lab analysis determined was of "mixed caucasian and negroid extraction." Jackson was said to have had a white grandmother. Jackson also confessed to killing Ramona.

But his "confession" was problematic. He said he had known her for some time and had been in her home on several occasions. On the night in question, he had gone to her apartment and they got in an argument over money and he "accidentally" stabbed her. He also claimed he'd done it in the bedroom. He wouldn't tell them where he'd left the knife. Every time a different detective would talk to him the story would change a little, and he later bragged in prison about how he'd jerked the cops around on this killing.

Adam Hawthorne* lived with his parents in an apartment not far from Ramona's house. He was only 15 years old, but the neighborhood was well-acquainted with his history: child molestation, window peeking and a tendency to steal women's lingerie from clotheslines. He fit the physical description of the man seen jumping out Ramona's window more closely than Jackson, and he admitted to having been in her apartment on several occasions. He also said he had watched her through the windows of her home, stolen her clothing, and thought she was the grandest of all the girls he spied on in the neighborhood. But when asked if he had killed her, he would change the subject, ask to see his parents, or tell the investigators he couldn't remember.

What it boiled down to, confession or no confession, was evidence. The police didn't have any. With today's DNA technology this case would have been a cinch, but in 1962 it just wasn't possible. None of the witnesses could positively identify the man they saw leap into the darkness, the fingerprints investigators lifted from the venetian blinds were unuseable, and the knife was clean.

The case remains open and unsolved. Jackson died in California in 1992, but Hawthorne still lives in Des Moines.

THE FINAL JOURNEY

Mona's final trip south was made one bright morning early in May, 1962. The hearse wound its way slowly toward Moravia down old Highway 5 carrying her home. She was buried in a small cemetery just outside town in a family plot. Her headstone, which will be shared with her parents when they pass away, was flanked by two small evergreens. They are 20 feet high now, and provide a signpost to the grave that can be seen from the road. It was a large funeral; she had many friends and lots of family.

The Woodland Tap is gone now but Tommie's is still there. It doesn't do quite as much business these days as it did in 1962. It isn't nearly as loud there as it used to be either.

The house at 1526 was torn down in about 1980, but 1530 is still there. The rooms on the east side of the building that once looked down on Ramona's bedroom are still being rented, possibly to other young girls from other small towns.

Those young girls still come to Des Moines, too, graduation summer after graduation summer, to work in the insurance companies or banks or in hundreds of small businesses throughout the city. Things don't change all that much in Des Moines either, I guess. ✪

*Not his real name.

HONOR ROLL

CHARLES ANDREANO

Appointed: 31 August 1942
Died: 30 July 1964

On the afternoon of 30 July, Capt. Andreano and Lieutenant William Purdy were responding to a possible drowning on the city's south side. As their patrol car passed east through the intersection of Army Post and Indianola Road, it was struck by a northbound car that failed to stop at the stop sign.

The driver of the other car, Mrs. Norma Fleming, died shortly after arriving at the hospital. Her passenger, Mrs. Nellie Farr, died the next day.

Lt. Purdy, the driver of the patrol car, was not seriously injured. Capt. Andreano suffered a skull fracture and was taken to a local hospital. He died that day.

None of the four people involved in the accident were wearing seat belts. ✪

"Just because you wear a badge doesn't mean YOU are important . . . But the badge is a symbol of the law. If people show disrespect for the law, they ignore what is sacred to us in America."
Tony Mihalovich

Des Moines' first Meter Maids, left to right: Beverly Borlin, Hazel Martin, Betty Hassell, Anne Martin and their smiling supervisor, Patrolman Tony Mihalovich.

Looks like a noisy Fourth of July

Left: For the first time in 47 years, liquor by the drink became legal in Iowa on July 4, 1963.
Reprint: The DM Register, May 8, 1963

IN CASE YOU DIDN'T KNOW TONY

D.M. OFFICER MIHALOVICH KNEW THE MEANING OF "COMMUNITY"

BY TOM ALEX

He was voted 'friendliest person in Des Moines' and called 'the busiest good Samaritan in Iowa.'

It was 2 am one day last year and Des Moines Police Sgt. David Murillo was walking through Mercy Hospital Medical Center when a wizened old man in a wheelchair motioned to him. Murillo walked over, and the man said, "Officer, you look like you're proud to wear that uniform."

"I am sir," Murillo said.

The old man said his name was Tony Mihalovich, and added he'd been a police officer in Des Moines many years ago. They talked about police work for some time, and as Murillo walked on, the man said, "May God always be with you, Sgt. Murillo."

Murillo responded, "May God always be with you, Officer Mihalovich."

LEGEND AT HEADQUARTERS

Tony Mihalovich, a legend at police headquarters and around central Iowa in his time, died last week at age 85 of complications of leukemia.

He was Tony. No need for a last name.

Editors at the *Des Moines Register and Tribune* saved ink when Officer Mihalovich was in the news; on no less than eight occasions, headlines referred to him only as "Tony."

In the 1940s, '50s and early '60s it seemed he knew almost everyone. But to the generation that grew up without him, he managed to outlive much of his fame.

"Of course I'd heard of him," said Murillo. "Everyone has heard of Tony Mihalovich. I'm glad I got to meet him before he went to that big cop shop in the sky."

Tony Mihalovich. Some cops think he was over-rated, others thing he was the best ambassador the police department ever had.

FESTIVAL OF GOOD PRESS

You could not make up a fictional character like Tony Mihalovich because no one would believe you. His clip file in the newspaper morgue is a festival of good press. It is an orgy of kind remarks and remarkable accomplishment.

Once called "the busiest good Samaritan in Iowa," he patrolled the city on a motorcycle for more than 20 years.

"Just because you wear a badge doesn't mean YOU are important . . . ," he once told a reporter. "But the badge is a symbol of the law. If people show disrespect for the law, they ignore what is sacred to us in America."

Mihalovich, whose family emigrated to the United States from Yugoslavia when he was one year old, wasted little time making a name for himself once he was on the police force:

1947—Mihalovich begins annual good-will tours with the Des Moines Chamber of Commerce, taking with him 10,000 peppermint candy sticks and 10,00 balloons. He keeps an inexhaustible supply of goodies in the back of his motorcycle, dispensing them like confetti.

1947—Mihalovich is voted "friendliest person in Des Moines."

Sept. 14, 1949—Mihalovich, irked at a motorist who failed three days in a row to show up in traffic court on a reckless driving charge, locates him at home and drags him into court. But after the judge fines the man $75, Mihalovich asks the judge to reduce the fine because "he's married and he's got a little boy and not very much money." The judge reduces the fine to $30.

1951—Mihalovich is selected for the *Tribune's* 1951 Community Service award, which notes Mihalovich has made hundreds of visits to hospitals to cheer the sick and disabled; obtained building materials from Des Moines merchants for families whose homes were destroyed by fire and flood; organized trips for the handicapped; obtained athletic equipment for underprivileged boys and girls; obtained free medical service for needy people; outfitted a Cub Scout troop with fishing equipment; obtained autographs from athletes for polio victims.

Jan. 1, 1952—"A CBS program Monday night will salute Patrolman Tony Mihalovich." A list of his accomplishments is read to listeners of the Rex Allen Show.

Aug. 30, 1954—Box Car Betty, queen of the hobos at Britt's annual Hobo Convention, gives $5 to Mihalovich for use in his work with underprivileged children.

Aug. 7, 1961—The 14th annual Tony Mihalovich baseball game for handicapped children and handicapped adults at Sec Taylor Stadium is announced.

June 11, 1962—The children and Golden Age Club from Wilkie House surprise Mihalovich with a birthday gift, a decorative driftwood creation made by the father of one of the children. It is accompanied by letters thanking Mihalovich for helping make available tickets and transportation to circuses and variety shows.

LOST BADGE, LITERALLY

When Mihalovich misplaced his badge in 1965, it was news. When it was returned to him, the headline above the second story said, "Tony gets Badge Back."

True to form, Mihalovich didn't just drop the badge. It came off while he was helping at a fire which partly destroyed Des Moines General Hospital. The badge was found in the debris during clean up.

The only time he openly refused an assignment was in 1959, when he told supervisors he would not provide security for Nikita Khrushchev while the Russian premier was in Iowa. He said his friends in Slavic nations "just wouldn't understand."

In 1964, Mihalovich gave 78 speeches to groups and organizations, an average effort for him. In 1955, when it was announced he was to emcee an event, the *Cedar Rapids Gazette* noted, "We have seen him in action directing traffic at Des Moines' busy Sixth and Locust and if he can perform as an emcee like he does there, he's got it made, brother. He controls the traffic at his corner like any leading maestro."

Rest in peace, Tony. ✪

143

THE MYTH OF THE ELEVATOR RIDE

GOING UP!

BY RICHARD CROOK

PHOTOS BY DEB BARBER

He could have been anyone, but for the sake of this story we'll call him Lugnut Bales. Since he was little, Lugnut had been sort of hard to handle; nice enough, but still a little hyper and sort of pushy.

In grade school and in junior high (middle schools hadn't been invented yet) he'd been the one who told the other kids what they were going to do and when they were going to do it. If there was ever anyone around to be picked on, it was usually Lugnut and his friends who did the picking.

By the time he got into high school, he'd learned what girls were and all about beer drinking. When he turned 18 he'd gotten his first car, a 10-year-old 1955 Ford Fairlane with a pea-green paint job and not much chrome. That car got Lugnut acquainted with certain Des Moines police officers.

One night during the summer, Lugnut and a couple of his buddies were busy "scooping the Loop," drinking beer and raising a little bit of hell, but not really bothering anybody. They got a major surprise when they were nailed by a Des Moines police patrol unit.

We'll call the patrol officer "Curly,"—because the top of his head was bald as a baby's butt. Curly knew Lugnut's old man and was inclined to cut the boys a little slack; the kids had only been drinking beer, after all. Everybody did that when they were teenagers, didn't they?

"Dammit ta hell anyways, Lugnut. Get outa the Loop an' get ridda that beer. Yer plenty lucky it was me that pulled you over. If it was anybody else you woulda been on yer way to the drunk tank by now." Curly had never seemed to be too bad a guy, even if he was a copper.

Lugnut was a notoriously slow learner, though. He did leave the Loop that night and

The padded elevator cell

he did get rid of the beer, albeit not necessarily the way Curly had in mind. The truth was, he didn't stay out of the Loop or cut back on his beer consumption. He and his buddies were back on the street again later that week doing the same old things that Curly had warned them about.

TWO-GUN TOOMEY

Around the patrol unit offices, Curly's partner—we'll name him Two-Gun Toomey—needed to be as heavily armed as possible just in case a running gun battle ever came up. Two-Gun lived for an armed insurrection. When he was in uniform, the space that he had available to put things into, sort of limited the numbers and types of weapons that he could carry. It was a different story when he was off-duty.

When he was in street clothes, Two-Gun favored Marlon Brando-style leather motorcycle jackets with zippers all over the place. Those jackets were sturdy enough to let Two-Gun tote all sorts of stuff around. He always had two or three handguns stashed in different places, along with a knife or two and a sap in his back pocket. He'd heard that someone had invented a spray can with some sort of gas in it that you could spray into a mope's face and it would knock him down and leave him wallowing around on the ground screeching. He didn't know its name but Two-Gun was keeping his eyes open for it. He hoped those spray cans were small enough to fit in his motorcycle jacket with the rest of his arsenal.

In spite of all that, Two-Gun was a straight-arrow sort of cop. He'd been around long enough to know that if you did everything by the book, no sergeant could bust your chops. So when Two-Gun saw the beer in the car, Lugnut and his boozy buddies

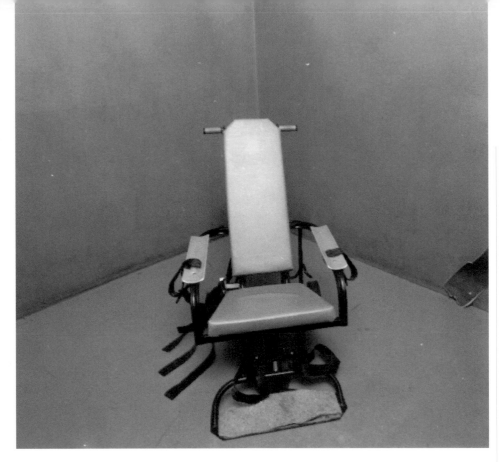

The time-out chair, in a padded cell

were all going to jail. When Lugnut pulled over, his buddies bailed out and took off as fast as their legs would carry them. Lugnut felt like doing the same thing except it was his car; he couldn't just leave it sitting there. He was the only one of the bunch arrested that night.

FIRST TIME

Back in those days, there was a large overhead door on the east side of the police station. A police unit could drive straight into the building's basement, then it was a step or two to the elevator and upstairs with a prisoner without ever having to go outside. For Lugnut it was a scary trip. This part of the basement was dingy and dark, with just one bare light bulb hanging over the elevator door. Back in the darkened garage he could see parked vehicles, and further back there were some rooms used by mechanics or janitors.

This was the first time that Lugnut had ever been inside the police station, but he'd heard all about it. Two-Gun and another officer were going to take him "upstairs" on that old elevator. This was the place where he'd heard that everybody got the crap beaten out of them for absolutely no reason at all. His insides were feeling a little squishy as he stepped inside the elevator car, one officer in front of him and one in back. One of the cops was telling the other about some kind of spray can that he wanted to get hold of. Neither officer seemed to be paying attention to him at all. What was this all about?

The elevator stopped at the first floor and they stepped out into the hallway. Down the hall Lugnut could see a large, barred door. Behind that was the drunk tank or "bullpen." He saw several hairy, dirty-looking men standing inside and he supposed that was where he was going to be spending the night. He made up his mind that if any of those guys in there started anything funny he

was going to whack him right in the chops.

After he'd been booked and printed, Lugnut was deposited in the bullpen for the night. He edged up against one wall so that he could keep an eye on the rest of his roommates. In a few minutes one particularly grungy looking character sidled over to him.

"Hey, kid," the man grinned. "You ain't got a cigarette you can let me have, do ya?"

"Ha," Lugnut thought and nailed the man in the forehead. He went down as though someone had dropped a rock on his head.

The jailer heard the commotion and came into the bullpen. "I jist asked the kid fer a cigarette and he cracked me right between the eyes," the man whined.

It made no difference to the jailer who started the ruckus—no fighting allowed on this jailer's watch. Lugnut was going to have a room of his own for the rest of the night.

So he was taken back onto the elevator, where he began to regret having smacked that old guy in the bull pen. Nothing had happened to him on his first trip up on the elevator but if these cops thought he was a smart mouth, they might decide to teach him a lesson, and there would be no one around to see it happen. All they'd have to do was stop the car between floors to do their business and no one would be the wiser.* Happened all the time, he'd been told.

*TODAY'S ST. LOUIS CELL

Today the elevator has a video camera mounted in the ceiling just in case someone complains. It's been there since the early '90s. A lightly-barred door was installed some years ago that divides the car into two sections. Officers taking someone "upstairs" can lock their prisoner behind that door and, in effect, have him in a cell by himself for the trip.

All they'd have to do was stop the car between floors to do their business and no one would be the wiser.

St. Louis Cells, about five feet across and eight feet long, just big enough for a steel-slatted bunk

But not this time. The car got to the second floor without incident and Lugnut had made up his mind to keep his mouth shut and stay cool for the rest of the night. The elevator door opened and he looked out into a large room with a block of small cells in the center.

These were the St. Louis cells, 10 of them in all, named for the company that had built them years before, the St. Louis Jail Co. They were old, narrow and musty, their paint was peeling and they stank. They were about five feet across and eight or so feet long, just big enough for a steel-slatted bunk (no mattresses, sheets, blankets, pillows with pillow cases, or fuzzy bedroom slippers with little bunny heads were provided);a sink; a commode at the rear; and the smell that came from that chemical toilet. They looked much like the jail cells you'd see in old prison movies. They were not a place where anyone in his right mind would want to be. Lugnut never spent a longer night in his life than the one he spent in that St. Louis cell. The upside was that he didn't get beaten up on the elevator ride.

But that that wasn't what he told his pals.

Any self-respecting jailbird who rode "upstairs" on the elevator in Des Moines' police station had to come out with a story about how he'd withstood everything that the coppers could throw at him—a stand-up guy in every sense of the word. Lugnut was no exception. He'd gotten considerably braver since they let him go, and he told all his friends about how he'd taken the worst the cops had to give during that ride. The myth continued, and the boys who'd been in the car that night with Lugnut almost wished they'd stuck around to see their buddy in action.

Did things happen on the elevator the way the stories say? Probably not. Ever since the back elevator was installed, stories had been circulated by would-be bad guys about the time they'd been taken "upstairs." If as many people had been tromped, stomped, and beaten as had been claimed, the poor old elevator car would have required hosing out every half-hour.

It's possible that over the years an occasional officer might have found it necessary to whack a drunk on the head to get his attention, but such occasions were very rare exceptions to the rule. In his younger days, this writer was asked to ride "upstairs" on the old elevator once. He'd been drinking a little and shooting his mouth off and a couple of officers got a little tired of listening to his b.s. They decided that he needed a little time to himself in a place of his very own, and took him up to the second floor to spend the rest of the night. Like Lugnut's trip, his elevator ride was uneventful. "Except, of course, for when they kicked me, punched me around, pointed their fingers at me, yelled at me, poked me with a night stick, handcuffed me, chewed me out, pinched me, and threatened to shoot me or at least shoot at me if I ever showed up down there flapping my lip again. Lucky for them there were too many of them for me to handle. If there'd only been one or two of them, they'd have been plenty sorry. I'da probably kicked their butts good. Ya believe me—don't ya?" ✪

EXPLORER POST HISTORY

BY SPO CHARLES GUHL

One of the most viable and nationally-recognized youth programs ever created by the Des Moines Police Department was Explorer Post 21, begun on April 1, 1966, when the Boy Scouts of America officially chartered it.

The program was designed to provide youth in the community with a better understanding of what law enforcement is all about, and to carry this knowledge with them in whatever career choices they might make in the future. Youth from ages 14 to 21 were invited to join the police Explorer program. There were 50 original members in the Explorer Post, and their advisor was Des Moines Police Officer Larry Youngs.

The Des Moines Police Explorer Post members were the first law enforcement explorers in the nation to change their uniforms from the Boy Scout green to a more police-oriented uniform that included blue pants and a light blue uniform shirt with the Des Moines Police patch on their shoulder.

It was also during this time that the Explorer Post received their first bus— a 1947 Flexible which was donated by a local business. This bus, and the ones that have replaced it since, have been used by Post members to take trips from one end of the country to the other. It is estimated that Post 21 members have logged over 100,000 miles travelling to schools, conferences, and recreational trips.

In 1970, the Explorer Post held its first Explorer Academy at the Iowa Army National Guard Base located in Camp Dodge, IA. Our department's Explorer Academy was one of the first in the nation to include firearms training for the explorers, and it was the first to have a military-style academy. Explorers from all over the country have attended the Des Moines Explorer Academy.

The Des Moines Police Explorer Post was instrumental in the organization of the National Association of Law Enforcement Explorers. The first national chairman, and first national advisor of this association were both from the Des Moines Police Explorer Post. The "Standard Operating Procedures" guidelines created by the Des Moines Post have been adopted nationwide as the example for how to organize an Explorer Post.

As an illustration of the success of this program, many members of the Explorer Post have gone on in life to become law enforcement officers in Des Moines, West Des Moines, Wichita KS, Mt. Pleasant IA, Greenfield IA, Polk County Sheriff's Department, Iowa State Patrol, US Attorney's Office in Minneapolis MN and the United States Secret Service. Other former members have become Certified Public Accountants, and directors of security for national companies.

In 1998, the Des Moines Police Explorer Post became known at the Metro Police Explorer Post. This change was made in order to expand the program into the surrounding communities and police departments. There are currently forty youth involved in the program. Police Explorers assist with parking at the Iowa State Fair and other major events, along with providing traffic control for dignitary visits. ✪

Explorers, left to right: Richard Wolfe, Lorrie Kelleher and Phil Cross

147

Above: **Patrolman Arthur Nelson warns motorists about the hazardous glaze of ice and snow covering the 7th Street hill into downtown, 1963**

Above: **Herman Hansen and Bill Wilson on patrol, 1967**

Right: **Patrolman Wallace Sidmore helps Moore Elementary School students across the busy intersection at Merle Hay and Douglas, 1964**

U.S. HISTORY	LOCAL HISTORY
1960 *U-2 shot down over Russia*	**1960** *First polygraph examinations by DM Police*
1961 *Yuri Gagarin—first man in space*	1961 *First use of tear gas by DM Police*
1962 *Cuban Missile Crisis*	1962 *Ramona Cox murder*
1963 *John F. Kennedy assassinated in Dallas*	1963 *"Liquor by the Drink" legalized, Tact Unit begun*
1964 *"Beatlemania"*	1964 *Harold Hughes elected governor*
1965 *Pres. Johnson sends troops to Vietnam*	**1965** *6th Ave. Bridge collapses, Saylorville Dam begun*
1966 *Truman Capote publishes In Cold Blood*	1966 *Blank Park Zoo dedicated*
1967 *Thurgood Marshall—1st black in US Supreme Ct.*	1967 *DMPD begins using portable radios*
1968 *M. L. King and Bobby Kennedy assassinated*	1968 *Pamela Powers abduction*
1969 *Neil Armstrong steps onto the moon*	1969 *Drake Bulldogs win 2nd NCAA Basketball*
1970 *M*A*S*H & Doonesbury start*	**1970** *DM Police Station bombed*
1971 *Joe Frazier beats Muhammad Ali*	1971 *State buys Terrace Hill*
1972 *Watergate break-in*	1972 *Phyllis Henry—first DM Patrolwoman*
1973 *14 states restore death penalty*	1973 *DMPD buys 2 helicopters*
1974 *President Nixon resigns*	1974 *36-story Ruan Bldg opens, DM flag adopted*
1975 *Jimmy Hoffa disappears*	**1975** *Southridge Mall opens*
1976 *US Bicentennial Celebration*	1976 *Local All Stars in Little League World Series*
1977 *"Star Wars" debut*	1977 *Valley West Mall opens*
1978 *911 die People's Temple, Jamestown Guyana*	1978 *Bloody Sunday murders*
1979 *Iran Hostage Crisis*	1979 *Riverview Park closes, Pope John Paul II visits*

"I've got a traffic jam out by the fairgrounds that you guys aren't going to believe"

Above: **The National Hot Air Ballon Championship races were first staged from the fairgrounds in August 1970. Thousands of people bound for the Iowa State Fair stopped and gawked causing a major traffic jam.**

Reprint: **The DM Register**, August 25, 1970

149

A Christian Burial

BY PAMELA SHAPIRO

Christmas Eve, 1968. Ten-year-old Pamela Powers was at the YMCA with her family for a wrestling tournament in which her older brother was participating. Dressed in orange slacks, vinyl boots and a striped shirt, she roamed about the gym enjoying the activities.

At about 12:30 pm, Pamela asked her mother from some money to buy something at the concession stand. Ten minutes later, she returned with a candy bar and some chips which she shared with her mother. Then she left again to go to the restroom. When she hadn't returned by 1:00 pm, her mother went looking for her.

Pamela Powers

Anthony Erthell Williams, alias Robert Anthony Williams, was born in Kansas City on March 19, 1944. In December 1968, he was 24 years old and had already stood trial on two separate counts of the sexual molestation of a child. He was found not guilty by reason of insanity and sentenced to the state hospital in Fulton, Missouri. He walked away from that facility in July 1968, and had been staying in room 724 at the Des Moines YMCA since October 26.

Williams claimed to be studying to be a preacher, and had joined the congregation at the Forest Avenue Gospel Temple, where he worked mostly with the youth groups. Just a few days before Pamela disappeared, the pastor of that church had received several complaints from members regarding "Reverend Anthony" and his inappropriate behavior toward their young daughters.

Pamela's frozen body was found wedged against this concrete culvert

Back at the Y, a little after 1:00 pm, they were paging Pamela over the intercom system. About ten minutes later, Physical Education Director Don Hannan saw Anthony Williams "coming around the corner" from the elevators and heading for the front door. In his arms was a large bundle wrapped in a blanket. Hannan called for another employee, John Knapp, and they ran after Williams. A little boy at the front door held it open for Williams, then followed him to his car and opened that door for him as well. He told the police that as Williams was putting the bundle in the car, the blanket fell away and he saw someone's bare leg. At that moment, Hannan and Knapp arrived at the car and attempted to stop it, but Williams pushed them away and drove off. Other witnesses at the scene said they saw no movement from the bundle.

On Christmas morning, Merle Killinger was cleaning the men's restroom at Rest Stop #80, located on I-80 eastbound, west of Grinnell. In the trash can he found a stained towel from the Des Moines YMCA, a man's suit coat and pair of pants (with the name "Anthony" on the trouser pocket), two small white socks, and a pair of orange corduroy slacks.

Early in the morning of December 26, Henry McKnight, Williams' attorney, called the Des Moines police to say he had spoken with Anthony. Anthony was in Davenport, and McKnight told him to go to the Davenport Police Department

Anthony Williams

and turn himself in. At 8:45 am, he did. The officers there advised him of his right to remain silent, which he invoked, saying he would return to Des Moines and speak with his attorney before he talked to the police. He asked to use a telephone and call Mr. McKnight, and he spoke with him briefly.

At 11:00 am, he was taken before Judge Metcalf at the Municipal Court and again advised of his rights. Williams requested a private hearing with Judge Metcalf, where he was advised a third time of his right to remain silent. Upon leaving chambers, he noticed a local attorney, Thomas Kelly, in the courtroom. After asking Kelly if he was a lawyer, the two of them were allowed to meet privately, after which Kelly told the police that Williams still had no statement to make, but would wait until he got back to Des Moines.

At 1:45 pm, Capt. Cleatus Leaming and

HE TOLD THE POLICE THAT AS WILLIAMS WAS PUTTING THE BUNDLE IN THE CAR, THE BLANKET FELL AWAY AND HE SAW SOMEONE'S BARE LEG.

Det. Arthur Nelson arrived in Davenport and took charge of the prisoner. Capt. Leaming asked Williams if he had been advised of his rights. Williams said yes, and Leaming said he had to inform him again. So Williams was told, for the fourth time, that he didn't have to talk to the police.

They walked Williams to the car for the long trip back to Des Moines. Leaming told Nelson to drive, as he was going to sit in the back with Williams and "you and I are going to be visiting."

What happened next would take them all before the United States Supreme Court.

Williams asked Leaming if he hated him and wanted to kill him. Leaming replied that he would be more likely to pray for him than hurt him. They spoke briefly of religious matters, then Williams asked Capt. Leaming if he believed he had killed Pamela. Leaming said yes. He added that he knew she was dead when Williams carried her out of the Y, and Williams said, "Yes, that's right." He also said he was certain Pamela had been in Williams' room. Williams agreed to that too.

Then, according to his report, Leaming said,

"I want to give you something to think about. I don't want you to answer me right now but I want you to think about it as we go along. I want you to observe the weather. It is raining, it's freezing, the visibility is very poor, it's going to get dark early tonight and they are predicting snow, and I'm afraid that if we don't find that girl's body tonight and it gets snow on top of it, maybe even you can't find it again because you have only been there once, and I feel that this girl's parents have a right to get this body back and have a funeral and a Christian burial for their little daughter who was snatched away from them on Christmas Eve. And also since we are going right by the spot anyway on the way into Des Moines, why shouldn't we stop and recover the body now rather than driving back out this same way again tomorrow?"

After this speech, Leaming and Williams talked of other things. They stopped at a gas station for coffee and removed Williams' handcuffs for a little while so he could stretch his muscles and drink his coffee. Shortly after they resumed travel, Williams said, "I am going to tell you where the body is. . . it's by Mitchellville."

He led them south from the Mitchellville interchange onto a gravel road. They were joined by several agents of the state Bureau of Criminal Investigation (BCI) who had been following their car. Williams told them he had left her body in a concrete culvert. After checking several such locations, Agent Jutte of the BCI spotted a flash of color at the bottom of a ditch. Wedged against the culvert, as Williams had said it would be, was the frozen body of Pamela Powers. She was taken to a Des Moines funeral home, where an autopsy by Dr. Leo Luka would reveal she had been suffocated.

Williams claimed he had entered his room at the YMCA on the afternoon of December 24 to find Pamela lying dead on his bed. He panicked because he was an escapee from the mental hospital in Missouri, so he wrapped her body up in a blanket and disposed of her. He claimed that a janitor at the YMCA, Albert Bowers, was the man they should be talking to. However, he could produce no witnesses other than a YMCA resident who claimed he heard strange noises coming from Bowers' room on the afternoon of the murder. The jury didn't accept his story, and he was convicted of first-degree murder on May 7, 1969.

Claiming that his rights had been violated by Capt. Leaming in what would become known as "The Christian Burial Speech," Williams filed an appeal with the Iowa Supreme Court. They upheld the conviction, so he tried again in 1974, when U.S. District Judge William Hanson ruled that his rights had in fact been violated. Hanson ordered a new trial, a view echoed by the 8th U.S. Circuit Court and the U.S. Supreme Court. The second trial was moved to Cedar Rapids, where Williams was again found guilty in July 1977.

Capt. Cleatus Leaming

In 1979, Williams filed another appeal. The Iowa Supreme Court affirmed the second conviction, as did U.S. District Judge Harold Vietor again in 1981. In January 1983, the U.S. 8th District Court of Appeals overturned Vietor's decision, but in June 1984, the U.S. Supreme Court again ruled, this time upholding the second murder conviction.

Williams tried again in 1985, claiming his lawyers hadn't done their job. In October 1991, the Polk County District Court ruled against him, and in 1993, the Iowa Court of Appeals again denied his request for another trial. He is still an inmate of the Iowa prison system, where he has devoted much of his time to studying law. It is unknown if he ever completed his ministerial schooling. ✪

BY ANNA KINGERY

BOMBING
OF THE POLICE STATION

All that spring, the word on the street was that something big was going to happen in Des Moines. The Black Panthers had been inciting civil unrest for quite some time, and planting bombs and creating general havoc was a favorite tool of urban terrorists. The prediction came true, but it hit closer to home than any police officer could have imagined.

In the cool and stormy predawn hours of May 13, 1970, someone crept along the south side of the Des Moines police station and planted a bomb containing a lethal 14 to 28 sticks of dynamite. The bomb was placed next to the building's power transformers, near where the telephone lines entered the building. Fortunately for employees inside the station, the device was not placed by a person particularly knowledgeable about explosives. The main force of the bomb shot away from the wall to the south, and the building sustained surprisingly little damage.

Most employees inside the building initially thought the blast was lightning striking the transformer. As they watched in amazement, a hole appeared and flames shot up the side wall of the building. Most of them were lucky; only one person was injured in the blast: custodian Willie Wells was treated and released at Broadlawns Hospital for cuts on the back of his legs from flying glass.

The blast ripped a hole three feet square in the south wall of the building, and shattered windows in the station and nearby businesses. In addition to losing primary power, the blast knocked out the station's emergency power generator in the basement. Communication between dispatchers and street officers ceased from the time of the blast at about 4:35 am, to 6:50 am when telephone company workers rigged up an emergency system consisting of mobile communications equipment and walkie-talkies. Despite the communications problem, Chief Nichols

later said, "The city was never without adequate police protection, although there was about 20 minutes of fires, confusion and other things before the situation leveled out."

A ball of fire greeted officers as they arrived at the police station in response to the blast. Several cars in the south parking lot were ablaze. One car, a mostly-restored 1930 Model A Ford, was owned by rookie officer Tim Cunningham, who reported to work that day to begin his first shift as a Des Moines police officer. The first day that Officer Jack Rickman drove his brand-new car to the station was also unfortunately the day of the bombing.

The rookies who were to begin their careers as police officers on the morning of May 13, 1970, were assigned to guard the perimeter of the station after the blast. Many of them were Vietnam veterans, and they had the calm stare of soldiers who had already seen much more than a damaged building. Veteran officers, many of them in plain

This photograph from May 13, 1970, shows the damage done to the Des Moines police headquarters in a bomb blast that morning.

clothes, moved around the crime scene while the rookies guarded the corners and the back of the building.

Investigators linked the explosion to the May 5 theft of about 285 sticks of dynamite and 600 blasting caps from the Quick Supply Company northwest of the city. Since less than 30 sticks of dynamite went off at the police station, the bombers still had plenty of explosives left, and Chief Nichols predicted the station would not be the last hit. His warning was right on target.

Within the next six weeks, there were three more bomb blasts. Dynamite bombs exploded at the Ames Police Department and City Hall on May 22; the Greater Des Moines Chamber of Commerce on June 13; and Drake University's Harvey Ingham Hall of Science on June 29. Ten people were injured in the Ames blast, but no serious injuries were reported in any of the other explosions. Other bombings occurred in Nebraska, Minnesota and Canada, and law enforcement officials speculated that the dynamite for all of them came from the Des Moines.

Investigators believe Ames Municipal Judge

*Cars parked near the Des Moines
police station sustained serious
damage from the bombing*

John McKinney may have been a particular target in the Ames explosion. Judge McKinney had presided at the trial of Roosevelt Roby and Black Panther leader Charles Knox, on charges of resisting arrest after a tavern brawl. Both were acquitted. On April 27, Judge McKinney discovered an incendiary device in his garage. At the time he blamed black militants for putting it there.

The Ames Police Department bomb detonated at 9:00 am on Friday, May 22. Although Judge McKinney usually parked his car at around 9:00 am and entered the building through a door near the blast site, on that particular day he had taken his car to a garage to be serviced and walked to work, entering through another door.

Two days after the bombing of the Des Moines police station, four people, including a 15-year-old boy and a woman, were charged with illegal possession of incendiary devices. The charges were filed after the four were stopped for a faulty taillight during a routine check for suspects in three recent armed robberies. While searching the car, officers found about 40 electrical blasting caps used to detonate dynamite. The blasting caps were identical to those stolen from Quick Supply. Three cases of dynamite were found in the apartment of one of the men arrested.

When the woman who was arrested appeared in court for arraignment, she raised a clenched fist and shouted "Black Power" several times. She also complained about the cold temperature in the station's second-floor courtroom. The room was drafty because the windows shattered in the bomb blast had not been replaced.

On June 22, 1970, Des Moines Police Officer Jack Morton opened a booby-trapped bomb found under a concrete pedestrian overpass that spans the MacVicar Freeway at 23rd and Cottage Grove. When Morton found the package, a gray metal toolbox, he opened it and lifted a tray in the box, which triggered a mechanism designed to detonate two sticks of dynamite. The device malfunctioned because a small sliver of wood dropped between a clothespin and a larger block of wood intended as a trigger. The toolbox also contained loose nuts and bolts, making it a potentially deadly fragmentation device.

No one was arrested in the bombings, and officially they remain unsolved. Unofficially, documents released years ago by the FBI under the Freedom of Information Act, show that a prime suspect was a 19-year-old youth who lived at Black Panther headquarters in Des Moines at the time of the bombings. ✪

A Scandal in the Department

BY ANNA KINGERY

10-X

The story begins when 10-X Manufacturing Company reported to the Des Moines Police Department that between November 2 and November 17, 1971, 829 snowmobile suits, 12 bush jackets, and other merchandise valued at over $46,000 had been stolen. In response to that theft Doug Durham, a former police officer and undercover agent for the department, was hired by 10-X as an investigator. He worked in concert with the police department to determine if the thefts were internal or external. Posing as an employee of the company, he worked out of a shipping warehouse at 3rd and Court (three blocks from the police station).

Durham contacted several officers about purchasing unsaleable merchandise. Written permission had been given by both the chief of police and the 10-X company for officers to purchase items from a small inventory of damaged and therefore unsaleable sportswear—hunting jackets, vests, pants, and snowmobile suits—for prices ranging from $1 to $10. In all, about 25 items exchanged hands for about $100.

Shortly after the initial purchases in March 1972, Chief Wendell Nichols discovered that several boxes of items that were marked unsaleable (but were probably firsts or seconds) had been delivered to a sergeant's home by Durham. The sergeant later sold these items at a garage sale. When Nichols learned of this activity, he forbade future purchases and ordered all items that had been purchased earlier returned, even the items he had given permission for the officers to buy.

Concerns arose that officers had purchased and/or resold stolen merchandise. The rumors flew and on April 6, 1972, the Policeman's Burial Association, a group representing nearly all the officers on the force, held a secret meeting in which members were told that Chief Nichols was being unresponsive to their demands for an internal investigation. The association, concerned that all members of the department would become suspect by the public, requested a complete outside investigation. Their resolution said, in part, "It is our desire that such disclosure will reaffirm in the public's mind that their police officers are honest and trustworthy."

On April 12, 1972, Chief Nichols turned the 10-X investigation over to the Polk County Grand Jury. Later, the special investigation by the Policeman's Burial Association proved that the items purchased by the officers were not part of the $46,000 worth of merchandise reported stolen by 10-X.

In June, after hearing 65 witnesses, the grand jury completed their investigation. They found that although the merchandise purchased by the officers was not stolen, a large portion of it was "firsts or seconds," not "soiled and unsaleable." They recommended that 10 policemen be disciplined for "misconduct and/or poor judgment" in connection with the case.

The grand jury censured Chief Nichols and City Manager Tom Chenoweth and concluded that Chief Nichols "failed to conduct a proper investigation following standard police procedures." Members of the grand jury also accused Chief Nichols of practicing a double standard of discipline within the department.

"An example of this double standard is the discipline amounting to two days off having to be worked with-out pay by officers found guilty of rules infraction in not wearing their hats when on duty, while the officers listed on this report received no discipline whatsoever."

After reading the report, Chief Nichols responded by saying that the grand jury gave the police officers a "clean bill." Taking full responsibility for the incident, Nichols said:

"....the Grand Jury went far beyond that and made recommendations which I consider completely out of their bailiwick...for censuring anyone but me. And if anyone is totally responsible, I've got to be the man.

We are reaching the area of a civilian review board, which I and every other police administrator knows is wrong. This is very, very close to a civilian review board."

With two council members calling for Nichols' dismissal, City Manager Chenoweth ordered Chief Nichols to reopen the internal investigation and recommend disciplinary action against the police officers who participated in purchasing the 10-X clothing. A five-member "Chief's Advisory Committee" was named to investigate the 10-X case and recommend disciplinary action for any officers who were deemed to have violated city or police department regulations.

Finally, in late June, 1972, eight months after the story began, eight police officers were disciplined in the 10-X case. The discipline ranged from working four days off for seven of the officers, to a 30-day suspension and a demotion for the one sergeant involved. Two officers were exonerated.

The original theft at 10-X was never solved. ✪

"IT IS OUR DESIRE THAT SUCH DISCLOSURE WILL REAFFIRM IN THE PUBLIC'S MIND THAT THEIR POLICE OFFICERS ARE HONEST AND TRUSTWORTHY."

DIRTY, ROTTEN COP, SIR

BY ANNA KINGERY AND PEGGY SCHLEUGER

During the late 1960s, public sentiment turned against law enforcement. Police officers were held in low esteem as a result of the "anti-establishment" craze founded by young radicals of the era. The morale at the police department was low and officers felt they might be better rewarded, both financially and emotionally, by seeking other employment.

A young lieutenant by the name of Billie Wallace (who later became chief of police) was extremely frustrated by the fact that Des Moines police officers were receiving very little support from the community they served.

Lt. Wallace approached a friend, Dick Gerdes, who was the marketing director of a local business. Mr. Gerdes, along with a copywriter named Dick Kelly, and an area artist came up with a campaign entitled "Dirty, Rotten Cop, Sir" to market the Des Moines Police Department. The campaign was funded by the business community. Richard Olson, who was to become mayor of Des Moines in 1972, was part of that funding effort.

The "Dirty, Rotten Cop, Sir" campaign focused on the good things the Des Moines Police Department was accomplishing and profiled five heroic acts by department members These profiles ended with the remark, "Maybe it ought to be Dirty, Rotten Cop, Sir."

The campaign was presented to the business community who funded it, and to all members of the Des Moines Police Department. Although skeptical at first, it was eventually endorsed by both.

Rod Serling, one of the best known writers in television history, agreed to do radio spots of the profiles at no charge. These spots ran on area radio stations for six weeks. Billboards profiling each courageous act were placed throughout the city.

"Dirty, Rotten Cop, Sir" turned out to be one

Dirty, rotten cop.

Dirty, rotten Des Moines cop Larry Worthington was first on the scene after an explosion in a house on the north side. A man and his wife and three of their children were burned and in shock on the front lawn. The father said another child was still in the Larry went into the still-one room and then another house. Without hesitation dirty, rotten burning, gas filled house. He searched until he found the 6-year old boy unconscious across the foot of his bed. He carried him to safety. The family is understandably grateful. Somebody even recommended Larry for a citation. And yet when he stops somebody for ignoring a school crossing sign he's a dirty, rotten cop.

Maybe it should be dirty, rotten cop, sir

of the most powerful campaigns in the history of the Des Moines Police Department. It forced the community to take a better look at what the police department was doing for them and spoke of the enormous risks officers take daily to protect the citizens of Des Moines. ✪

FOOT PATROL

BY SPO CHARLES GUHL

With all of the talk today about the "new" community policing programs that departments around the country are adopting, it is interesting to note that Des Moines' community policing began years ago.

In May 1976, as a result of community actions to bring more police protection and service into high-crime area neighborhoods, the Neighborhood Foot Patrol Program began.

Community and federal grants funded this program, with the remaining costs being authorized by the city council. As the debate for approval of this program was being conducted in the city council, there were some opponents who felt the money should go towards training teams of police dogs and handlers rather than a neighborhood foot patrol. One council member even stated that they would be sentencing a policeman to death by having them walk foot beats in high-crime areas.

The original goals of the program were to increase citizen cooperation with the police, reduce crime in targeted neighborhoods and

increase the satisfaction of officers working foot patrol. This program also acted to combat the citizen alienation that resulted from impersonal law enforcement. The police officer would no longer be seen as just a person in a blue uniform driving around in a patrol car.

The original Neighborhood Foot Patrol was divided into two areas—the Woodland/Wilkie neighborhood, and the Model Cities neighborhood. Each of these two neighborhoods was provided with a foot patrol squad that consisted of one sergeant and four officers. The Model Cities officers worked out of a building located at 11th Street and College Avenue, while the Woodland/Wilkie officers were housed in a building at the corner of Harding Road and Cottage Grove. The Woodland/Wilkie office later moved to 855 17th Street.

The original foot patrol officers worked from 10:00 am until 6:00 pm, and in July 1978 a third squad of foot patrol officers was added to the program working from 7:00 until 3:00 am.

The officers originally patrolled their areas with two of them walking foot beats, while the other two officers used three-wheeled enclosed motor scooters. Shortly after the program began, the department purchased six CJ7 Jeeps for the officers to use on their patrols. While patrolling on foot was still the primary duty of these officers, it became necessary, due to the large geographic area, for the officers to have the Jeeps so they could respond to crimes within their beats immediately.

The Neighborhood Foot Patrol Program received national attention in March 1977, when United Press International ran a story about the Des Moines program entitled "Police Walk Beats, Meet People". This story was published in newspapers around the country, and it reported on how successful the program had been, along with its outstanding acceptance by the people in the neighborhoods.

Besides the visible impact of the foot patrol officers, this program provided many other services to the community such as Operation ID, Neighborhood Watch, security checks

Foot patrol officer

Motor scooter used by the foot patrol

OFFICER BRIAN MELTON

BY ANNA KINGERY

HONOR ROLL

BRIAN CHARLES MELTON
Appointed: November 19,1973
Died: April 21, 1977

and many public service talks to community groups and business organizations.

It was the foot patrol officers who were the first to arrive on the scene of one of the deadliest fires in the city's history. On February 9th, 1977, the five-story Coronado Apartment building caught fire, killing four people and injuring nine. One of the foot patrol officers, Russell Underwood (now a captain on the police department), was the first to arrive at the scene. Just as Officer Underwood arrived, a man who was clinging to his top floor fire escape let go and fell towards the ground. Underwood ran towards the falling man, however, he was only able to get close enough to have the man's belt buckle rip through his hand. Despite the fall, the man survived his injuries.

All of the officers involved with the foot patrol program felt they received much less hostility and more support than the squad car patrol officers. This is the same attitude exhibited today by people in the neighborhoods who get to know their police officers on a first-name basis.

Around 1980, the department changed the name of the Neighborhood Foot Patrol to the Special Area Crime Unit, however citizens and officers alike still referred to the officers who worked this assignment as the "foot patrol" officers.

In February 1988 the foot patrol program was disbanded, due in part to the expiration of the federal funds that helped support this program. ✪

It started like any other bizarre situation—completely routine.

On April 21, 1977, Officer Brian Melton and several other officers responded to a complaint that a group of intoxicated people were gathering outside in the Highland Park area of the city. When officers arrived, David Welton and Paul Bell were sitting in a car near Bell's house listening to music. Both men were arrested for intoxication, and officers were in the process of escorting the men to the paddy wagon when a scuffle ensued between Welton and the officers. It is not exactly clear how it happened, but another officer's gun apparently slipped from his holster. Welton retrieved it and shot Melton.

Melton managed to get back to his feet and run to his patrol car to radio for assistance. He then slumped to the street while the other three officers struggled for the gun. Two officers tried to administer first aid to Melton while the others put Welton in the paddywagon.

"I can't die," Melton told Sgt. Joe Fusaro as he was being placed in an ambulance."I've got a wife and two kids." He was 25 years old when he died. Although Melton, a police cadet for two years who was promoted to police officer in 1973, was usually consistent about wearing his bullet-proof vest, he was not wearing it the night of the shooting.

David Welton, 22, was charged with murder in the case and bond was set at $500,000. At the time of the shooting, Welton was on probation for a charge of assault with intent to commit rape. He had pled guilty to the rape charge and was sentenced to two years probation in June, 1976.

It came as a total shock to most people when Welton was found innocent of the murder by a jury in Scott County, where the trial was held in a change of venue. His lawyer,

Alfredo Parrish, contended that Welton was the victim of police brutality prior to the shooting and the fatal bullet could have been fired by an officer during the struggle for the gun. Judge A.B. Crouch had instructed the jury that if they found police used unreasonable and excessive force in arresting Welton, he had the right to resist, defend himself, and "repel force with force." Later, jurors said they had "reasonable doubt" that the state had proven Welton was guilty.

Des Moines police officers and Melton's family members reacted with bitter disappointment."Brian died in vain," his widow, Karin, said as she cried in the hallway outside the courtroom. When contacted at his home, the normally vociferous Chief Wendell Nichols said in a quiet and subdued voice: "No comment. We have got to live with it." Even Alfredo Parrish, Welton's attorney, said he was "very surprised" by the acquittal.

After an internal investigation that cleared officers of the excessive force charge, the Des Moines Police Department sadly closed the book on this fatal shooting with no satisfaction that the killer had been punished. ✪

AMBUSH OF OFFICER DENNIS HILL

BY ANNA KINGERY

Two days after the acquittal of David Welton in the shooting death of Officer Brian Melton, two more police officers were shot, one fatally. Officer Dennis Hill died several hours after he received a shotgun wound to the head. A five-year veteran of the Police Department, Officer Hill was ambushed in a residential area on the north side of Des Moines.

The incident began about 4:00 am on August 29, 1977 when Ronald Davis and Donnie Buckner refused to give Anthony Clayburn a ride home from a party. Clayburn left, then returned minutes later with a Browning 12-gauge semi-automatic shotgun and shot Davis in the lower back. Stray pellets wounded Buckner in the right shoulder. An unidentified woman telephoned the police to report that there had been a shooting.

As Officers Dennis Hill and John Meeker sped to the scene in their patrol wagon, Clayburn apparently hid behind nearby bushes. When Hill, the driver of the van, pulled to a stop next to the wounded men, Clayburn shot three times, shattering the driver's window and striking Hill in the left side of his head. Clayburn ran across a nearby vacant lot toward an alley between Washington and Mondamin Avenues.

After Meeker put out the call that an officer had been shot, officers responded immediately to assist. A search for the shooter ensued. As Officer Larry Cramer rounded the corner of a garage on Washington, he spotted Clayburn coming towards him and told him to halt. Clayburn raised his shotgun and fired three times, striking Cramer once in the knee. One blast also knocked his hat off his head, but he received no head injury.

As Cramer was going down, he fired four rounds at Clayburn. At the same time, Officer Dan Catalfo and Officer Dean Emary rounded the corner and both opened fire on Clayburn. Officer Emary fired once with his shotgun and Officer Catalfo fired one round with his service revolver. Clayburn was dead on arrival at Broadlawns Hospital. Cramer was treated at the hospital and released.

Chief Wendell Nichols termed the incident as a "senseless shooting." He said that Hill, "had no defense. He never even got out of the car."

The scene was one of bitter grief at Mercy Hospital where doctors attended to Officer Hill. His wife, Cynthia, sat quietly in a waiting room with other family members, while officers lined the hall outside the waiting room. At 8:55 pm, Officer Hill passed away. He was also survived by two children, Todd, age 5, and Denyce, 18 months and his parents, Earl and Marella Hill. Earl Hill was a sergeant on the force and had been a Des Moines police officer for 27 years. He retired shortly after his son's death.

A local evangelical movie company later produced a film about Officer Hill. The film, entitled "Heaven's Heroes," focused on Officer Hill and his friendship with his partner, Officer Wayne Lunders. The film was shot in Des Moines and was distributed primarily to religious organizations for showing to church members and at some commercial theaters. ✪

POLICE CADET PROGRAM

BY SPO CHARLES GUHL

The Des Moines Police Cadet Program began in 1970 as a part of the Personnel and Training Section.

This program was initially financed by the federally funded Model Cities Program, and was sponsored by the Des Moines Police Department in cooperation with other community organizations.

The purpose of this program was to provide employment for youth in the community, to promote interest in police work and ultimately help create future police officers. Persons with low incomes, as well as minority groups, were particularly recruited for this program. In order to be eligible for this program, the applicant must have good character, integrity, initiative, and be in good physical condition, and at least 10 years of age. All

CHIEF WENDELL E. NICHOLS

BY ANNA KINGERY

On Thursday, August 17, 1978, Chief Wendell Nichols announced his retirement after 36 years with the Des Moines Police Department, 10 of them as chief of police. His intention was to remain on the job until a new chief was appointed, but on September 28 he was making his farewell address to his men. His abrupt departure came about as a protest of the city council's action to dismiss City Manager Richard Wilkey. Ultimately, Wilkey was not fired, but Nichols went ahead with his retirement plans and officially ended his career on September 30, 1978.

Wendell Nichols

Nichols, the son of a coal miner, was born March 30, 1918 at the Hocking mining camp near Albia. He attended Pershing Grade School in Marion County and graduated from Attica High School in 1935.

He was working for a meat packing company earning about $64 a week, when he decided to take a pay cut to become a policeman for $144 a month. In those days, training to become a police officer consisted of one week of class work and one week divided between class work and traffic duty.

After 18 months as a Des Moines police officer, Nichols joined the Navy during World War II and served until 1945 before returning to police work. Nichols worked under eight different police chiefs and served as chief himself longer than any of them. Nichols was promoted to sergeant in 1954, lieutenant in 1958, and to captain in 1961. He served as acting chief for three months before replacing Vear Douglas as chief in July 1968.

Although Nichols never avoided controversy, not even his harshest critics ever accused him of being dishonest. A tough-talking realist, he never minced words when he was chief. He never ducked an issue, seldom said "no comment," and usually had a colorful (and quotable) remark ready. That made him a favorite of local reporters.

During his tenure as chief of police several controversies arose, both internally and externally. Several major internal investigations in the early 1970s led to retirements, firings and suspensions. Nichols did not hesitate to take disciplinary action when he felt the integrity of the department was at stake. As a member of the department in 1960 when several officers were caught participating in illegal activities, he experienced the extra scrutiny the public placed on the department after that incident. He did not want that same type of shadow cast on the department during his tenure as chief.

In his first two years as chief of police, there were racial disturbances, anti-war protests, buildings burned and community tensions heightened. In 1970, he led the investigation into the bombing of the Des Moines Police Station.

His creation of a foot patrol squad in the inner-city area of Des Moines was successful, and he created the first narcotics squad for this department. He implemented many of the suggestions made by the International Association of Chiefs of Police (IACP) after a study of the department in 1969. While both were captains, Nichols and Harold Fryman devised a plan in which Des Moines was divided into sections with police officers under a sergeant assigned to each area. The plan was lauded by the IACP, and later adopted by other cities.

In 1972, Chief Nichols had the pleasure of appointing his son, Douglas Nichols, to the Des Moines Police Department. Following in his father's footsteps, Doug rose through the ranks over the years and is now an assistant chief.

Wendell Nichols retired to become a full-time farmer in Martensdale, Iowa, just south of Des Moines. He left a proud legacy during his 10 years and three months as chief of police in Iowa's largest city. ✪

---

applicants must undergo the same basic testing as police officers prior to employment. Current cadet applicants must also have at least 15 semester hours of college credit to be eligible for employment, and they must be accepted for the position of police officer within five years after becoming a cadet.

Police cadets perform a variety of jobs with varied hours within the department, to include administrative support, crime prevention, traffic control, report writing, and minimal patrol duties.

The success of this program is evident by the number of cadets who have gone on to become police officers. In fact, The Department currently has former cadets who have attained the ranks of captain, lieutenant, and sergeant. The cadet program continues this day with 14 cadets employed by the police department. ✪

BY TOM SUK

BLOODY SUNDAY

FEBRUARY 19,1978

began as a normal, quiet winter Sunday in downtown Des Moines, but changed to a day of horror when Ira Hockenberg stepped through a doorway at 10:50 am and saw the bodies.

"There were three of them lying like soldiers in a row, face down in what I first thought was red paint. Then I realized it was blood," the 70-year-old restaurant supply salesman said.

"It was tragic. It was an especially grisly scene with the bodies side by side—young bodies," veteran Polk County Medical examiner Dr. R.C. Wooters said later.

The boys—brothers Gerald Hoffman Jr., 15, and Jeff Hoffman, 14, along with their 14-year-old friend Jeff Beavers—had been

"THERE WERE THREE OF THEM LYING LIKE SOLDIERS IN A ROW, FACE DOWN IN WHAT I FIRST THOUGHT WAS RED PAINT. THEN I REALIZED IT WAS BLOOD." Ira Hockenberg

Patrolman Roger Rowley waits inside police lines set up at 510 Grand Avenue Sunday while homicide detectives and the coroner finish their investigation into the shootins of three teen-age boys, 1978

THE CITY HAD BEEN STUNNED BY THE

dropped off about 90 minutes earlier.

The West Des Moines teens were making pocket money by doing clean-up work for the Hoffman boys' father, who was remodeling the building at 510 Grand Avenue.

Most residents thought Des Moines was a safe, small midwestern city. After Hockenberg found the three teenagers—gunned down execution-style with each shot in the head from close range while lying face down, side by side—Des Moines became something else. Newspaper headlines called February 19, 1978, "Bloody Sunday." Des Moines was dubbed "Little Detroit."

The city had been stunned by the discovery of yet another victim the same day, less than three blocks away from where the boys were murdered.

William Baldwin, 30, a clerk at an adult bookstore, was found dead of a gunshot wound to the head shortly before 5:00 pm. There was $160 missing from the store's cash register.

All four victims had been shot with a .38-caliber handgun. Police believed the same person was responsible for all the murders.

There was not only shock in the city, there was fear.

"It kind of makes you worry. It was more like some of the big cities—not like Des Moines," a clerk at a downtown clothing store said the next day.

Dave Berlovich, the operator of a popular downtown eatery, said his customers were "apprehensive. I'm apprehensive."

Employees of downtown businesses walked in pairs or small groups to their cars. Parents warned their teen-agers not to go downtown.

Polk County Attorney Dan Johnston said the fear was understandable. "All we know is that somewhere, whether still in Des Moines or someplace else now, there's a man capable of making three young boys lie down, and blowing their lives away."

Despite the largest manhunt in the city's history, authorities could do little to reassure the public.

A small army of detectives, up to 60 investigators from the Des Moines Police Department and Iowa Division of Criminal Investigation, was assigned to the case. They worked around the clock putting in 12 to 16-hour days.

"I wish I had a lot of confidence, but this one really looks tough. We need a break. We really need a break," Des Moines Police Chief Wendell Nichols said.

The investigation was intense. Hardly a person in the downtown area before 7:00 am or after 6:00 pm had not been questioned or studied in some way by a police officer.

Roadblocks were set up in downtown Des Moines on two consecutive Sunday mornings. Motorists were stopped and asked if they had seen anything, anything at all.

Officers combed through the alleys, vacant buildings, railroad yards and construction sites in downtown Des Moines. Dozens of derelicts were questioned about their whereabouts on the morning of Sunday, February 19.

Investigators received information from snitches, psychics and psychologists, as well as hundreds of tips from the public. The officers grilled people with records of being robbers, muggers, drug dealers, burglars and those with known violent tendencies. They were asked to account for their time on Sunday morning, February 19. Many were given polygraph tests.

For weeks, police radios crackled with messages asking officers to locate persons to be questioned in "the homicides."

"Anybody brought to jail for anything is asked THE question—do you know anything about the February 19 slayings," Sgt. Phil Vander Meide said.

Detectives checked records of gun sales and thefts of .38-caliber handguns.

Progress of the investigation was plotted on

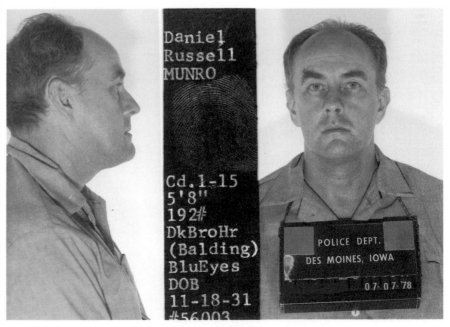

Daniel Russell Munro's mug shot and fingerprint card

DISCOVERY OF YET ANOTHER VICTIM THE SAME DAY

large cardboard sheets reaching from the floor to ceiling in the Crimes Against Persons office on the third floor of the police station. Leads to be followed, leads that had been checked and new leads were posted on the placards.

Despite the massive investigation, evidence was sparse. Police had six spent .38-caliber slugs recovered from the crime scenes or the victims' bodies. They also had a number of vague descriptions of people seen near the crime scenes.

But sleep-deprived detectives with sour stomachs from subsisting on irregular fast-food meals for weeks, continued running down every possible lead.

"If dedicated effort, sincerity and persistence mean anything,one of these days we are going to put the right key in the right door and the door will open for us," Chief of Detectives Billie B. Wallace said.

The key came when a detective walked into a pawn shop in the east loop of Des Moines. He discovered a .38-caliber, five-shot Smith and Wesson revolver had been redeemed Friday, February 17. A total of five shots had been used to kill the three boys.

Records showed the man who pawned the gun had identified himself as Jerry Meeks. He listed a third-rate downtown hotel as his address. He had pawned the gun for $50 in December and redeemed the gun two days before the murders.

"Jerry Meeks" had disappeared the day after the murders. He had not gone to work as a maintenance man at a suburban manufacturing company the day after the murders. Investigators learned he led a transient existence working odd jobs.

Co-workers said he was a loner. They believed he was a Southerner who had recently gotten out of prison.

"IF DEDICATED EFFORT, SINCERITY AND PERSISTENCE MEAN ANYTHING, ONE OF THESE DAYS WE ARE GOING TO PUT THE RIGHT KEY IN THE RIGHT DOOR AND THE DOOR WILL OPEN FOR US." Chief of Detectives Billie B. Wallace

Meeks had a tendency to get mean when he was drunk, which was often.

The Friday before slayings, the same day he redeemed the revolver, Meeks invited two co-workers to go drinking. He also asked one of the men to buy a box of .38-caliber ammunition for him.

The man bought a box of Winchester Western 158 grain ammunition. It was the type of ammunition used in the murders.

Meeks and his co-workers went drinking in the bar of a cheap hotel. Meeks uncharacteristically bought most of the drinks. When they left the hotel only a few blocks from the police station, Meeks had the .38 caliber revolver tucked in the waistband of his pants.

Meek's jacket was open and the handle of the gun was protruding from his waistband when a police car passed. His companions urged Meeks to zip up his jacket so police would not see the gun.

"Hell no, if they give me any trouble I'll just shoot them," a drunk and belligerent Meeks replied.

When Meeks woke up the day before the murders he was broke. He had spent his meager paycheck redeeming the gun from the pawn shop, buying ammunition, buying drinks and paying his rent.

Police soon determined Jerry Meeks was an alias but did not know the real identity of the suspect. All avenues to answer that question led to dead ends.

Investigators played a long shot. Police took his two drinking companions on a tour of Southern prisons.

First in Kentucky, then Tennessee, the men flipped through prison mug shots of men who had recently been released or escaped. No luck.

Then, while sitting next to Des Moines Detective Clarence "Laddie" Jobe in the records office of the Kilby State Prison just outside Montgomery, Alabama, one of the men saw a familiar face on a prison mug shot.

Jerry Meeks was Daniel Russell Munro, a 46-year-old escapee.

Fingerprints from some tools Munro had used and paychecks he had cashed in Des Moines confirmed that Munro was the man using the name of Jerry Meeks in the city.

Munro had been given a life sentence in Alabama for a brutal robbery at a Mobile shoe store in February of 1968.

A clerk in the store, who offered no resistance, was tied up when Munro sat on his back, slashed his throat with a hunting knife and stabbed him 16 more times.

In a desperate struggle the clerk managed to partially break free from his restraints and was able to kick Munro in the groin, causing him to drop the knife and flee. Two passing Navy medics managed to stem the clerk's blood loss until he could be transported to a hospital, and were credited with saving the man's life.

Other passersby alerted by the clerk's calls for help saw Munro leave the shoe store and followed him, leading to his arrest a short time later.

INVESTIGATORS PLAYED A LONG SHOT. POLICE TOOK HIS TWO DRINKING COMPANIONS ON A TOUR OF SOUTHERN PRISONS.

CHIEF BILLIE WALLACE

BY TOM ALEX

Munro was given a life sentence after being convicted in the attack, largely on the testimony of the surviving clerk.

Even with the life sentence, Munro became eligible for parole and was placed in a work release program. On March 17, 1977 he left the prison on a work assignment and did not come back.

Police believed he led a migratory existence before arriving in Des Moines sometime in November of 1977.

Murnro became the subject of a nationwide manhunt. He was nearly placed on the FBI's Top Ten Most Wanted list. Police also feared Munro would destroy crucial evidence and possibly go on a violent crime spree if he learned he was wanted for the Des Moines murders.

FBI agents checked transient hotels and shelters throughout the nation. On April 28, 1978 they showed a photograph of Munro to the operators of a Salvation Army transient lodge on the edge of downtown Little Rock, Arkansas.

They identified the man as a shelter resident known as Steve Smith, who also did janitorial work for them. He came to the shelter broke and hungry on April 5, they said.

A short time later, Munro walked into the shelter and was arrested without resistance.

Taken back to Des Moines, Munro was convicted of the murders of the three boys on a case based largely on circumstantial evidence put together by prosecutor James Ramey. He was sentenced to three consecutive life sentences.

Munro has maintained his innocence throughout the years since his conviction.

The murder of the bookstore clerk was never prosecuted but police said they were certain Munro was his killer.

Authorities said it appeared robbery was the motive for all the murders. The wallet of one of the three teenaged victims was taken. It contained $2. ✪

Billie Wallace and the man who appointed him chief of police, City Manager Richard Wilkey, both denied that the successful investigation of the so-called "Bloody Sunday" killings launched Wallace into the top spot in the state's largest police department.

But the conviction of Daniel Russell Munro, an Alabama prison escapee, in the slayings of three West Des Moines teenagers, put then Chief of Detectives Wallace in the spotlight just as former Police Chief Wendell Nichols was stepping down.

Billie Wallace

Nichols walked out of police headquarters as chief for the last time in October 1978. Wallace took a seat in the big chair in the northwest corner of the first floor in February 1979.

City Manager Wilkey said he selected Wallace because of his reputation for honesty and for being thorough. That police got a conviction in the difficult Munro case was seen as further proof that Wallace paid attention to detail. But many detectives, evidence gatherers and county prosecutors also worked hard to solve it.

But as an administrator he had earned a reputation. Thirty-seven of the 42 murders that occurred on his watch as chief of detectives had been solved. The numbers were big enough to be convincing.

Once in office, Wallace got a break. While there were 29 homicides in 1978, there were less than half as many during his first year at the helm. Homicides continued to drop during the next five years while he was in office, but burglaries were beginning to skyrocket, jumping by 500 break-ins his first year in office. The trend would not swing around for seven years.

Wallace recognized the cause. It was drugs, and he said in an interview that he intended to attack the problem with all the resources at his disposal. But the increasing popularity of cocaine made it difficult to gain control.

Robberies were staying at high levels, banks and armored cars were increasingly popular targets and larcenies also were climbing. Illegal drugs were gaining ground across the country.

During his term, the deep-voiced chief sometimes answered the telephone "Billie B." The B stood for Blair. In 1979 as he took office at age 53, Wallace told a reporter that he had sometimes managed to place second in his life, second in golf, second in command at the police department. But this was the first time he could remember finishing first.

He had been on the force about 30 years when he became chief. The son of Charles O. Wallace, also a Des Moines officer, he joined the department on July 1, 1949. He was a Lincoln High School graduate and Navy amphibian pilot during World War II. He earned a bachelor's degree in accounting from Drake University in 1949. Wallace was promoted to sergeant 10 years after joining the department. He made lieutenant in 1963, captain in 1968 and assistant chief in 1974.

Over the years, Wallace earned a reputation both inside and outside the police department as being rather close to a dollar. One of his favorite questions during oral examinations of lieutenant candidates was, "So you want to be a supervisor who works with budgets. What is the budget of the Des Moines Police Department?"

The question caught a lot of sergeants flat-footed. Some reportedly stumbled on the questions, blurting out guesses in the hundreds of thousands of dollars, when the actual answer was some $16 million. But the question was not designed to elicit the correct answer. It was designed to determine how a candidate could deal with a difficult question. ✪

22 POUNDS OF EQUIPMENT CARRIED BY
SPO FRANK SCARCELLO WHILE ON DUTY, 1999

Left to right on belt: **two 9mm 15 round clips, mace, radio holder, flashlight, PR 24 nightstick holder, handcuffs and holder, police radio with microphone and speaker, cell phone, handcuffs and holder, hat, holster, keys with police whistle**
Left to right below belt: **PR 24 nightstick, wallet, knife, and 9 mm Semi-automatic Beretta with one bullet in the chamber and a 15 round clip**
Right: **SPO Frank Scarcello's badge**

RECORD HOLDING CHIEF
WILLIAM H. MOULDER

BY ANNA KINGERY

As the Des Moines Police Department's longest-serving, Chief William Moulder ushered in the age of computers, mentored the Des Moines Police Department's community policing program and is dealing with Iowa's drug threat of the 1990s: methamphetamine.

He was appointed on September 4, 1984. The only chief of police to be appointed from outside the ranks of the department, he served his first career with the Kansas City Police Department, retiring as a major to come to Des Moines and be the chief of the Des Moines Police Department. While many officers were skeptical of him at first, he proved himself through his quiet but strong leadership, and his intense loyalty to them and the Des Moines Police Department.

Chief William Moulder

He inherited one of the most tragic cases in the history of Des Moines: the disappearance of newspaper carrier Eugene Martin. In August 1984, Eugene was delivering newspapers early in the morning on the south side of Des Moines when he dropped from sight. Sadly, he has never been found and the case remains open to this day.

Moulder's innovative community policing program, "The Municipal Approach," was begun in 1986. It has been instrumental in allowing the citizens of Des Moines to solve problems they experience in their neighborhoods. Several local "housewives" became community activists when they realized that through this program they could make a difference in their lives and in their neighborhoods. These women, Neila Seaman, Neva Jorgensen-Wells and Doloros Thomas, were profiled on a national television news show.

In conjunction with the Municipal Approach, he formed the Neighborhood Area Resource Coordinator's office. This office assists neighborhood groups in problem solving and allows for a central point where citizens may exchange information with the police department. He advocated for other City departments (zoning, building, public works, parks) to come on board and offer assistance to residents in cleaning up neighborhoods.

Instrumental in his Municipal Approach concept was a series of meetings that brought together representatives from neighborhood associations, the police department and other City entities. These meetings were facilitated by a professional who assisted the participants in brainstorming about the problems they perceived in their neighborhoods and possible solutions.

In 1990, Chief Moulder received the NAACP's President's Award," for his untiring leadership in the Municipal Approach to eradicating drugs in the city of Des Moines and for keeping the community informed by the special meetings and forums held periodically."

Controversy over an arrest in 1991 led to the City Council holding several forums around the city to allow citizens to express their views about the Police Department. Many neighborhood association leaders and other citizens came out in support of the chief of police and the Police Department.

A proponent of allowing citizens to see first-hand the varied duties of police officers, Moulder established a Citizens' Academy. Over 130 citizens have participated in this training. Additionally, he developed and implemented a program where community leaders were invited to spend eight hours in a patrol car with a police officer on duty.

Staying abreast of law enforcement trends has allowed him to implement several innovative programs during his tenure as police chief. He has been asked to sit on several boards and committees regarding subjects such as sentencing procedures, juvenile crime, education and drug abuse. Recognized nationwide as a leader in the policing community, he has been asked to address a sub-committee of the United States Senate and the International Association of Chiefs of Police regarding issues confronting law enforcement.

As drug issues confront police departments all over the country, Des Moines and the entire state of Iowa have been most impacted in the 1990s by the manufacture, sale and use of methamphetamine. Chief Moulder has worked closely with the federal Drug Enforcement Administration to form a working relationship that allows joint investigations and loans of Des Moines officers to the federal agency.

Because it is a crossroads for two major interstate systems, Des Moines sees more than its share of drug dealers who are transporting drugs all over the country. In response to that phenomenon, the SAF-T Squad (Strategic Anti-Felon Team), comprised of officers from Des Moines and other area law enforcement agencies, was formed. These officers train hotel and motel employees to recognize the signs of drug use and and sales. Arrests are made each year from tips from these hotel and motel workers, and many of the arrestees are from far-reaching locales.

As one of the most recognizable leaders in City government, Chief Moulder is often approached by Des Moines residents. An avid traveler, Chief Moulder has had strangers introduce themselves to him aboard a ship in the Atlantic Ocean and on a mountaintop in Colorado; in airports across the country and in local grocery stores. ✪

Reprint: *The DM Tribune,* July 28, 1981

PAST COMES BACK AS WALLS CRUMBLE AT POLICE STATION

BY TOM ALEX

Bits of history are falling out of the walls of the Municipal Court and Public Safety Building—usually called the Des Moines Police Station—as workmen hammer away at the structure that is more than 60 years old.

In the walls on the second floor pieces of newspapers from 1920 were found; out of a judge's rostrum fell a tobacco tin nearly as old as the building and in judge's chambers there were notes and documents dated 1921.

In the first phase of the $2.1-million project, which won't be completed until 1985, workers are tearing apart the basement where traffic court and clerk's offices used to be and the second floor that once housed the District Associate Court and small claims and clerk's offices.

The original floor plans of the building at E. First Street and Court Avenue point to a way of life long forgotten in today's age of television, oil shortages and jet-age travel. The pace was a little slower in the years following World War I.

When the building was opened in 1920, there was a barbershop on the first floor. That room eventually became a janitor's closet.

There was a doctor's office where the radio equipment room is now elsewhere on the first floor were sanitary department offices, four relatively large areas labeled "public space," a bedroom and the inebriant room.

Police still have an inebriant room, although located in a different spot—but now it's called the drunk tank.

The second floor is virtually unchanged since the building was constructed, which probably accounts for the pieces of memorabilia turning up in nooks and crannies.

On the third floor, now reserved mostly for detectives, was a tailors shop, a doctor's office, operating room, hospital office and corridor, men's lodging rooms, men's and women's reading rooms, showers and a gymnasium.

While Assistant Police Chief Donald Knox, Capt. Charles Backstrom and other officers wearing blue jeans and T-shirts struggled with record shelves last week to get them from the third to the first floor, workmen were knocking out walls with sledge-hammers. Among the items collected were pieces of cigarette papers made in Paris and a Tuxedo Tobacco box, probably used by a judge in the late 1920s.

Also on the third floor, when the building opened, was a Bertillon room. Named for the anthropologist Alphonse Bertillon (1853-1914), the Bertillon system was an early means of identifying people by recording body measurements, marking deformities, coloring etc.

That system later became the fingerprint and photo section, now known as the ID or identification section.

Also long gone from the third floor are the delousing stalls.

A few things remain the same. The office of the police chief is in the same location now as when the plans were drawn in 1918.

And in the little section in the basement, originally designated the "confiscated liquor room," there still are many bottles of confiscated liquor.

During the remodeling the chief's office is to be moved to the third floor and other offices are being moved to various sections in the building. Police are going to have a lot more space in their building than when it was shared with the Municipal Courts. Even the jail will be taken out once the new Polk County jail is completed.

The extra space was made available when many of the offices in the Polk County Courthouse were moved to the County Administrative Building and District Associate Court, Traffic Court and the clerk's offices were moved from the police station to the courthouse.

Most of the second floor and much of the basement in the police station already have been torn out to make way for additional and larger offices.

Gordon Evans, project superintendent with Breiholz Construction Co., said the police building is constructed well "but there was a lot of wasted space when they built it. You couldn't afford to build a building like this today."

As the walls come tumbling down in the basement and on second floor, workmen can easily tell which areas have been changed through the years.

Police used to park squad cars in the basement and the gas pump also was located inside the building at one time.

When the remodeling project is complete, there will be little left to remind an old-timer of the way it used to be—except for the press office. It will remain in the same stuffy little room where it's been for years. ✪

Editor's note: During remodeling, the old main stairway was walled off permanently. Reporter Tom Alex placed a stack of 1981 Des Moines Tribune *newspapers on the landing to be discovered at some future date.*

JOHN MONROE BRANCH INCIDENT
HIS TIME IN HELL

BY PAMELA SHAPIRO

Discharge of firearms - permitted: When the employee reasonably believes that such force is necessary to protect himself or another person from the use or threat of use of deadly force.
—Rules and Regulations Manual, DMPD 1994

Police recruits, when still in academy training, are sometimes asked a question: Of the incidents you will respond to as an officer, what percent will involve a gun?

Sometimes they get it wrong, because the answer is 100%. Every time an officer enters a situation, be it a robbery, domestic assault or theft of a bicycle, there is at least one deadly weapon at the scene: the officer's.

Officer James Harkin

They are told never to forget that, because one moment's disadvantage is all it takes for that gun to end up in the wrong hand. That is what nearly happened to Officer Jim Harkin, and for him, keeping his gun ended up being almost as bad as what could have happened if he hadn't.

A SURPRISING REACTION

It was about 7:00 pm on August 14, 1982. Still plenty of light in the sky, even though it was drizzling. Officer Harkin, wearing his uniform and driving an unmarked Volkswagen Rabbit, was cruising in the 2400 block of Garfield, an area that had experienced a rash of car burglaries lately, when he noticed a tall, black man standing in a driveway. The man was motionless, just staring into space, and caught Harkin's attention. He stopped his car and called out to the man, asking him if that was his house.

According to Harkin's testimony, his question elicited an unexpected response. The man, John Monroe Branch, ran up to his car, swearing and yelling. Harkin told him he didn't want any trouble and decided to leave immediately, radio for help and come back with a partner to talk to Branch. But when he tried to drive away, Branch reached inside the car and grabbed at him.

Harkin continued trying to drive away so he could get on the radio and call for backup, but Branch wouldn't back off despite his repeated requests that he do so. He continued interfering with Harkin's attempt to drive the car, which had a manual transmission, and hitting Harkin in the face. Harkin pulled out his nightstick, but as soon as he got it in his hand, Branch took it away from him.

He began hitting Harkin in the head with the nightstick. The car stopped and Harkin tried to get into the passenger seat, away from his attacker. In response, Branch opened the driver's side door and came in after him, swinging the nightstick. He hit Harkin so hard he fell on top of him, and as Harkin pushed him off, he grabbed at the officer's gun. Harkin deflected the attempt, pulled his gun and told Branch to back off. When Branch reached for Harkin's gun, the officer testified he said to himself, "He's going to kill me." The potential was certainly there: Branch was, at 6'6" and 180 pounds, nearly a foot taller and 30 pounds heavier than the 5'7" Harkin.

Branch stepped back from the car. Then he bent down and tried to come at Harkin again. At that point, Harkin "fired as fast as I could... I wasn't going to let him come in on top of me again with the chance of him knocking me out or getting my gun away from me like he almost did."

He fired all six shots in his .38 caliber revolver, reloaded as he had been taught to do, then radioed for help. He did not approach Branch, now lying on the lawn, until backup arrived. Branch was pronounced dead on arrival at Mercy Hospital; the autopsy would later show he was hit with four bullets.

Public reaction was immediate and furious, with people claiming Harkin had shot Branch for no reason other than the color of his skin. The next day, NAACP President Larry Carter was already talking to Des Moines Mayor Pete Crivaro about setting up a citizen's review board. Officer Harkin's mental fitness was called into question: two days later, Branch's mother filed a $1 million dollar civil suit in Polk County District Court alleging that negligence and lack of training were what led Harkin to fire "six shots into an unarmed man." It further stated that Harkin's action "was an irrational act of an individual with a deranged and mentally sick mind."

Over the days, the anger grew. A teenaged girl was interviewed in the paper on August 16, claiming to be a witness and seeing Harkin shoot Branch in the back as he walked away from the car. Members of the black community picketed city hall, demanding Harkin's immediate suspension.

Harkin was, in fact, on medical leave, recovering from the injuries he received at Branch's hands, and getting repairs to dental work damaged when Branch hit him in the side of the head with his nightstick. The dozens of newspaper stories about the incident and subsequent unrest bear one eerie consistency: none of them show a photograph of Officer Harkin. The department was so uncertain of his safety, they didn't want anyone to know what he looked like.

TROUBLED PAST

The Grand Jury convened less than two weeks later—its job, as is customary whenever an officer shoots a citizen, was to determine if evidence indicated Harkin had acted improperly. When their decision on August 30 was a refusal to indict him, tension flared anew. County Attorney Dan Johnston released a summary of the Grand Jury's findings, as their transcripts must by law be kept secret, which indicated that Branch had a history of mental illness severe enough that he was taking Lithium. That is, he was supposed to be taking Lithium.

His mother, Beatrice DeVan, had him involuntarily committed to Broadlawns Hospital in July 1981, because he was not taking his medication and was consequently a danger to himself and others. In the month before he was killed, Branch was involved in three incidents where he either "assaulted or threatened to assault individuals without provocation."

His physician, psychiatrist Dr. Oscar Barillas, described his problems as the sort that "the mood is unpredictably replaced by irrationality and unprovoked irritability. He might distort what was going on around him and explode." This description fit well with what Officer Harkin described: "It was a rage that I had never seen before. He was frantic.... I've seen violent gestures, I've heard violent language, but he was not listening to anything I was saying to him. . . "

WHAT REALLY HAPPENED

The family's lawyer, Alfredo Parrish, objected to the jury's being given information about Branch's mental condition. "What difference does it make what his mental problems were? The fact remains the man was unarmed. He was away from the car."

County Attorney Johnston was quoted in the Tribune saying, "It is wrong to call a man wielding a billy club 'unarmed.'" Investigators estimated that the first bullet was fired at a distance of three feet away from Branch, while Harkin lay on his back in the front seat of the car. The autopsy also showed that Branch was struck with four bullets, each of which penetrated either the seats or the side of the car—separating the lead slug from the jacket so that he was actually hit eight times. According to his testimony, Harkin did not draw his gun until after Branch had hit him hard enough to make him dizzy. Contrary to the teenaged witness' statement, all four shots entered Branch from the front or side. He was not shot in the back.

SUIT DENIED

In December 1982, Branch's mother filed a suit in U.S. District Court, asking for $1.5 million in damages for the violation of her son's civil rights. On 14 November 1983, the trial to decide her Polk County suit began. The verdict came in on November 22: Harkin was not liable. On 24 July 1984, the $1.5 million suit was dismissed by U.S. District Court. She re-filed in Polk County, but the denial was upheld.

The 8th Circuit court of Appeals upheld the original ruling in 1985, and later that same year, the U.S. Supreme Court declined to review the appeal.

AFTERWARD

In October 1981, two months after the shooting, four policemen were injured (one had his leg broken) in a brawl at a tavern. The manager of the bar said he believed that current racial tensions had escalated what was really a minor incident. Two days later, Melvin Harper arranged a meeting with several area residents and some of the staff at black radio station KUCB, wherein they drafted a heartfelt plea to "parents and youths to stop this kind of thing." In October 1982, Mayor Pete Crivaro established a committee to examine race relations in Des Moines. The following month, for the first time in years, NAACP Chapter President Larry Carter was challenged in his bid to continue as president of the organization.

Slowly, race relations improved. The headlines quit blaring news of the latest transgression, and life returned to normal in Des Moines. But for those closest to the incident, things would never be the same.

Like so many other items a police officer carries on the job, the gun is a tool of the trade. I have yet to meet an officer who looks forward to some day having to pull that trigger. Mrs. DeVan probably didn't know how right she was when she said of Officer Harkin, "He has to live with my boy's death for the rest of his life." ✪

U.S. HISTORY	
1980	Reagan elected, Three Mile Island accident
1981	IBM introduces "Personal Computers"
1982	Space shuttle Columbia flies
1983	Cable TV and videotapes catch on
1984	Michael Jackson makes "Thriller" video
1985	"New Coke" fails
1986	Space shuttle Challenger explodes
1987	Iran-Contra Affair
1988	Pan Am 747 blows up over Lockerbie, Scotland
1989	Baseball bans Pete Rose; Berlin Wall falls
1990	Lech Waleska elected President of Poland
1991	Persian Gulf War
1992	"Murphy Brown" vs. Dan Quayle
1993	Hubbell space telescope fixed by astronauts
1994	Ex-president Nixon dies
1995	Oklahoma City bombing
1996	Microsoft stock rises 88%
1997	"Titanic" top-grossing movie of all time
1998	Presidential impeachment hearings

LOCAL HISTORY	
1980	Old Bankers Trust Building demolished
1981	Locust Street Mall opens, IA Cubs created
1982	Terry Branstad elected governor
1983	Iowa's slogan State of Minds
1984	Bill Moulder appointed chief of police
1985	DM Register sold to Gannett Corp.
1986	Prairie Meadows Race Track passes
1987	New Iowa State Historical museum
1988	DM Police adopt 9mm pistols
1989	United flight 232 crashes in Sioux City
1990	44-story Principal Financial Bldg—801 Grand
1991	First black police Capt., Richard Sanders
1992	Drake Diner murders
1993	Downtown DM floods
1994	Gateway Park plans announced
1995	Prairie Meadows casino opens
1996	State Fair funnel cake murders
1997	Preston Daniels, 1st DM African-Am. Mayor
1998	Tom Vilsack elected, 1st Dem. Gov. in 30 years.

First Superglue Fingerprint Conviction
Murder Will Out:

BY PAMELA SHAPIRO

William Helm showed up at his mother's place a little before 11:00 am on September 2, 1990. He needed to go to his estranged wife's house to get some tools he had left there, and wanted his brother to come with him. He and his wife had a volatile history, and his lawyer had advised him against seeing her without another person being present.

They arrived at Susan's at about 11:45 am. They knocked at the front door and there was no answer. William went around to the side of the house and beat on a window. He could see his 15-month-old son, Chucky, in his crib, but neither Susan nor her older son, Derrick, were in sight. He went back to the front door, which was finally unlocked by Derrick, who was four years old. William picked up the baby from his bed and, followed by his brother, checked the other bedroom.

Susan lay on her back in bed, partially covered by a blanket. She wasn't moving, so William checked her right wrist for a pulse.

Lt. James Trotter

There was none. His brother called the police from the phone in the kitchen.

Officers arrived within minutes and took charge of the scene. Over the next 12 hours, identification technicians gathered a fair amount of forensic evidence from the house, including hair and fiber samples. And from the skin of Susan's upper abdomen, they took something else: a handprint.

History of Fingerprinting in America

Fingerprinting as a means of identification isn't new—the Chinese were using thumbprints on legal documents over 2000 years ago. But as a way to convict a criminal, fingerprinting was regarded as something akin to voodoo until the early part of this century. Sometimes the wheels of justice turn slowly, and it took awhile for America's court system to see the usefulness of a means of identification that is unique to each human being, and will never change—unlike height, weight, hair color, or handwriting.

Once the law enforcement community succeeded in getting fingerprints admitted into court as evidence they quickly became,

along with photographs, an integral part of any arrestee's identification folder. Many a burglar and car thief was successfully locked up because they left fingerprints at the scene.

In 1924, the federal government established in Washington a central bureau where all fingerprints are recorded and kept. A classification system in which a series of numbers is assigned to the loops and whorls of each print, makes possible a fairly quick determination of possible matches on a suspect. In 1988, the state integrated the Automated Fingerprint Identification System (AFIS), which sped up identification even more, as it is a computer that reads the prints.

A Discovery

"Superglue" was invented by accident in the late 1950s, in the labs of Eastman Kodak. The official name for it is "cyanoacrylate ester adhesive." Cyanoacrylate ester has unique abilities besides bonding surfaces in seconds: a factory worker packaging the product one day happened to notice that when it is heated in an airtight container, its vapors bond to the faint oily residue left behind by a finger contacting with a surface. As the vapors harden and build upon that residue, it becomes visible as a fingerprint.

And such residue can be left on many types of surfaces: metal, wood, plastic, human skin....

Give it a Try

After Identification Technicians Lee Shaklee and Nancy Lamasters had completed the standard gathering of evidence from the crime scene at Susan Helm's house, their boss, Lt. James Trotter, decided to attempt the "cyanoacrylate fuming" process on the body. The idea was pretty new, and no one had yet been successful in prosecuting a murder based on that sort of evidence, but Lt. Trotter figured it was worth a try. From the appearance of her body, it looked like she had been either strangled or stabbed, so it was very likely that the killer had touched her.

Using plastic pipe and a clear plastic drop

Des Moines Police Squad car

Reprint: *The DM Register,* December 12, 1990

FOR OFFICER, AN ARRESTING CAREER IS OVER

BY TOM ALEX

cloth, they constructed a tent over the body and sealed it with duct tape. They poured superglue into two aluminum dishes, placed each one on a hotplate inside the tent, and turned them on. After 30 minutes, they checked the body and found they probably hadn't gotten a high enough concentration of fumes to do the job. So they turned up the temperature and tried again.

This time it worked. On Susan Helm's abdomen, just below her right breast, they could see the print of someone's right palm. They photographed the print and attempted to lift it from the body. They were unsuccessful in that, but the photos were very clear. The print itself would not be necessary.

WE'VE GOT IT

The primary suspect, from the beginning, was Susan's husband, William Helm. Det. Rahn Bjornson obtained a search warrant that enabled him to collect fingerprints from William Helm.

When a "latent" print (one taken from the scene of the crime), is compared to the known prints of a suspect, the technician is looking for "points of comparison": tiny curls, breaks and ridges in the lines of a fingerprint that are exactly the same in both the latent and the suspect's prints. When technicians Robert Baker and Jerry Wilson compared William Helm's prints with the photos of the print on Susan Helm's body, they needed eight points of comparison to prove that the latent was William's. They stopped counting at 96.

ONE OF A KIND

On August 23, 1991, William Helm was sentenced to life in prison without parole for the murder of his wife Susan. The case remains the only one in the world where a murderer was convicted by a palm print found on the body itself, using the cyanoacrylate fuming process. ✪

Over the years he's had a lot of nicknames: Dad, TAT, The Nose, and The Old Man.

Starting in January, they can call Thomas A. Teale retired.

When Teale, an assistant Des Moines police chief and commander of the uniform division, hangs up his uniform, it will end a career spanning more than 39 years.

"You know you have to do it. It's just a matter of identifying a date," Teale said of his retirement. "I hate to leave. I don't know if I feel that way because it means I'm getting old or if I just like the job that much.."

Teale, a former teacher and one of the few older officers with a college degree, retires Jan. 25.

Teale was named assistant chief in 1970. He held the position for half of his career. Twice, he was acting chief while the city searched for a permanent chief.

SURPRISED

News of Teale's departure took some officers by surprise Monday. Others said they knew it was only a matter of time since he turned 65.

"You don't replace a person like Teale," Police Lt. Neil Leighter said. "He's a legend. His plans for opera-

tions, like handling the Pope's visit (in 1979) are used by larger police departments as models. He's not always easy to get along with, but you have to respect him."

The department went through some "integrity problems a few decades ago," recalled one of the other assistant chiefs, William McCarthy, "but there was always one constant, someone who stood for integrity and honesty. Tom Teale.

"You did it legally or you didn't do it," McCarthy said, "because you knew if Teale found out about it, it wouldn't fly."

REMINDERS

In his early days on the force, however, the Mount Ayr native required an occasional reminder of proper police procedure. It is said Teale, who fought the Nazis on the rhine River with George Patton in World War II, once removed a motorist from a car without bother-

Thomas A. Teale

DRAWING BY DAVE MURILLO

ing to open the door.

Not all the officers hold Teale in high esteem. Forgetting to put on a hat when leaving a squad car or forgetting to pin a badge on the outermost garment could cause a nose-to-nose confrontation with "Dad." Some critics said he kept too tight a rein on the captains under his command.

But he'll be remembered fondly for being among the first to go into a building after a gunman, Sgt. Kelly Willis said.

Speculation about Teale's retirement has been one of the chief amusements around the department for 10 years. He'll probably remain a topic of conversation, Leighter said.

"People will talk about him here 20 years after he's gone, he made that kind of mark here," Leighter said. ✪

171

THE BIRTH OF O.P.S.

BY RICHARD CROOK

"Today more than ever the public expects accountability by the police for their actions. The use of force by law enforcement officers is one of the greatest responsibilities and liabilities facing agencies. Every law enforcement administrator must recognize the public suspicion about internal review processes. A department must take whatever steps it can to be responsive to that suspicion and strengthen public confidence."

—From Police Administration, by O.W. Wilson

It can be called nearly anything. In Los Angeles, San Francisco and New York City, it's called Internal Affairs. In Chicago they have both an Internal Affairs Section and a Professional Standards Unit; in Philadelphia they have both an Internal Affairs Division and an Ethical Affairs Unit (now called IMPACT). The mandates are the same in all departments, however: to ensure their members maintain a high degree of professionalism and integrity; and to ensure that accusations leveled against officers are addressed in a timely and fair manner.

Before 1969, the Des Moines Police Department had no formal internal review process. Those were the days before Miranda, Escobedo, Garrity, reverse-Garrity and the myriad other legal decisions that define and govern the behavior of law enforcement officers all over the country.

In the '60s there were student sit-ins at University of California at Berkeley and Columbia University, among others. There were draft card burnings, bra-burnings and ROTC building burnings; free speech movements, filthy speech movements and free love movements. A fine line had to be walked between what was legitimate control of rioters or demonstrators, and what might be considered excessive use of force.

Things came to a head in the last week of August 1968. There was to be a presidential election in November of that year. Along with presidential elections come political party conventions. The Democrats chose Chicago for theirs. Vietnam War protesters, civil rights activists, Black Panthers, free speech movement activists, Students for a Democratic Society, yippies and about every other social protest group in the country, mainstream or fringe, wacko and relatively sane, decided they were going to show up in the Windy City at the same time. The result was some of the worst rioting the city had ever experienced.

These days, lots of self-proclaimed experts believe that the "Days of Rage" mess happened because the Chicago Police Department went out of control. They have probably forgotten, though, it was the specific intent of many protesters to do whatever they could to incite the police to use extreme measures. However, regardless of where the fault for the Days of Rage lay it was the Chicago Police Department in particular, and any U.S. police department in general, that caught the heat.

Most dispassionate people realized that most police officers were more concerned about the misuse of police powers than the average citizen. It also had long been the practice to hold police officers to a higher standard of conduct than the average man on the street, but no one had officially laid down and defined those higher standards. A few quasi-police associations around the country, such as the International Association of Chiefs of Police and the Commission on Accreditation for Law Enforcement, took it upon themselves to address the questions.

By 1969, all the polls, surveys, appraisals, studies, planning and strategizing were complete. A new code of ethics for police officers was written and a new organizational concept was born—one that the experts hailed as being the answer to law enforcement's image problem. It was called Internal Affairs.

The idea was that police agencies should establish an internal unit whose members were organizationally separate from the traditional police hierarchy; a unit that was answerable only to the chief of police. That unit's sole and specific purpose would be to ensure that all other members of the department operated within a set of precise ethical and moral guidelines.

In December 1969, such a unit was established within the Des Moines Police Department. It was manned by one police officer whose main function was to investigate complaints.

In the early spring of 1991, an incident occurred in Southern California that brought the issue of police conduct back to the public's consciousness. At about 12:30 am on March 3, two California Highway Patrol officers, Tim and Melanie Singer (husband and wife), were driving on the Foothill Freeway in the Pacoima area of Los Angeles' San Fernando Valley.

As they neared the Sunland Boulevard off-ramp, they spotted a car speeding up behind them. The two officers began to follow the car west toward the Foothill Boulevard intersection with the Simi Valley Freeway. They clocked the white Hyundai at almost 115 miles per hour during their nearly six-mile chase.

What happened after the car was stopped immediately attracted international attention. Rodney King's name became known in every household in the country. Whether the incident involved police brutality or the use of force necessary under the circumstances was, in a sense, irrelevant. The focus of the nation's attention was back on police conduct once again, and every police agency in the country would feel it.

In Des Moines several months later, officers were involved in a "use of force" incident that resulted in a reorganization of the department's Internal Affairs Unit. At around 7:00 on the evening of December 28, 1991, a woman living in a large old home in the

172

Riverbend neighborhood on Des Moines' near north side answered a knock at her front door. There were two men standing on her front porch. One of them asked if he could come in and use her phone. The woman declined, but volunteered to make a call for them, if they needed help. The man responded by saying, "Call the police. This man's been hurt bad." The woman could see that the other man did indeed appear to have been injured. She later told investigators that his left eye was swollen and there was blood on the left side of his face.

Her 911 call was received by the DMPD at 7:06 pm and dispatchers sent a call out to officers who were in the area. The call was received by Sgt. Joanne Pollock. Two other officers in the area driving a police van normally used to transport prisoners, Thomas Heller and Thomas Strawser, also responded to the scene.

When the officers arrived a few minutes later, they saw two men walking toward their vehicles; one appeared to be helping the other. Officer Strawser took one of them, James Harvey, aside to talk with him and left the second man, Larry Milton, with Sgt. Pollock and Officer Heller.

As they talked with Milton, it became apparent to Pollock and Heller that the man was either drunk or high on some drug, maybe both. Milton later admitted that he had both been drinking for much of the day, and had also used some "crack" that afternoon. The officers asked Milton to move over to the police van so that they could search him for weapons prior to taking him to the hospital to be treated for his injuries. He began acting peculiarly, yelling that someone was trying to kill him, and the officers attempted to place him under arrest before he hurt someone.

Milton let out a loud scream and began to act even more erratically. At that point, the officers took him to the ground to handcuff him. Milton began to resist and the fight was

on. Even though both Pollock and Strawser were on top of him, Milton continued to struggle. Pollock determined that the force necessary to subdue the man would have to be escalated. She grabbed her mace canister and sprayed it directly into Milton's face. The only thing that happened then was that he spat, as though he didn't like the taste of the chemical. It turned out that Strawser was affected much worse by the mace than was their intended prisoner; Milton just continued to struggle. He managed to take the mace canister away from Pollock for a few moments, but she wrested it back from him before he could spray anyone.

By now, the officers had taken Milton to the ground several times but he managed to get back up again each time. They were able to wrestle him to the ground once again, but this time Milton grabbed for Strawser's gun. Strawser shouted a warning, "Gun!" and Heller immediately hit Milton in the head several times with the flashlight that he had been carrying. It was a clear justification for the use of "deadly force."[1] Heller could just as easily have shot Milton at that point, but the officer chose to continue trying to subdue the man.

As required by departmental policy and procedures, the officers prepared reports of the incident and submitted them to their watch commander, Captain Richard Sanders, and the incident review process began. After reading the written reports, Sanders interviewed each of the officers, affixed his approval endorsement and sent them on to Assistant Chief of Police Kayne Robinson, the Uniform Division commander. Their finding was that the amount of force that had been used to subdue Milton was justified. Independent investigations by the Iowa Citizens' Aid/Ombudsman office and by a Polk County grand jury subsequently confirmed the department's findings. The officers had clearly done what was necessary under the circumstances.

The Office of Professional Standards is

now responsible only for investigating allegations of police misconduct. The results of their investigations are forwarded to the appropriate unit commanders for review and recommendation. The unit has no responsibility for defining degree of guilt or recommending punishment; they merely investigate and report.

Within the DMPD, there are two categories of complaints that can be lodged against an officer: Procedural complaints are those involving minor acts of misconduct such as use of profanity, rudeness or certain policy violations. Standard of conduct violations are those that involve more serious breaches of the rules. Complaints that could result in criminal charges against an officer, such as the use of deadly force, are investigated by the officers of the Des Moines Police Department's Criminal Investigation Division. Departmental disciplinary actions can range from a verbal reprimand to dismissal from the force.

[1] Deadly force is defined in Iowa Code 704.2 as being:

1. Force used for the purpose of causing serious injury,

2. Force which the actor knows will create a strong probability that serious injury will result.

3. The discharge of a firearm in the direction of some person with the knowledge of the person's presence.

4. The discharge of a firearm at a vehicle in which a person is known to be.

There are four categories of findings that can be reached when a complaint is investigated.

- A sustained finding means that the alleged acts occurred and were inappropriate.

- A non-sustained finding means that not enough evidence was available to prove or disprove the alleged act.

- An exonerated finding means that the act was justified, legal and proper under the circumstances.

- An unfounded finding means that the alleged act did not occur.

Upon receiving a complaint, Office of Professional Standards personnel will investigate the allegations, take statements from appropriate persons—both within and without the department, and assemble all pertinent information relative to the allegation. The resulting report is forwarded to the commander of the division to which the accused officer has been assigned.

The division commander is then responsible for reviewing the report and making appropriate recommendations. Those recommendations are then forwarded to the chief of police, who then determines the findings and sanctions.

The reports that document the completed investigation are then passed on to a review committee whose members include the City Manager, the city's Human Rights Director, the Corporation Counsel, the Chief of Police and the commander of the Office of Professional Standards. The committee may concur with the original findings, or they may order further investigation. If they concur, they will also provide an opinion as to the applicability of the sanctions that were originally proposed by the division commander. It ultimately becomes the responsibility of the City Manager to make the final determination as to the disposition of the case.

The message has gotten across. In the period 1992 through 1997, the Office of Professional Standards opened formal investigations into a total of 670 complaints against officers. Of that total, only about 25% involved standard of conduct allegations. During those five years, only 10 allegations resulted in sustained findings. Des Moines can boast of having one of the cleanest departments of any major city in the United States. ✪

Above: **View looking into holding tank at Des Moines City Jail**
Right: **Phone used by prisoners**

CHILD ABUSE TRAUMA TEAM

BY CAPT. DALE PATCH AND
PAMELA SHAPIRO

The Des Moines Police Department, Polk County Attorney's Office, Department of Human Services, Judicial Department of the State of Iowa's Juvenile Court, and local medical personnel formed the United States' first Child Abuse Trauma Team.

Police work is a tough business, and its never harder than when a child is harmed. Investigating allegations of child abuse is a difficult, emotional process often made even more complicated by the structure of the very system designed to protect those children. Police, prosecuting attorneys, child protective investigators and medical personnel all must come together if a case of child abuse is going to be handled properly. But these agencies have their own needs, tasks and rules, which can make it too easy for the necessary swift response to get bogged down in bureaucratic red tape.

Until 1992 in Des Moines Iowa, that is. In January of that year, the Des Moines Police Department, Polk County Attorney's Office, Department of Human Services, Judicial Department of the State of Iowa's Juvenile Court and local medical personnel formed the United States' first Child Abuse Trauma Team. This coalition works as a single unit, sacrificing departmental self-interest and one-upmanship in favor of a true team approach.

When they get the call on a possible child abuse case, their response is immediate. There are no more long delays for the child protective investigators when they request the court's permission to remove a child from an abusive home, while crucial evidence and witness testimony needed by the police evaporate.

The County Attorney's office plays an important role on the team, as their representative has special legal powers not available to the other agencies, and immediate access to the court system. Their presence at the initial stages also enables that attorney to become involved on the ground floor of the investigation, and be aware of all the evidence gathered and its potential relevance to the prosecution of the case.

As the Child Abuse Trauma Team operates today, all personnel on the team are immediately contacted when severe trauma cases occur. Since the team is each member's highest priority, they respond immediately upon notification. Each member's special training and jurisdictional authority, when combined with the other team members, gives the team more power to act in the investigation and protect the victim.

Since its inception, the Child Abuse Trauma Team has been a resounding success. Working as a unit instead of as separate entities with fragmented and diverse goals and duties, investigations have gone more smoothly, faster and more effectively than before. In the first year of the Child Abuse Trauma Team, 99% of charges filed resulted in a conviction. In the first three months of 1993, Detectives Ken Moon and Tom Follett raised their conviction rate on 30 offenders to 100%.

The team has been profiled on "CBS Nightly News with Dan Rather," and "America's Most Wanted." Following this national media exposure, they have been contacted by representatives of law enforcement from nearly every state in the union. They are a little surprised by this attention—all the job requires is a willingness to roll out of bed when the phone rings at 2:00 am, and the capability to set aside ego and the bureaucratic temptation of "my department is more important than yours."

They maintain that this kind of a team can be created in any jurisdiction willing to expend the effort. It requires no special funding, since its members are already working for their individual government offices. Their impressive success is the result of a single quality: in the words of Assistant Polk County Attorney Melodee Hanes, who was involved in this group at its inception, "The reason it works is cooperation." ✪

Each member's special training and jurisdictional authority, when combined with the other team members, gives the team more power to act in the investigation and protect the victim.

92-51577

BY PAMELA SHAPIRO

A few minutes before 7:00 on the night of November 30, 1992, a young man carrying a large handgun walked up to the cashier in the noisy, crowded Drake Diner and pulled the trigger.

Cara McGrane, 25, slid to the floor, her skull shattered by the .44 caliber bullet that tore through her brain.

As most of the restaurant's occupants hit the floor, manager Tim Burnett, 28, who was helping his wife decorate a Christmas tree about 20 feet from the register, came running toward Cara. Another shot, and he, too, lay dead.

The gunman ordered a second girl standing beside the register to open the drawer. Stunned, horrified, and splattered with her friends' blood, she did as he said without looking at his face. He grabbed a handful of cash and walked calmly past several members

AS MOST OF THE RESTAURANT'S OCCUPANTS HIT THE FLOOR, MANAGER TIM BURNETT, 28, WHO WAS HELPING HIS WIFE DECORATE A CHRISTMAS TREE ABOUT 20 FEET FROM THE REGISTER, CAME RUNNING TOWARD CARA. ANOTHER SHOT, AND HE, TOO, LAY DEAD.

of Drake University's basketball team as they were coming in the door, unaware of what had just happened. He disappeared into the dark around the south end of the building.

The 911 call came in at 6:55 pm. At 6:57, Officer Deb Farrell was the first to get to the scene. She examined the bodies and spoke with a few witnesses. Other officers arrived and she turned to her next task: as the initial responding officer, her job was to write up the basic report of the incident. She pulled out a blank form and called into dispatch for a

case number: 92-51577.

Det. Jim Rowley was summoned from home and arrived at the diner at 8:30. He would become the lead investigator on this case. A police officer since 1968, and assigned to the Crimes Against Persons section of the Detective Bureau for the last 16 years, he had seen enough homicides. But he was sufficiently shaken by what he saw to note in a report that "it set me back one full step. . . to look at what had happened to these two people."

But there was work to be done. More than 40 eyewitnesses milled about the diner in varying states of shock. Patrol officers were out knocking on neighborhood doors. Detectives, uniformed officers, identification technicians, and supervisory personnel filled the restaurant. Patrons were providing various descriptions of a young black male. He was 5'7" or 6'1". He wore a black sports parka with a hood; or a green jacket with a hooded sweatshirt underneath and a stocking cap; or a purple coat and baseball cap; wire-rimmed glasses or goggles; no glasses, but "wild-eyed"; a ski mask pushed up above his forehead or over his eyes.

There were two things agreed upon by the few people standing nearest him: he had a space between his two front teeth, and as he left the restaurant, they heard him say, "Merry Christmas."

A RARE GUN

The first break came from the State of Iowa's Division of Criminal Investigation (DCI) laboratory. Lt. James Trotter of the DMPD Identification section told Det. Rowley on the night of the murders that they were dealing with an unusual gun: a .44 magnum

The Des Moines Register

DES MOINES, IOWA ■ MONDAY, NOVEMBER 30, 1992 ■ PRICE 35 CENTS

2 are slain at Drake Diner

Robber shoots while patrons dive for cover

Police receive tips on possible suspects and interview witnesses late into the night.

By HOLLI HARTMAN and KELLYE CARTER
REGISTER STAFF WRITERS

Two Drake Diner employees were shot to death Sunday evening by a man who robbed the popular Des Moines restaurant.

Cara McGrane, 25, of 3120 Beaver Ave., and Tim Burnett, 28, of 5540 N.W. 61st St. Place in Johnston, both were managers at the diner. They were shot at point-blank range while standing at the cash register area at the front of the restaurant, said police Sgt. Raymond Rexroat.

INSIDE
A look at the two victims.
Page 2A

Rexroat said that the sequence of events remained unclear late Sunday, but that McGrane and Burnett did not resist the robbery.

The assailant fled out the front door of the restaurant and ran east through a parking lot and behind an apartment building, witnesses said.

Search for Gunman
Police continued early today to search for the gunman, who was described as a black male adult, about 6 feet tall, wearing a dark athletic jacket and dark trousers with a gray hooded sweat shirt, Rexroat said.

The man used an automatic handgun and fired two shots.

Rexroat said detectives were getting numerous calls about possible suspects . . .

Cara McGrane
The first of 2 killed

Tim Burnett

INFORMATION

A grief-stricken Phyllis Burnett is taken from the Drake Diner where her son, Tim Burnett, 28, and Cara McGrane, 25, were shot to death.

| Blacks kill 4 whites at club

SCENE OF SLAYINGS

◆**ABOUT 40 PEOPLE WERE** in the Drake Diner when the shootings occurred.

1. A man shoots and kills Drake Diner managers Tim Burnett and Cara McGrane.

Patio service area

Kitchen

Bar

Table dining

Counter

South parking lot

Booths   Cash register   Booths

2. The man walks calmly past patrons waiting to be seated and leaves through the main door on the west side of the diner.

Main entrance

3. The man runs to the south end of the diner, and flees east through a parking lot and between apartment buildings behind the diner.

◁ North

West parking lot

---

automatic. Similar shells had been recovered in Des Moines just 10 days before when a man named Isaac Newsome was shot in the groin. His assailant was still unknown.

They found out just how unusual that gun was when they received DCI Criminalist Robert Harvey's report: the gun that injured Isaac Newsome was the same gun used at the Drake Diner—an L.A.R. Grizzley. There were only 450 of them in circulation in the U.S.

The Federal Bureau of Alcohol, Tobacco and Firearms provided the department with a list of every gun shop in America that had taken delivery of an L.A.R. Grizzley. Each investigator was assigned a state or two, and they began the laborious work of contacting each shop owner to verify that the guns they ordered had arrived, if they were sold, and to whom. They would then contact the customers and see if the gun had been re-sold, stolen, or was still in their possession. This would have to be done 450 times or until someone got lucky.

Meanwhile, guns were being photographed for the 10:00 news, composite drawings were being published in the paper, and phone leads were being received by the hundreds. Each lead, no matter how bizarre, was carefully noted on a numbered slip, along with the names and phone numbers of those willing to give them; the notation "Anonymous" if they were not. In all, over 800 of those pieces of paper would be handed over to the thirteen officers who made up the core crew of investigators.

THE FIRST ANONYMOUS CALL

On December 3 at 1:42 pm, Det. Rowley's phone rang. The caller refused to give a name and would not allow the conversation to be recorded. Rowley picked up his pen to take notes on the case's 56th interview.

The caller began describing an incident at a home on Washington Avenue in Des Moines. The police had been called to the house when the homeowner returned to find

a fresh bullet hole in her kitchen floor. Officers located a spent slug in the basement. The caller said this shell came from the gun that did the Drake Diner, and that it had been fired in the house accidentally just a few hours after the murders. The caller named "Freddy C" as the shooter at the restaurant, and said that Freddy and his cousin Joe, "from Texas," had done the job together.

The caller also described a party at the Downtown Holiday Inn on the night of December 1 at which Joe, who never had any money, paid for a group to rent the Presidential Suite—then going for $167 a night. There was one adult in the party, a 21-year-old named Barbara Hogan, who signed the register.

The caller said Freddy C and Joe were gang members, and they had said that anybody who "snitched" would die.

THE SECOND ANONYMOUS CALL

After this conversation, Rowley and his partner, Officer Rick Singleton, went to the Holiday Inn, where they quickly learned that Barbara Hogan had indeed rented the Presidential Suite on December 1 for a party of four, and checked out the next day at noon. The bill was paid in cash.

Officer Singleton interviewed the night clerk, who remembered the group consisting of two young men and two girls, with two other visitors who came and went.

Ultimately, the hotel surveillance tape would show Barb Hogan and another male entering, signing in and leaving again, to return approximately 15 minutes later with two other couples for a total of six people: three males and three females.

After two days of more interviews, more lead slips, and trying to learn just who Freddy C and "Joe from Texas" actually were, the anonymous informant called again. With Rowley asking questions on one phone and Singleton taking notes on another—again, no tape recorders—the second interview began on December 5 at 11:55 am.

They again discussed the episode at the Washington Avenue residence. The caller said Joe had the gun in his hand that night when it went off. The caller identified "Freddy C" as Alf Freddy Clark, and said he also had a gun a lot like it. The caller said a third male at the residence claimed Freddy and Joe had told him they did the Drake Diner, but neither one had admitted this to the caller directly.

The caller was very disturbed by Freddy and Joe's behavior after November 30. Both were acting "paranoid," and Freddy wouldn't change his clothes. They would yell at anyone who mentioned the Drake Diner to "shut up." Also, Joe had said the two victims got what they deserved.

Rowley asked the caller directly if they had any idea who actually did the shooting. The caller said it was hard to say, but Freddy sure was acting strange.

The caller provided descriptions of Freddy and Joe. Both were the same basic height and weight, but one thing stood out: Freddy had a gold tooth. When asked if Freddy had a gap in his two front teeth, the caller said no, but Joe might.

TWO SEARCH WARRANTS

With this information, Rowley and Singleton contacted the Polk County Attorney's office and obtained two search warrants: one for the house on Washington, and the other for Freddy Clark's house at 2212 Carpenter.

At 4:30 pm on December 5, the police set out for both residences. In an upstairs bedroom at 2212 Carpenter, they found Joseph Hodges White, Jr., age 17. Det. Rowley's report notes that "the first thing you notice about Mr. White is the gap in his front teeth." White was taken to the station to be interviewed, along with his aunt and guardian, Zella Williams—Freddy Clark's mother.

While Officers Ralph Roth and Larry Harris interviewed Joe and Zella, Rowley and Officer Kenny Moon sat down with Barbara Hogan. She was able to verify for them the anonymous caller's version of events at Washington Avenue and the Holiday Inn. She also said that Joe had a lot of cash at the motel.

Meanwhile, Roth's client wasn't being quite so cooperative. A great deal of time was spent discussing rights, who was going to talk, and the fact that Joe was not under arrest.

Once they finished the preliminaries, Joe stated he'd been in Des Moines about two months, that he'd come here from Seattle and hadn't been to school since January of 1992 or 1991, he couldn't remember which. He told them he had an ulcer he sometimes took medication for, and that on the night of November 30, he was with Freddy at Freddy's girlfriend's house for awhile. He didn't know the address or her last name. They got

Joseph White

home—2212 Carpenter—at 6:30 pm and stayed there the rest of the night.

A minute later, he said maybe they went home at 3:00 pm. They were smoking weed, so he didn't really know. He described the night at the hotel, but didn't recall having been in a house where a gun accidentally discharged—until he was reminded by Lt. Trotter that he wasn't the only person the

police were talking to. Then he suddenly remembered: one or two nights ago, he'd been examining a .38 or .44 revolver at the Washington Avenue house and it accidentally went off in his hand.

The interview lasted two hours, with much hemming and hawing from White, and a few answers straggling through. Of greater help was all the information he couldn't provide. They took a photograph of Joseph White that evening and placed it in a photospread with five other people. Three Drake Diner eyewitnesses picked out White as the shooter. On the evening of December 5, White was booked into the county jail on suspicion of two counts of murder.

GRIZZLEY HUNT

Rowley was pretty sure he had the killer, but where was the gun? It would be another four days, December 9, before Officer Bill Boggs, who had been assigned the state of Washington on that long list of L.A.R. Grizzleys, would call Fall City Firearms and

L.A.R. Grizzley

learn that their one specimen, sold to a Roger Cline in April 1992, had been stolen from his home in October.

Fall City High School, located in King County Washington, was the last school Joe White had attended. He was expelled in January 1992 for behavioral problems. Despite the fact that the members of the King County Sheriff's Office patrol over 200 square miles of the largest county in the United States, the name Joseph White was a familiar one to many of them. Aside from the usual encounters between police and a teenaged gang member, one incident stood out.

On October 17, 1992, at 4:30 pm, Fall City officers were called to the projects where White lived, on a report of shots being fired. The caller, the apartment manager, heard a series of gunshots and could hear spent shell casings striking the guttering along the edge of the building's roof. Knowing it was where White lived in the building, and White's history, the police decided that if he had a gun, they wanted to get it away from him. They went to his apartment, where they were met by Joe and another young man. While they talked to him, his mother, Sharon James, came home and gave permission for them to search the apartment.

In a bedroom, they found a leather shoulder harness minus the holster, a .44 caliber clip, and a brass .44 magnum shell. Out on the roof was another spent shell. They confiscated these items with Ms. James' permission, even though Joe claimed they had been there since he moved in—that he found them out on the roof. After the call from Des Moines, one of Fall City's officers remembered the incident and called Roger Cline into his office to take a look at the items. Cline tried on the shoulder harness, which he said looked like the one he had purchased specifically for use with his Grizzley. It fit him. He also turned over to the police some spent shells from his collection that he believed were fired by the Grizzley. These were sent to Des Moines for comparison with the shells from the Drake Diner.

On January 3, 1993, Rowley and Boggs flew to Seattle to do some first-hand interviews with people who had known Joe White. Police in Fall City had gathered a list of young people known to have associated with White. On January 6, Rowley sat down to talk to one of them, a 16-year-old named Kim Anders. Kim said she knew Joe a little, having met him through a mutual friend, Marlin Curry. She said Joe had dated a girlfriend of hers for a little while in the fall of 1992. Her friend's name was Johanna Cline.

Rowley, Boggs, and their local contact, Officer Seltzer, went to Mt. Si High School in Snoqualmie, WA. to meet with Roger Cline's daughter.

Johanna verified Kim's story: that she had met Joe White in early October 1992, and that over the next month he, Marlin and Kim spent the night at her house several times while her parents were away for the weekend. She explained that her father kept his guns in a room that was "usually locked," but the fact that neither she nor her father could say the room was definitely locked 100% of the time explained why Roger Cline's L.A.R. Grizzley came up missing some time between October 8-15, with no sign of forced entry to the house.

When confronted with the fact that a .44 magnum clip, ammunition and a shoulder harness that fit her father were found in White's apartment, Johanna agreed with the officers that even if they couldn't prove White had stolen the gun, he'd very likely had control of it at some point.

By the time Rowley returned to Des Moines, an answer had come back from the DCI on the shells Mr. Cline had given to the King County officers: they were from the same gun used to kill Cara McGrane and Tim Burnett.

THE TRIAL

During the trial, Joe White admitted to bringing the gun to Des Moines from Seattle, then claimed he had sold it to a gang member for $300—that was where he got the money for the hotel. The jury instead believed the three eyewitnesses who had picked White out of the photospread on December 5, and pointed him out again in the courtroom. On Friday, May 21, 1993, Joseph White was convicted of the Drake Diner murders. On July 20, in the middle of the greatest flood Des Moines has ever seen, he was sentenced to mandatory life in prison without possibility of parole. Alf Freddy Clark was not charged.

EPILOGUE

The box that contains the files of DMPD Case no. 92-51577, weighs 42 pounds. Every sheet of paper in it is a testament to the time spent solving this case—time that literally hundreds of officers spent walking the streets, dialing and answering phones, talking with witnesses, and writing, always writing. That, and so much more, was what the lives of two human beings were worth to this department. To Joseph White, they were worth $427.00.

In December 1993, Drake Diner employees planted a Christmas tree outside the restaurant, to honor the memories of Cara McGrane and Tim Burnett.

In August 1996, Joe White and three fellow prisoners made a brief escape while being transported to a prison in New Mexico. After two tense hours they were captured, and he was returned to the custody of Iowa's penal system, where he remains today and is considered one of its most difficult inmates.

And on the wall beside Jim Rowley's desk, is a framed, 15x19 inch color photograph of an L.A.R. Grizzley. Roger Cline's gun was never found. ✪

BY CHIEF WILLIAM H. MOULDER

IT IS POLICE OFFICERS TAKING RESPONSIBILITY TO KNOW THE PEOPLE ON THEIR BEAT, THEN WORKING WITH THEM TO SOLVE THE MATTERS THAT DETRACT FROM QUALITY NEIGHBORHOODS.

THE MUNICIPAL APPROACH

Community policing is not a new idea. Des Moines, and most other departments, were doing community policing at the start of the 20th century. They didn't call it community policing. They just made a point of knowing the residents of their area, along with the businesses there. It was a good way of policing.

Then technology got in the way. Cars equipped with radios made it possible for officers to cover bigger beats. They didn't have time to get acquainted, and the advent of vehicle air conditioning created yet another physical barrier between them and the public they served. As officers disconnected with the people of their beats, police management embraced the concept of "Professional Policing:" that police officers were trained professionals. They knew when an area needed additional police attention and what was needed to address the crime problems. They did not need or want input from citizens.

There was also concern over corruption. If the beat officer became too familiar with the people of his area, he might overlook petty crime like bootlegging. Modern police managers took it as an act of faith that to combat corruption, officers needed to be moved around with some regularity. They were also transferred with little notice so they could not cover up corruption.

Police departments became very rule-oriented. A police officer's discretion was narrowly structured. The model for corruption-free "Professional Policing" was depicted in the popular television series Dragnet. The show, set in Los Angeles, was based on a "strictly by-the-book" Sgt. Joe Friday. He was only interested in the facts and could quote the rule book or the state code for any situation. There was no emotion. The crooks went to jail. The police officers were the professionals—they knew what was needed. Policing was done "to" the citizens, not "with" the citizens.

Des Moines was no exception. The depart-

Capt. Bill Tigue and neighbors at National Night Out at Drake Park, 1991

ment took pride in developing clear rules to address the myriad of challenges the officers faced. Legend has it that Assistant Chief Don Knox, who retired in 1992, once testified that the Des Moines Police Department had a procedure for every contingency. He was asked, "If a submarine appeared in the Des Moines River, would the department have a procedure to deal with it?" Assistant Chief Knox paused, thought for a moment, and responded, "No, but we would have a procedure the next day!"

Although Des Moines embraced the "Professional Policing" model, it did not walk away from some forms of community policing. The Special Area Crime Unit (SACU), commonly referred to as the foot patrol, was a federally funded unit begun in 1976. Eight officers and two sergeants were sent out to walk and drive distinctly-marked Jeeps in the Woodland-Wilkie and Model Cities neighborhoods. They regularly attended meetings with neighborhood

groups and various advisory boards. Their mission was to meet with people and develop good relationships. SACU ended in 1988 because of a lack of funding, not because citizens were dissatisfied with the service.

During the social unrest of the late 1960s and early 1970s, police agencies rediscovered the power of listening to the people. More police officers were college-educated, and it was no longer possible to tell officers that they should not think for themselves. Officers knew that the problems they encountered would not always lend themselves to a by-the-book solution.

As police agencies became more skilled at solving problems, the expectations of the police as problem-solvers grew. Police departments became identified as the ones to call "if something is going on that shouldn't be going on and somebody should do something about it." Police agencies took on the surrogate parent role by starting Explorer Scout programs. Police Athletic Leagues formed inner-city baseball, football and basketball teams to give kids in distressed neighborhoods a healthy outlet and a closer association with police officers.

School liaison officer programs were initiated to solve problems of disruption in school and school violence. As drugs became more prominent, anti-drug programs like DARE (Drug Awareness and Resistance Education) programs were started everywhere.

Police agencies developed other educational programs to address personal safety, especially programs for women. Those programs focused on defense in the event of sexual assault or purse snatching. The Neighborhood Watch Program called upon neighbors to look out for each other.

What goes around comes around. At the end of the 20th century, Des Moines and most other police departments are doing community policing. The emphasis is on people that live in an area getting to know their police officers. In Des Moines, the current term for community policing is "The Municipal Approach." The Municipal Approach was initiated in 1986, mostly as a result of the influx of drugs, street crime and street violence.

The department encouraged neighborhood groups to form. The neighbors identified the issues that were important to them, not the issues the officers thought were

National Night Out at Nollen Plaza, 1993

important. They met with the officers who worked in their area. They organized social events to encourage interaction with the officers policing their neighborhoods. The Drake Park Neighbors held a party to celebrate the recovery of Drake Park, and officers were treated to cake and coffee. The Riverbend Association held coffees to get acquainted with the officers on each watch. The first party was held in a parking lot across the street from a problem bar and drug houses, and demonstrated to the thugs that something new was happening.

Citizens not only identified the problems, they joined in crafting solutions. People used their parks and public spaces, making them less attractive to criminals. They harassed prostitutes and their customers. They held sit-ins at businesses, usually bars, that were havens for

criminals. They walked the streets with cellular phones and called the police when a street crook was doing business. Neighborhood associations lobbied the city council for alcohol bans and curfews in the parks, and better lighting to make streets and parks less attractive for criminal activity. They even convinced the city council to close a street in order to route traffic away from drug houses.

The success of the neighborhood groups is rooted in committed residents and the Police Department's Neighborhood Area Resource Coordinator Program (NARC). Riverbend residents Neila Seaman, Doloros Thomas and Neva Jorgensen-Wells worked with the first NARC officer, Sgt. Larry Cramer, to develop a new concept in community policing. The police officers worked with the residents to empower them, to help them take charge of their destiny. The concept was so powerful that 42 neighborhood groups formed in just three years. The group published a "how to" handbook that has been reprinted many times and adopted by police agencies across the country.

As the 20th century closes, community policing is back to the point it was at the start of the century. It is not the NARC sergeant or the SACU Program, or even School Resource Officers. It is police officers taking responsibility to know the people on their beat, then working with them to solve the matters that detract from quality neighborhoods. ✪

Community Relations Bus

THE FLOOD

Reprint: *The Blue Line,* Vol. 3, Ed. 5

*Above: **Flood waters threaten the police station, 1993***

This was no FEMA tabletop exercise in a prearranged classroom command center; this was the real thing. Mother Nature threw everything she had at us. For the most part we had little warning, and certainly expected much less than she ended up giving.

At 10:30 am on Sunday, July 11, 1993, a staff briefing was being held at the headquarters of Public Works on East 5th south of Court Avenue. We had just been notified that the Des Moines area was being threatened by increasing flood waters. The normal Police Emergency Operations Center (EOC) in the roll call room at the station was also in jeopardy and not nearly large enough to accommodate the growing number of government officials becoming involved. Added to the problem was the reality that city government was about to lose internal telephone lines from flood waters rising in the basement of the city's Armory Building.

City Manager Cy Carney gave the police department the responsibility of establishing a suitable site for the city's emergency operations. Within a half hour, East High School had been chosen and we were making arrangements with school authorities. They turned their entire school over to our control. Less than three hours later, the first 30 telephone lines were installed and operational in the school cafeteria, and the EOC began receiving tenants prior to the scheduled 3:00 pm staff briefing.

All of these emergency workers needed to be fed and supplied with water. We contacted Red Cross, and they began serving meals immediately. Some have said that because of Red Cross efforts, this was the best-fed disaster in history. A gym was set aside to serve as an eating area and a place to get away from the adrenaline-charged atmosphere of the command center.

Each support system at the school (water, electricity, telephone) had at least one backup system installed. Cellular telephones had to be used when telephone service was interrupted. Electric power was lost twice, but portable generators had previously been set in place to feed power into the center. Water-cooled air conditioners had to be manually filled by either bottled water or on-site tankers.

The Des Moines Emergency Operations Center was lauded as one of the finest and most organized EOCs in the country by representatives from HUD, FEMA, and perhaps most importantly, by two police officers from Homestead, Florida, who had gone through Hurricane Andrew and were here to critique our operation center.

One of the secrets to such a successful operation was the supervisory and command staff of the Administrative Services Division, who worked 12-hour shifts at the EOC managing the facilities and resources throughout the flood emergency. This was the first time that any EOC was managed in such a manner. Usually police help staff such an operation, but no formal police management staff had ever before been created to ensure things run smoothly.

We may never experience a disaster of this magnitude again, however, someone will. Our lessons learned, knowledge gained, and our story told will hopefully serve other communities who have yet to go through a "Flood of '93." ✪

*Below: **Skyline view of Des Moines during flood of 1993***

FLEUR DRIVE

BY LT. BEN BISHOP
Reprint: *The Blue Line,* Vol. 3, Ed. 5

If cases of Old Milwaukee, rock 'n roll, sand and water sound to you like the makings for a great beach party, you're right; but Fleur Drive might not be the ideal location.

During the early stages of the flood emergency, the Traffic Unit reorganized into two, 12-hour shifts and was responsible for public safety and traffic control at the sandbagging operation established on Fleur Drive, directly in front of Holiday Inn South—the temporary southern edge of the Raccoon River.

At the water's edge, Public Works deposited dump truck after dump truck of sand. Volunteers filled the bags and then the bags were trucked back across the viaduct, where the National Guard loaded them onto helicopters and deposited them on the levee surrounding the pumping station inside the Des Moines Waters Works plant.

The operation went around-the-clock for six days. The intent was to raise the levee so the water could be pumped out from inside its perimeter, retrieve the pumps, repair and replace them; thus restoring running water to a quarter-of-a-million central Iowans. In addition to the orderly flow of traffic in an area heavily congested with dangerous machinery and fatigued workers, police personnel tended to general public safety issues and cared for several whose toil drove them to heat exhaustion.

One member of the Traffic Unit, Sgt. Barry Arnold, significantly contributed to the morale of the thousands of volunteers who took part in this effort. When Sgt. Arnold arrived for his first 12-hour shift at the Fleur sand extravaganza, the sun was about gone. "I've never seen people working so hard and having such a good time," Lt. Ben Bishop told Sgt. Arnold.

But the sun was all but down, the night air cool, and the crowd of 1500 that had packed the temporary beach during the afternoon was dwindling. Then the Minneapolis Television satellite truck cut their floodlights, and the work site that had been as bright as the beaming faces of the volunteers was instantly dark. The laborers groaned, the festive mood dissipated. It was apparent to Sgt. Arnold an ingredient had to be added to this mix of dirty, back-breaking work to hold the volunteers' spirit, or their bodies were soon to follow. Music seemed a logical solution to the sergeant. Within minutes, Sgt. Arnold dispatched members of his squad to recruit a radio station that was willing to broadcast live from the site.

KGGO answered the call. They not only came as soon as physically possible, but they stayed day and night until the operation was completed. Sgt. Arnold related that when the platter player came that night, his first comment over the air was, "The police said they needed us, and when the police say they need us we are going to be there."

Lt. Bishop thought his day sergeant, Kelly Willis, had gone a bit too far with the party motif when he arrived at the site at 5:25 pm the next day. He was accompanied by Mayor John "Pat" Dorrian, who was to be interviewed by Dan Rather of the CBS Nightly News from the top of the Minneapolis satellite truck at 5:30 pm.

Lt. Bishop parked his squad car behind a long line of dump trucks that were waiting to deposit their loads at the water's edge. He and the mayor walked up, approximately a city block, from behind the trucks. When he came out from behind those trucks the first thing he saw was 150 cases labeled "Old Milwaukee" and filled with amber, quart bottles. He thought, "Oh no, Kelly, this is not a good idea. Somebody was trying to do a very nice thing, but, Kelly, we got to stop this right away; it wouldn't take much for this to get out of hand."

When he saw some juveniles drinking from the quart bottles, his anxiety rose. Then he saw officers drinking out of them, and realized the unlabeled bottles contained water only seconds before he made a fool of himself.

Bishop later said,

"They sure gave me a start, but more important, they did a great job. I've never been prouder of a unit than I was the Traffic Unit during this emergency. Gas leaks, fires, levee breaks, evacuations, one emergency after another, and almost daily changes in assignments and duty hours; each and every member of the unit responded with 100% effort 100% of the time. I have never received more job satisfaction, nor worked with more dedicated people than I did during the great flood of '93." ✪

DEPARTMENTAL ORGANIZATION IN THE 1990S
ALL THE PUZZLE PIECES:

Over the years, the organization of the department has changed both drastically and often. Officers have shifted from one division to another, units have come and gone, and ranks (Patrolman, Police Woman) have vanished into the mists of time. Currently, the Des Moines Police Department is organized into three divisions: Patrol, Administrative Services, and Criminal Investigation. Each division is under the command of an Assistant Chief of Police, all of whom report to the Chief of Police.

PATROL DIVISION

This is the largest and most visible division. It houses the "front-line" officers, the Traffic Unit, Tactical Unit and Animal Control Unit.

ADMINISTRATIVE SERVICES DIVISION

The Administrative Services Division employees provide critical support services to both citizens and police officers. Personnel and Training, Records, Detention, the Community and Media Relations Section, Information Management, Communications and Property Management make up the services offered by this Division.

Information Management

The Management of Information Services Unit (MIS) enters data from case reports daily in the National Incident Based Reporting System (NIBERS). The state-of-the-art technology used provides statistics unrivaled in accuracy and in uniformity, and has become a model for reporting agencies nationwide. The MIS Unit also manages the department's internal PC-based network.

Communications

When a citizen calls 911 at any time of the day or night, the Des Moines Police Department responds swiftly through the Communications Unit. Twenty-four hours a day, seven days a week, 38 civilian dispatchers on three shifts receive 911 emergency calls, information requests for vehicles and drivers licenses and wanted requests for persons and property.

The Communications Unit receives over 600,000 telephone calls a year that generate over 230,000 "trips" (service requests where police units are dispatched). The telephone equipment consists of eight enhanced 911 lines and four trunk lines, and 12 administrative lines for receiving requests for both police and fire service. These two systems are administered through the use of Computer Aided Dispatch (CADS), a program developed in the city's mainframe computer.

The Des Moines Police Department Communications Unit radio equipment consists of six channels within the 450 MHz range.

Property Management

All property brought into the police department, including confiscated, found or seized items, is inventoried and secured in the Property Management Section. This includes drugs, weapons, and all other property pertaining to a variety of cases.

The Property Management Section is also responsible for the issuance of officers' clothing and leather goods; furnishing office supplies to all divisions of the police department; assisting the city's zoning department with the beautification ordinance; junk vehicle impound and coordinating the department's Biological Hazard Protection program.

This section notifies owners and lien-holders of vehicles that have been impounded and not returned to the owners within 48 hours. Auctions of abandoned motor vehicles are held every two weeks.

Police Information Officer

Probably the most visible member of the department, the Police Information Officer (PIO) is responsible for providing information to the media on events of concern to the public

Des Moines Police Department Communications Center, 1999

184

that the department is involved with. The PIO (actually a sergeant) coordinates press releases and press conferences on current criminal cases as well as internal investigations.

Records and Detention

Over 30 employees are assigned to the Records and Detention Unit. Through computerized systems for indexing, uniform crime reporting and for the booking of prisoners, this unit provides support services to all other divisions, sections, and units of the department in record storage, retrieval, and dissemination. The Records Unit provides valuable information to various public entities and private businesses.

The Records Unit staff processes over 55,000 investigation reports per year. It processes and/or transcribes over 300,000 pages of supplemental reports. Over 12,000 requests for copies of trips, cases, photos, accidents, and loss verification reports are handled annually by this office, and it completes over 1600 requests for criminal records checks.

The Detention Unit is responsible for the welfare of over 8,000 male prisoners annually, held temporarily prior to arraignments. Transportation and booking procedures are conducted under constant video surveillance, to insure the prisoner's safety while he is in the custody of the Detention Unit. (Female prisoners are booked and housed in the county jail.)

Community and Media Relations

The Community and Media Relations Section provides programs and services aimed at community safety issues and disseminating the Des Moines Police Department's concept of community policing.

The Victim Resource Office responds to the scenes of violent crimes and deals directly with the victims, families, witnesses and affected neighbors of a crime victim.

Section personnel also have regular contacts with local media representatives on a

Jail Security Officer Mel Ferguson viewing jail cell observation cameras

variety of crime prevention-related programs, services and topics. Examples are "Crime Beat Focus," "Today in Iowa" and "Metro's Most Wanted," which is a 30-second television public service announcement that highlights a different fugitive each week.

The Community and Media Relations Section offers the community presentations on many crime prevention topics. By taking a proactive approach, we hope to make Des Moines a safer place to live, work and play.

RESEARCH AND DEVELOPMENT

The Research and Development Section was established in 1969 as a result of the management report by the International Association of Chiefs of Police (IACP). The IACP report recommended, among other things, that such a section be created to organize research and planning activities to support the entire department.

Police agencies had begun to realize the benefit of using and applying common business practices to police service. At the same

time, federal grants were becoming available to support improvements and innovations in law enforcement.

The use of computers by police departments was also becoming possible with potential benefits in many areas.

The section became responsible for managing and coordinating planning, research, grant and computer projects. Several years later, responsibility for managing the operating budget and capital improvements budget was added.

In addition, the section manages the written directive system, conducts staff studies, manages special projects and acts as staff to the chief of police.

CRIMINAL INVESTIGATION DIVISION

The Criminal Investigation Division consists of employees responsible for follow-up investigations of criminal cases. Over two-thirds of the department's approximately 55,000 cases per year will be examined by the 52 officers and support staff assigned to this division. These investigators prepare cases for prosecution and provide expert witness testimony to the courts.

Division Headquarters

The assistant chief directs the activities of the Criminal Investigation Division. This section consists of a chief of staff, advanced projects development supervisor and support staff. It also includes two specialized investigators: the senior services coordinator and a juvenile crimes resource officer.

Senior citizens are often victims of crime directed toward them as a group. The senior services coordinator is an expert at investigating such crimes and working with seniors to prevent new offenses.

The Seniors and Law Enforcement Together (SALT) program is a liaison developed by the police department with various agencies and groups throughout the city whose common goal is the welfare of our elderly citizens.

The juvenile crime resource officer works closely with the juvenile court and other juvenile justice agencies to provide a coordinated approach to the prevention of juvenile crime and the punishment and rehabilitation of juvenile offenders. It also assists other youth agencies in developing meaningful juvenile crime deterrent programs and provides instruction on juvenile procedures.

Identification Section

This section is the forensic, "crime lab" arm of the department. It is comprised of technicians who process crime scenes to locate and photograph trace evidence, latent fingerprints, and other facts as needed. Since its inception in the late 1800s, the Identification Section has become more diverse and more specialized than any other section in the department.

The task of identifying persons, gathering and analyzing evidence at crime scenes, and then presenting that evidence in court has transformed the identification technician into a quasi-scientist, evolving with advancements in technology. What used to be a crude system of measuring a person's body parts for identification has now evolved to a computerized fingerprint identification system, DNA-marking, retinal scanning, voice spectography, and thermal imaging.

The most basic identification system, the Bertillon system, began around 1883, and consisted of exact measurements of various parts of the body. A flaw in the Bertillon system was discovered in 1903 when two people were found to have the exact same body measurements. Des Moines police used the Bertillon system until around 1908, when we adopted a more exact system: fingerprint identification.

We continue to use fingerprint identification as it is the most accurate, widely-accepted, understood and cost-effective method of identification. This system has, however, also evolved along with modern technology, specifically by the use of computers.

The newest computerized system, AFIS (Automated Fingerprinting Identification System), contains a database of over 4 million fingerprints in the state of Iowa. The Des Moines Police Department's system, purchased in 1998 at a cost of $137,000, can run a print in a matter of moments—a feat that would take one technician a lifetime to complete. This computer will soon be hooked up to a multi-state database, and will eventually evolve into a nationwide system.

For those prints that must still be analyzed manually, the department has developed a Latent Fingerprint Analysis and Recording System. This uses technology from today's medical science field to combine high magnification and high-resolution optics with a color monitor and video/digital printer to create a state-of-the-art system that can magnify a fingerprint from 34 to 1,437 times its original size. This provides an easier and more accurate way to spot the minute discrepancies in fingerprint patterns than the old method of one technician with a hand-held magnifying glass.

Crimes Against Property

The Crimes Against Property Section investigates burglary, arson, hate crimes, theft and other related crimes. A Property Recovery Unit concentrates on locating and returning stolen property to victims. The section monitors pawn shops and investigates fencing operations. Crime patterns are analyzed and detectives employ surveillance and undercover techniques to intercept criminal activity.

Intelligence Section

The Intelligence Section gathers, analyzes and disseminates criminal intelligence information on major crimes, ongoing criminal enterprises, criminal gangs, and supremacist groups. Its detectives conduct undercover investigations and form a close liaison with

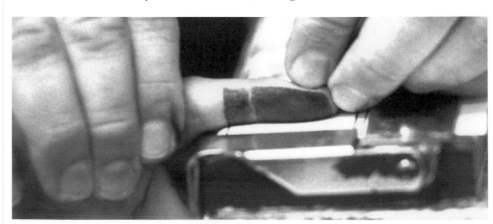

Rolling a fingerprint

186

Left to right: **Police Chiefs William Moulder, Billie Wallace and Wendell Nichols**

Special Assignment Section

The Special Assignment Section investigates check and credit card forgeries, frauds, confidence games, embezzlements, car theft, and computer crimes. Section personnel also identify and arrest fugitives from other jurisdictions, do handwriting and document analysis, and provide training for businesses and consumers.

Sexual Violence/Intra-Family Conflict

This section investigates crimes in two main arenas: crimes of a sexual nature and child abuse.

The sexual cases include sexual abuse and attempts, enticing children, child exploitation and obscene communications.

The section also investigates child abuse. The Child Abuse Trauma Team is an emergency response team dedicated to the discovery, investigation and prosecution of child abuse.

other units of the department, as well as outside agencies. They coordinate protection with federal officials whenever a dignitary comes to town.

The team consists of members of this section working in unison with the Polk County Attorney's Office, Child Protective Services and the medical community.

Crimes Against Persons

This section's homicide detectives have achieved a success rate far above the national average. This is due both to the extensive experience of the detectives, and excellent cooperation from the people of Des Moines.

In addition to the more high-profile homicides, this unit handles cases involving assault, robbery, threats, harassment, domestic abuse, kidnapping and all DOAs.

The Des Moines Police Department currently has an authorized strength of 498 people. Of these, 357 are sworn police officers and 141 are civilian employees. In the battle against crime, we like to think that our force is actually strengthened as we rely on the eyes and ears of the 200,000 citizens within our community. ✪

	MAYORS	POLICE CHIEFS
1980	Pete Crivaro	Billie B. Wallace
1981	"	"
1982	"	"
1983	"	"
1984	"	William H. Moulder
1985	"	"
1986	"	"
1987	John P. Dorrian	"
1988	"	"
1989	"	"
1990	"	"
1991	"	"
1992	"	"
1993	"	"
1994	"	"
1995	"	"
1996	Arthur Davis	"
1997	Robert D. Ray	"
1998	Preston Daniels	"

THE PATROL OFFICER WAS, AND STILL IS, THE FIRST LINE OF DEFENSE BETWEEN THE CITIZENS OF DES MOINES AND THE CRIMINALS WHO PREY ON THEM.

PATROL DIVISION

BY SPO CHARLES GUHL

When the Des Moines Police Department began in 1886, the officers were given a badge and a billy club and told to go out and patrol the streets of this growing city. This basic instruction is the primary function of the police department to this day: Go out and patrol the city.

The patrol officer was, and still is, the first line of defense between the citizens of Des Moines and the criminals who prey on them.

Patrol officers are found on the streets of this city 24 hours a day, 365 days a year, protecting the life and property of the citizens of Des Moines. Because of this responsibility, the patrol division has been, and always will be, the largest division within the police department.

Throughout the years, this particular organization has been identified as the Patrol Bureau, Patrol Division, Uniform Division, and is currently known as the Patrol Services Division.

The familiar blue uniform of the "beat officer" has been the single most identifiable representation of the police department, and the men and women who wear this uniform are also the most easily-recognized entity of City government. They are the "thin blue line" between crime and the citizens of the community.

Throughout the decades, the patrol officers have performed their duty on foot, horseback, wagon, trolleys, streetcar, motorcycles, boats, helicopters, bicycles, and, of course, in automobiles.

Patrol officers currently respond to over 260,000 calls for police service annually. These calls can range from a barking dog to a homicide, and from debris in the street to the entire city being flooded in 1993.

The city is divided into three basic patrol districts—west, south and east. Each of these patrol districts is divided into individual territories. Depending on the time of day, there can be as many as 27 individual patrol territories throughout the city. The patrol officers who work these territories patrol in either one-officer or two-officer cars. In addition, officers from

PHOTOS BY CHRISTINA LYNCH JONES

Working the streets in the 1990s

the Traffic and Tactical Units work as a supplement to the regular patrol officers.

Throughout history, there have been many sections and units that have been a part of the Patrol Services Division. Typically, this division has been divided into three separate patrol watch sections—First Watch, from 10:30 pm until 6:30 am; Second Watch, from 6:30 am until 2:30 pm; and Third Watch, from 2:30 pm until 10:30 pm. Another section within the division is the Special Operations Section. The Special Operations Section is divided into several units: the Headquarters Unit, Traffic Unit, Tactical Unit, and the Animal Control Unit.

An assistant chief of police is the overall commander of the Patrol Services Division, with each section being commanded by a captain. The Traffic and Tactical Units are commanded by a lieutenant, with the

Patrol cars in police garage, 1990

Headquarters and Animal Control Units being supervised by a sergeant.

Overall there are 246 sworn officers, including supervisors, assigned to the Patrol

Services Division who carry out their duties for the citizens of Des Moines, 24 hours a day, 365 days a year. ✪

Providing assistance on Interstate 235

*Patrolman George Kachelhoffer
stands guard during Premier
Khrushchev's visit, 1959*

*President John F.
Kennedy guarded by
Anthony Andreano*

190

DIGNITARY VISITS

BY SPO CHARLES GUHL

Left to right, **Des Moines Police Officer Max Cleveland, unidentified, Harold Grossnickle and President Harry Truman**

Throughout the history of the Des Moines Police Department, as with any law enforcement agency, there are occasions when a President or some other prominent dignitary comes to town for a visit. Over the years, almost every President of the United States has visited Des Moines at some time, either by campaigning during the first-in-the-nation Iowa caucuses or during their term in office.

On April 28, 1902, President Theodore Roosevelt arrived in Des Moines to give a speech at the Iowa Statehouse to a crowd of 100,000 people (Des Moines' population at the time was approximately 62,000 people). The speech was preceded by a horse and buggy tour of the city.

On August 29, 1927, Colonel Charles Lindbergh and the Spirit of St. Louis visited the city. Colonel Lindbergh circled the city and the Iowa State Fairgrounds before landing at the Municipal Airport, which at the time was located near present-day Altoona. After landing, Lindbergh traveled 18 miles through the city streets by motorcade, thrilling the huge crowds that had gathered along the route. It was estimated that two-thirds of the city's population turned out to greet the famous aviator, and over 63,000 had gathered at the fairgrounds to view the colonel's fly-over. Nearly 300 soldiers and law enforcement officers were on hand at the airport to deal with the 50,000 spectators, and to protect the famous Spirit of St. Louis airplane from souvenir hunters.

Des Moines has also been fortunate enough to attract foreign dignitaries such as Russian Premier Nikita Khrushchev in September 1959, and Pope John Paul II on October 4, 1979.

During the visit by Pope John Paul II, the Des Moines Police Department used approximately 180 police officers to provide traffic control, security and logistical support for his visit to the city.

For the police department, a visit by the President or Vice President of the United States includes numerous briefings with the United States Secret Service. These planning sessions include intelligence support, explosive ordnance disposal support, motorcade vehicles and route selection, traffic control along the routes, and security positions for the various locations where the President will be visiting or staying.

Depending on the nature, length, and destinations of the visit, the police department could easily devote anywhere from 50 to 100 police officers in our effort to ensure the safety of the President or Vice President while visiting the city.

During the presidential campaigns for the 1988 election, the Des Moines Police Department assigned three Tactical Unit officers to each candidate whenever they came to Des Moines. Because of Iowa's prominence with the first-in-the-nation caucuses, Des Moines was soon overwhelmed with visits from presidential candidates. The costs to the city in overtime for the officers assigned to the candidates was exorbitant, and this practice was not repeated. Officers are now assigned to presidential candidates only when their assistance is requested by the United States Secret Service. ✪

*President Ronald Reagan
visits Des Moines, 1982*

WEAPONS OF THE DMPD

BY SPO CHARLES GUHL

The weapons carried by Des Moines officers throughout the history of the department have varied widely, and these weapons have evolved right along with the other equipment used by police officers.

The first patrolmen probably carried primitive percussion revolvers that required loading the powder and bullets by hand into the cylinder. These weapons were obviously very unreliable and had to be maintained on a daily basis. Other revolvers that were popular prior to 1870 were the single action Colts and Remingtons that were chambered for either the .45 Colt cartridge, or the .44-.40 Winchester centerfire cartridge.

Around 1870, top-break revolvers were introduced, with the most popular cartridges being the .38 Smith and Wesson (S&W)—not to be confused with the more powerful .38 Special—and the .32 S&W. These top-break revolvers were made by numerous manufacturers that included Smith and Wesson, Harrington and Richardson, Hopkins and Allen, Forehand and Wadsworth, Iver Johnson, and Merwin and Hulbert. Many of these revolvers were pocket-sized, making it easy for the officers to conceal them in the pockets of their heavy wool coats.

At the turn of the century, the weaponry of the era improved dramatically with the development of double-action revolvers. The term "double-action" means that every time the trigger is pulled, the revolver fires a cartridge. It was not necessary, as with the single action pistols, to manually pull the hammer back each time the officer wanted to fire the weapon. Almost all of these double-action revolvers could be loaded with either five or six cartridges in the cylinder.

The most popular double-action revolvers during this period were the S&W double-action and the Colt Model 1892 New Army and Navy, both of which were chambered for the .38 caliber cartridge. The New Service Colt revolver that chambered in either the

Two 9mm pistols and a shotgun, weapons used in the war on drugs, 1989

.44-.40, or the .45 caliber cartridge was also a popular handgun during this period.

For detectives, the S&W Safety Hammerless revolver in .32 or .38 caliber was very popular because of its size and the fact that there was no exposed hammer on the weapon that could become tangled in the officer's clothing. Detectives could literally fire this gun from inside their coat pockets.

In 1930, the Des Moines Police Department purchased a 1921 A-1 Thompson sub-machine gun. This gun was rumored to have been used during the infamous Bonnie and Clyde shootout near Dexter, Iowa in 1934, but that story was never substantiated. Other unique weapons owned by the department have included a Harrington and Richardson Model 55 Reising sub-machine gun; a .30 caliber M1 carbine; and the Marlin 336C lever action 30-30 rifle. These weapons are used for training and identification.

During the 1940s and 1950s, the S&W Hand Ejector revolver became very popular among Des Moines officers and was perhaps one of the most commonly carried weapons by officers during this time. This S&W revolver was known later as the Model M&P (Military and Police) and carried this name until World War II. After World War II, the S&W M&P evolved into the Models 15 and 19, both of which carried the .38 Special cartridge.

In the late 1950s and early 1960s, Colt Manufacturing introduced the Python and Trooper models of revolvers. Both of these models became very popular, and several officers on the department carry them to this day.

The primary shotgun used by the department prior to 1900 and up through the 1960s, was the Winchester Model 1897. Sometime in the mid-1960s the department purchased Winchester 1200 pump action shotguns and used these weapons until 1988, when they were replaced by the Remington Model 870 12-gauge shotguns with synthetic stocks.

The 1970 Departmental Rules and Regulations pertaining to the regulation sidearm carried by Des Moines police officers provided the following requirements that are, for the most part, still in place today:

"The regulation sidearm to be carried while on duty shall be the Colt or

S&W .38 special revolver or .357 Magnum revolver. Handles must be plain. No light colored, stag, bone or carved handles will be permitted. The metal finish shall be blue. Uniformed officers while on duty in uniform shall carry a revolver having a barrel length of four inches. Plainclothes officers may, if desired, carry a revolver with a short barrel. Only one handgun shall be carried while on duty in uniform or plainclothes."

Officers were required to carry .38 Special ammunition only in their revolvers, and their extra ammunition was carried in either leather dump pouches or in loops on their equipment belts.

It was not until April 1988 that the Des Moines Police Department, along with other law enforcement agencies across the country, responded to the need for additional firepower by authorizing officers to carry the 9mm semi-automatic pistol. They were finding themselves outgunned by criminals who had semi-automatic pistols capable of carrying many more cartridges than the six-shot revolvers carried by police officers.

Des Moines officers who wish to carry a 9mm pistol are required to complete a three-day orientation and transition school for the 9mm. While many veteran officers still carry their "old revolvers," the majority of officers today are armed with the 9mm pistol.

Those authorized by the department are the Smith and Wesson three-digit or higher models, Sig Sauer, Beretta, and Glock double-action semi-automatics. The *Departmental Rules and Regulations* were also updated at this time to include these pistols as being authorized for use by Des Moines officers. Officers are given several choices because the service weapon is a substantial investment which must be paid for by the individual officer. Officers also have personal preferences regarding safety, ease of handling and the general "feel" of a gun.

All Des Moines Police recruit officers beginning with the class of 1990 have been trained with the 9mm pistol. These recruit officers receive approximately 94 hours of firearms instruction during their academy training. Officers must qualify with their duty weapons twice each year during the departmental shoots. Any officer who fails to qualify must attend a remedial training course until they can attain the minimum qualification score.

In addition to the guns carried by patrol and plainclothes officers, the Tactical Unit uses more sophisticated weaponry, including the Remington Model 700 .308 caliber Varmint Synthetic Model bolt-action rifle, and Colt H-Bar .223 caliber semi-automatic rifles. The officers who use these rifles train monthly, and must qualify semi-annually with each weapon.

The police officers of today have federal, state and municipal laws governing the use of their weapon in the line of duty. Add to these laws the *Departmental Rules and Regulations and Administrative Manual* guidelines, which also regulate the use of their weapons. Every officer, prior to graduation from the police academy, is also required to memorize, verbatim, the deadly force policy of the Des Moines Police Department.

USE OF DEADLY FORCE:

1. This directive is for internal use only, and does not enlarge an Officer's civil or criminal liability in any way. It should not be construed as the creation of a higher standard of safety or care in an evidentiary sense with respect to third party claims. Violations of this directive, if proven, can only form the basis of a complaint by this Department, and then only in a nonjudicial setting.

2. The decision to use deadly force shall rest solely with the employee's individual judgement.

DISCHARGE OF FIREARMS— NOT PERMITTED

1. For the purpose of warning.

2. At moving vehicles except in self-defense, the defense of another Police Officer, or a third party.

3. Against the violations of shoplifting, theft of an automobile, theft, all classes of misdemeanors, traffic charges.

4. In cases where a warrant is on file, the identity is known to the employee and such escape would not be an immediate danger to innocent persons or the employee.

DISCHARGE OF FIREARMS—PERMITTED

1. At an approved range.

2. To destroy animals seriously injured or dangerous, when other disposition is impractical.

3. When legally ordered or authorized by a Commanding Officer.

4. When the employee reasonably believes that such force is necessary to protect himself or another person from the use or threat of use of deadly force.

5. When the employee reasonably believes that such force is necessary to effect the arrest of a person who, in the employee's mind, is known to have committed a felony if:

The person has used or threatened to use deadly force, and;

The employee has made a reasonable attempt to make known his official identity and intent to arrest, and;

That identity and intention, in the employee's mind, has been in fact transmitted to the person to be arrested, and;

All other methods of apprehension have been exhausted, and;

That employee reasonably believes that such discharge of firearms can be done without substantial risk of injury to innocent persons. ✪

BY SPO CHARLES GUHL

The origins of what is now the Tactical Unit began with a group of officers in March 1963. This group was originally known as the Fourth Platoon, and consisted of one sergeant and five officers. The Fourth Platoon worked from 8:00 pm until 4:00 am, and was originally designed to provide an additional group of officers to supplement the regular patrol officers. An additional benefit of the Fourth Platoon was that their hours of assignment overlapped Third Watch—what was, and still is, the busiest time for police calls from the public.

In 1964, the Fourth Platoon grew to seven patrol officers, while remaining under the supervision of one sergeant. In 1968, partially due to the Vietnam War and subsequent political and racial unrest throughout the country, this platoon expanded to seventeen patrol officers under the supervision of one sergeant and two lieutenants.

In early 1970, the Des Moines Police Department began to organize our present day Tactical Unit which, along with the Traffic Unit, became a part of the Special Operations Section. The original Tactical

TACTICAL UNIT

Right, **Tactical officers emerge from the Peacekeeper ready for action**

Left to right, **Sgt. John Meeker, Carolyn Taylor, Sgt. Allan Tunks and the "War Wagon,"** *a mobile communications center*

Tactical Officers Paul Little, *left,* **and Mike Moody,** *right,* **discuss an operation**

Unit was comprised of one lieutenant, two sergeants, and two squads of eight patrol officers each.

The duties and mission of this unit as outlined in the *1970 Department Ball Book* were, *". . . to work closely with other line units in the division; and be available for immediate deployment. This will be a highly trained group of officers who can meet the special demands of police services. The unit will not be directly involved in providing routine services ordinarily performed by patrol elements, but will instead be deployed in specific areas where it can produce maximum effectiveness in terms of crime suppression and criminal apprehension.*

"Personnel attached to this unit are handpicked and will have many demands placed upon them. Their assignments and working hours will be changed constantly due to the changing

The Entry Team for hostage situations, 1999

trends in criminal activities."

Because of the specialized nature of the duties of this unit, there was also the need to obtain specialized equipment. Some of this specialized equipment included boats, weapons, SCUBA equipment and motorcycles. There was also a 1969, 22-foot Winnebago motorhome to be used as a mobile communications center and is commonly referred to as the "War Wagon."

The special weapons provided to this unit during the early years included a 1921 Thompson sub-machine gun; a Harrington and Richardson Model 55 Reising machine gun; two Remington Model 700 BDL high-powered rifles in .243 caliber; a .30 caliber Inland M1 carbine; a Marlin 336C lever action 30-30 rifle and a Marlin Model 60 .22 caliber rifle.

A unique addition to the Tactical Unit occurred in 1973 with the purchase of two helicopters from the Iowa National Guard through the Office of Civil Defense and State Excess Property. These helicopters were 1957 and 1958 Hiller UH-12D models. The police department paid $200 for the old helicopters, and the city council granted the department $27,500 for equipment, maintenance, and the operation of the helicopters for six months or 500 hours of flight time. The helicopters were flown by police officers who were also pilots, with volunteer "observer" officers who were rotated every thirty days.

The helicopters were used for a variety of functions that included locating stolen vehicles, aerial surveillance of suspects, freeway patrol, patrolling high-crime areas, and monitoring high-speed pursuits. Once the helicopter located the fleeing vehicle in a pursuit, the patrol cars were called off by the watch commander until the ground units could surround the fleeing vehicle. Car prowls at the local shopping malls during the holiday season were at an all-time high until the aerial units began their patrols in these areas with 200-foot passes over the

A 1958 Hiller UH-12D helicopter owned by the Des Moines Police from 1973-1975

parking lots. Sgt. David Noel, who was one of the primary helicopter pilots for the department, stated that since they flew so low and slow at times, the department had to spend $1000 for a transponder so the radar at the Des Moines Airport could constantly track the helicopter's location. The helicopter crew also was rumored to have frequently gone out and picked up donuts for the air traffic controllers just to stay on their good side.

Obviously, being a piece of police equipment, it became necessary at times to land near the police station. The pilots would land the aircraft on the river levy just outside the front doors of the station. This practice, however, would startle the chief of police, and the pilots were soon ordered to obtain permission from the Uniform Division commander prior to landing so he could call the chief and give him some warning that the helicopter was landing.

The helicopter program was disbanded in 1975, after the money that was to be used for equipment maintenance was reallocated to

Above left: **Paul Stout in camouflage**
Above right: **Todd Taylor in ghillie suit**

purchase portable radios for the street patrol officers. So in 1975, police unit number 475 was never heard on the police radio again.

The officers of the Tactical Unit were all cross-trained in the early years for any type of

"SWAT" (Special Weapons and Tactics) operation they might encounter. There was no formalized training for this unit during the 70s, other than a yearly "mock incident."

In June 1990, a new team of officers called

Equipment of the Des Moines Police Tactical Unit

The Bomb Squad Truck

the Special Complement Against Thugs (SCAT) was created with one sergeant and nine officers. The purpose of this team was to counter the growing numbers of gangs and gang-related activity in the Des Moines area. This team gathered intelligence information on all active gangs and their members within the city, while directing their enforcement efforts toward this type of activity. The SCAT team was a federally-funded grant program and in 1994 changed its name to the Gang Unit.

The Tactical Unit continues to be a part of the Special Operations Section, and is comprised of one lieutenant, three sergeants and 25 officers who are divided into three different squads.

The officers who work within this unit are highly trained in specialized areas such as SCUBA, precision rifle marksman team, high-risk entry teams, chemical agents, bicycle patrol, motorcycle patrol, watercraft operation and river patrol, gang investigations and undercover assignments.

A large portion of the present day Tactical Unit's time and energy is spent in directed patrols within targeted neighborhoods to support the department's community policing effort. The officers patrol in plainclothes and unmarked vehicles as well as in uniform and marked police cars.

Possibly the smallest of the Tactical Unit's responsibilities is the Special Response Teams. Hostage and barricaded suspect situations are the most dangerous and volatile that officers face. The Entry Team and the Precision Marksman Team train on a monthly basis to keep their "edge."

Some of the more specialized equipment used by the Tactical Unit today includes a military armored vehicle called a "Peacekeeper," which we obtained in 1994. This vehicle is used for hostage rescue and barricaded person situations. Also included in the unit's inventory is a 1992 International Mobile Communications Center. This vehicle is 30 feet long and is used for all large special events, disasters, hostage and barricaded person situations. This modern-day "War Wagon" has telephone hookups along with communications equipment connected to every law enforcement agency in central Iowa.

The SCUBA Team uses a specially-equipped truck for all diving operations that contains all of the air tanks, wet suits, buoyancy compensators, weights, belts and Dive-Com underwater communications equipment.

The weaponry of the modern day tactical officer includes the 9mm pistol; Remington Model 700 Varmint Synthetic bolt-action rifles in .308 caliber; Colt H-Bar AR15 .223 caliber semi-automatic rifles; the Remington Model 870 12-gauge shotgun; and tear gas guns.

The predecessors of the modern day Tactical Entry Teams were probably the 1920s police "raid squads" with their sledge hammers, revolvers and pump shotguns. The equipment of the old raid squads was a far cry from the present-day ballistic armor, laser sights, night vision equipment, explosive devices, semi-automatic rifles and pistols, all capable of carrying large amounts of ammunition—unfortunately a sign of the times. And as technology grows so will the Des Moines Police Tactical Unit. ✪

Members of the water rescue and recovery squad left to right: **unidentified diver, Robert Crouse, Todd Taylor**

197

IN THE '90S THEY ARE CALLED METH, ICE, MOON ROCK, SPACEBASE, WIZARDS AND WOOLAH. ALCOHOL AND MARIJUANA REMAIN, AS THEY HAVE SINCE THE '60S, THE MOST COMMONLY-ABUSED DRUGS IN AMERICA.

BY RICHARD CROOK

NARCS

"The use of cocaine among the classes that the police have to deal with in Des Moines is noticeably on the increase. When I first became connected with (the Des Moines police) department ten years ago we never heard of cocaine being used."

Police Captain John Sneddin, quoted in the January 26, 1902 *Des Moines Capital.*

Drug use and abuse is not a new or even recent phenomenon in Iowa or anywhere else. People in societies throughout the world learned to use narcotic and hallucinogenic drugs thousands of years ago. The plants that produce naturally-occurring drugs: the coca plant, the opium poppy, hemp, the psylocibin mushroom, the peyote cactus and others have been grown for local consumption by village farmers since before recorded history.

Information regarding opium dens first began appearing in Des Moines newspapers in the early 1880s, but it wasn't until after the turn of the century that people began to realize drug use could develop into a major problem. By 1908, it had become a federal offense to import smoking opium into this country, but soon after, opium smoking became somewhat *passé*; the drug *du jour* of the early 1900s had become cocaine.

It's unclear exactly how cocaine first arrived in the United States. It's likely that the drug first became commonly used as a general tonic and for fighting sinusitis and hay fever. It was also touted for awhile as being a cure for morphine addiction. When people found that cocaine could be obtained cheaply and could provide a high vaguely similar to that of other, less easily obtainable drugs, its sale and use became nationwide almost immediately. For a period of time it was used in medicines, soda pop (hence the "Coca" in "Coca-Cola"), wine, cigarettes and cigars, tablets, ointments and sprays.

Eventually, however, it became commonly believed that prolonged use of cocaine caused insanity. Men and women who were chronic cocaine users were routinely committed to the state mental hospital in Mount Pleasant. Nevertheless, in Iowa it was not illegal to possess or use cocaine until after the passage of the Harrison Act by the U.S. Legislature in March 1915. After about 1908, though, it was illegal to traffic in drugs here. However, the $50 fine for "operating a disorderly house" didn't stop the peddlers. Drug

Robert Curtiss returning from raid

traffic was centered on the city's east side in an area bounded by the river to the west and about 4th Street on the east; and by Elm Street to the south and Walnut or Locust Street on the north.

By early 1914, the preferences of the city's drug users had changed once again. Cocaine had declined in popularity and it appeared that a new epidemic was underway—heroin had found its way to the capital city. Again, the trafficking seemed to be centered in the old cocaine neighborhoods on the east side, but heroin addicts could be found everywhere in the city. If the statistics of the day can be believed, there were over 1000 addicts in Des Moines out of a total population of 100,000. Clearly, the problem was out of control.

Heroin enjoyed a relatively brief period of popularity after WWI, but drug use in general seemed to decline somewhat by about 1930. Since the Great Depression was in full swing by that time, it is likely that most people couldn't afford to buy them.

After the Korean War marijuana became popular and heroin enjoyed a resurgence. But by no means were those the only drugs being used. By the mid-'60s, people had more money than ever to spend, pharmaceutical chemistry had advanced beyond imagination and air/sea transportation had improved to the point where a whole cornucopia of drugs became both easily available and affordable to most people in the United States. What was worse, it was now socially acceptable to be a druggie, too. Smack, yellow jackets, blow, white crosses, acid, black beauties, red devils, grass, hash, bennies and dexies—it was all popular for awhile in the '60s and '70s. Some

people even believed they could get high by smoking banana peels.

In the '80s and '90s the department saw crack, angel dust, cocaine (again), paint sniffing, glue sniffing and quaaludes. In the '90s they are called meth, ice, moon rock, spacebase, wizards and woolah. Alcohol and marijuana remain, as they have since the '60s, the most commonly-abused drugs in America.

In Des Moines prior to 1960, drug abuse was considered to be a vice and users were treated in much the same way as drunks and prostitutes: when they were caught they were fined. Police officers were seldom assigned to work specifically on drugs, drug houses or drug users. They were just as likely to bust a bootlegger or whorehouse madam as they were a drug trafficker. Liquor violations were of greater interest to police until about 1960; for awhile the DMPD had a large liquor squad whose responsibility it was to work nothing but liquor law violations.

Once the blue laws that governed the sale of booze in Iowa were relaxed, and once organized prostitution was more or less eliminated in the capital city, the focus changed. The old liquor and vice units were combined to form Vice and Narcotics Control. That section is comprised of five units totaling 31 people. The five units are:

The day and night narcotics investigation squads, which include a contingent of DMPD narcotics investigators, a forfeitures (seized property) administrator, a vice coordinator whose primary responsibility is the investigation of liquor law violations and two statisticians on loan from the Army National Guard.

The N.A.R.C. (Neighborhood Area

Resource Coordinator) office handles a wide variety of complaints from citizens.

The vice unit includes three DMPD officers and is primarily responsible for the investigation of liquor and prostitution violations.

The SAF-T (Strategic Anti-Felony Team) Unit is a task force that is involved primarily in longer-term narcotics investigations. In addition to DMPD officers, the unit includes agents from the FBI and the Drug Enforcement Administration, officers from suburban police jurisdictions and Des Moines' K-9 unit. The unit typically not only runs ongoing investigations of individual drug traffickers, but also works closely with airlines, trucking companies and bus lines in keeping the flow of drugs into the city at a minimum. The interdiction of drugs is an increasingly important part of their day-to-day work.

As part of a federally sponsored program to combat the growth of the manufacture and use of methamphetamine, the Narcotics Control Section has also been targeting traffickers who set up meth labs in the city. In 1998 alone, well over 200 such labs were seized.

The DMPD has recognized that narcotics are a major problem, one that will not go away of its own accord. An ever-increasing part of the department's resources are being dedicated to suppressing drug trafficking and use. The section commander, Lieutenant Clarence Jobe, and his men and women are very busy people. ✪

THE UNIT TYPICALLY NOT ONLY RUNS ONGOING INVESTIGATIONS OF INDIVIDUAL DRUG TRAFFICKERS, BUT ALSO WORKS CLOSELY WITH AIRLINES, TRUCKING COMPANIES AND BUS LINES IN KEEPING THE FLOW OF DRUGS INTO THE CITY AT A MINIMUM.

BY OFF. CYNTHIA DONAHUE,
PAMELA SHAPIRO, JOHN ZELLER,
ASSIST. CHIEF BILL MCCARTHY
AND ROBERT WRIGHT SR.

The ink on the Emancipation Proclamation was barely dry when, according to the *Iowa State Register* of 29 May 1878, George Johnson became "the first colored man that ever wore a policemen's star in Des Moines." What this means is that there were black officers in Des Moines before there ever was a police department, and over the years they have made substantial contributions to our history.

Des Moines' black community is an active one, and they have always expressed a desire for appropriate representation on the police department. According to a 1921 article in the Iowa Bystander, "The Negro knows the Negro better than any other race knows him." In an interview with the same journal, Jo Ann James adds,

> *"The black community wanted representation on the Des Moines Police Department because the black community identified with the black officer, the black community knew the black officer, and the black community respected the black officer."*

A glance through personnel records and newspaper stories gathered over the years reveals that respect was deserved.

Ira Jones joined the department in 1898. College-educated at a time when such an accomplishment was rare; he later became a successful businessman who ran for City Constable in 1906, and was very active in several local charities. Another

William Wilkinson, 1913

THE HISTORY OF DES MOINES' BLACK POLICE OFFICERS

James "Jamo" Allen

John Rhodes

J.G. Dillinger

educated officer, J.G. Dillinger, wrote and published an article on the importance of an officer's physical appearance and honesty in his ability to do the job well.

The lack of any such advanced schooling didn't slow down John Rhodes, who was appointed to the force in April, 1920. He had begun his police career as a mechanic, but proved a good cop as well—his personnel file contains letters of recommendation for his part in capturing a bank robber and two house prowlers, in addition to a robbery

James Thompson

suspect who had been terrorizing the entire community for 18 months. He was also known for his clarinet-playing and he, along with Officers Colonel Hill and Bert Powell, appear in a 1928 photo of the department's baseball team.

Another popular baseball player was James Allen, "Jamo" to his colleagues. Before joining the department in 1937, he actually played semi-pro ball for the Tennessee Rats. His skill as a pitcher seemed to translate well into skill with a gun, and he often walked away with the prize at marksmanship competitions. Probably, though, when the officers gathered to tell "war stories," he would have gotten the most mileage out of an event that happened in 1941: a murderer, desperate to escape capture, jumped into the Des Moines River. Allen simply jumped in after him, hauled him out and marched him off to jail.

Of course, all work and no play can be a real drag, and Ben Rich, who spent most of his police tenure (appointed in 1932) as a detective, was at the forefront of the fun and games reported in the papers during the 22 years of a pool-playing "feud" he had with dancer and movie star Bill "Bojangles"

Robinson. Several issues of the local rags sport photos of Det. Rich and Mr. Robinson in the throes of their festive rivalry—Robinson never let his tours pass through Des Moines without the two of them racking up at least once.

Charles Brinker

Frank Kaiser

The '50s and '60s were a time for "firsts": James Thompson and Paul Thomas became the first black traffic investigators in 1958. James Thompson went on to be the first black officer to serve as president of the Des Moines chapter of the Iowa State Policemen's Association. World War II veteran Frank Kaiser, who joined the department in 1951, became the city's first black sergeant (in 1961), and first black lieutenant in 1974. He served during some rough years and saw a lot of change, but was a good and respected leader of men. He revealed in an interview his no-nonsense strategy for success with those under his command: "Either follow my orders or go home."

In 1962 Richard Sanders, who would become the department's first black captain in 1991, joined the ranks. He was a veteran of the United States Air Force and attended Des Moines Area Community College.

Also working as an officer during those years and simultaneously enjoying the rigors of law school, was Robert Allan Wright, who joined the force in 1951 and received his law degree from Drake University in 1954. The next year he was joined by another part-time student, Thomas Spencer, who managed to work the streets of Des Moines in uniform (and be promoted to sergeant in 1969) at the same time he was earning a Bachelor of Science Degree and a Master's in Education from Drake; working as a student teacher at Dowling High School; and teaching science,

history, economics, forensics and criminal investigation and psychology at Drake, Grand View and Des Moines Area Community College.

Another "first" occurred in 1970, when the department implemented a Cadet Program under the administration of former officer Richard Anderson. Anderson, another Air Force veteran, had become an officer in 1967. After a few years he resigned to attend college, but returned to department employ in 1970 as a civilian in the Personnel Section. It was while he was in that office, that the Cadet Program was established—a plan whose goal was to recruit minority and low-income youth aged 18-21 who were interested in becoming police officers. Over the years, many cadets have made that transition—among them, the department's first female captain, Judy Bradshaw.

Anderson is still with the DMPD: since 1975, he has commanded the Property Management Section, the office whose formidable task is (among others) to keep track of the evidence generated by over 55,000 cases each year. ✪

Robert Webb

Capt. Richard Sanders

THE POLICE STATION PRESS OFFICE

BY TOM ALEX

The Des Moines police station press office is six paces long, four paces wide and will accommodate about six or eight police officers if they are really upset with the newspaper reporter.

The thing about having a newspaper office actually in the police station is that the reporter is instantly available to any officer for discussion about any story. And just to make sure officers know what's being written about them, *The Des Moines Register* provides several free copies daily to the station house.

It's worked like that for about 80 years. During most of those years the press office was equipped with mechanical typewriters. On busy days, stories were delivered by taxi cab from 25 East 1st Street to the Register-Tribune building at 715 Locust Street.

For a short time there were electric typewriters, then word processors, laptops and other computers. Currently a Macintosh computer with Internet access, national news wires, library archive access, instant messaging and storage for hundreds of articles sits atop the news desk.

The tiny office, furnished mostly with cast-off furniture from the newspaper building, once shared its space with a shoe-shine station.

Reporters did not get the space in the police building without some controversy. According to

Tom Alex, Des Moines Tribune *reporter, files story single-handedly after being injured while covering a story.*

The Des Moines Evening Tribune, in March, 1920 Judge Tom Sellars, a candidate for re-election to the bench, said he was opposed to the tax-payers of Des Moines furnishing free space in the new Municipal Building (later the Des Moines Police Department) to "representatives of the rich newspapers."

But Ben F. Woolgar, safety superintendent, said, "The newspapers are the only means of the tax-payers knowing where their money is being spent and every public official should be willing to have his work open at all times to the public eye." Woolgar con-

cluded that he would introduce a resolution before the City council making the room a permanent one by order of a city ordinance.

In those cramped quarters reporters covered Prohibition, the Great Depression, anti-gambling measures, stories of heroism, alleged police corruption and brutality, the dawning of the illegal drug era, civil unrest and anti-war demonstrations and union conflict. They wrote about officers gunned down in the line of duty, police chiefs in hot water with City Hall, hundreds of murders, thousands of robberies.

Officers didn't always like what they read in the paper, and more than once reporters had to clean tobacco juice from the pressroom door or take a hard bump while trying to negotiate a crowded hallway at shift change.

Until the *Tribune* folded in 1982, the two reporters who worked in the press office were fierce competitors. The *Register* reporter and the *Tribune* reporter had locks on their file cabinets to prevent each other from snooping while one or the other was away. The *Tribune* loved nothing more than scooping the *Register*, which enjoyed a larger circulation and a national reputation. And yet at 715 Locust, both newspapers existed side by side in the same newsroom and were part of the same company.

I was the police reporter for the

Ottumwa Courier in 1971 and 1972, the *Clinton Herarld* 1972-1976, the *Cedar Rapids Gazette* from 1976-1978, *The Des Moines Tribune* 1978-1982 and *The Des Moines Register* from 1982 to present.

Twenty years ago my long "hippie" hair and wire-rimmed glasses were seen by officers in Des Moines as proof of a liberal news bias and a bleeding-heart press. As time passed, the hair became shorter and grizzled. The "press" became "the news media" to include the ever-increasing importance of television news, and police attitudes shifted the point that officers prepared weekly newspaper columns to catch wanted criminals and regular television spots covering a wide range of topics.

In 1983, a public information officer was appointed to help the news media gather information. After that officers were appointed to help in other areas: a specialist was appointed to help crime victims weather tragedy, another officer was assigned to help senior citizens, another went to work with neighborhood associations.

These changes aside the general job description of the police officer has altered little, as human nature remains unaltered. And the tiny office on the main floor, six paces long and four paces wide, with one desk, three file cabinets and four chairs, has been a window to it all. ✪

Roll call briefing by Capt. William L. Johnson

Officers in Third Watch roll call

Reprint: *The DM Register,* October 31, 1998

FORLORN LITTLE GOBLINS GET TREAT FROM POLICE

BY LYNN OKAMOTO

Two Des Moines boys went trick-or-treating Friday night in style—riding in the back of a police car.

Officers Joe Widlowski and Sean Wissink said they were driving by Seventh Street and Indiana Avenue about 7:15 p.m. when they came across two brothers, who appeared to be about 8 and 9 years old.

One boy was dressed as an ape; the other was dressed as a werewolf.

"We asked how they were doing, and how much candy they'd got," Wissink said. "One of them started crying."

The officers learned that the boys were waiting for someone to pick them up to go trick-or-treating, but their ride had not shown up. The boys had four or five pieces of candy, and Beggar's Night would last only 45 more minutes.

Widlowski told the boys to jump in the back seat of the patrol car. At first, they didn't believe him. Then they ran to tell their parents, returned and hopped in the car.

The officers drove the boys around for 45 minutes, stopping the police car and turning on its amber flashing lights as the boys ran to houses to collect goodies. Some people doled out treats with both hands.

"They got a lot of candy," Widlowski said.

Some folks didn't believe the officers were really police. "They tried offering us candy," Wissink said, "but we kept on giving it to the kids." ✪

203

POLICE RADIO COMMUNICATIONS

BY SPO CHUCK GUHL AND WILLIS BASSETT

Des Moines Police Dispatcher Sgt. Pat D'Ostilio working at the computerized Police Communications Center

During the summer of 1931, a group of young businessmen called the Junior Chamber of Commerce started a campaign to equip the Des Moines Police department with a radio system.

In 1932, the city fathers found the money to purchase an RCA radio transmitter for the department. This first transmitter was located in the police headquarters in what was then called the telephone room. Chief radio operator Warren K. Norton built receiving sets for the squad cars using electric relays and wires that were salvaged from pinball and slot machines confiscated by the police vice squad.

On August 11, 1932, radio station "KGZG" officially went on the air for the first time, and in September of that year a radio section was established within the department. By the end of 1932, the department had 21 radio-equipped squad cars and eight radio-equipped motorcycles. These vehicles had only the radio receivers in them, so officers were unable to call from the car to police headquarters.

In 1935, the police radio operators constructed the first two-way radio sets for the department to try out, and by 1936, three more homemade two-way radio transmitters were constructed. In 1937, the department's first two-way radio system was put into operation, and four more two-way radio sets were built by the department's radio operators.

Up until 1938, no police department radio in the United States was recognized by the Federal Communications Commission. That omission was corrected that year, when the FCC assigned a series of radio frequencies to the Des Moines Police Department for two-way police radio communications. Police radio manufacturers were also improving their product during this period, and in response to the improved equipment that was available, the department purchased nine new squad cars equipped with two-way radios.

In 1940, the original radio transmitter was replaced with a new one, and a radio antenna was placed on the roof of the Municipal Court Building (headquarters). By 1943, we had radio receivers in 43 cars and motorcycles. Twenty-five of these vehicles had two-way radios, including the river patrol boat.

The first two-way radio system that allowed the officers in the patrol cars to talk to each other, as well as police headquarters, was installed in 1951. This system obviously enhanced the officers' communications ability and was a huge improvement to the police radio system.

By 1958, the department had only two radio channels, both of which were on low band VHF (Very High Frequency) mode. In 1968, the department installed a five-position radio dispatching console that could control three different police radio channels. The "Crime Alert" program also began during this time period. The Crime Alert number, 283-4811, soon became synonymous with the police department when a citizen needed to call for police assistance. It remained in place until the nationwide adoption of 911 occurred in 1984.

In 1970, the department decided to replace all personnel in the dispatch office with civilians. Until then, sworn officers had worked dispatch, but a new way of thinking led

Above: **Officer Robert Eastman**

department leaders to decide it would be better if they could be on the street where their training would be put to better use. Twelve civilians were originally hired to cover the three patrol watches. Of those 12, two are still working in dispatch, and four eventually became officers. By 1998, the dispatch office had grown to 38 civilian dispatchers.

In July 1973, several dramatic improvements in police radio technology were made. The department began using UHF (Ultra High Frequency) radio channels to replace the VHF channels used before. The city also installed six centralized radio repeaters,

Standing, left to right: **Asst. Chief Harold Fryman, Chief Wendell Nichols, Vince Davis, dispatcher is Sgt. Walter Armstrong**

along with six receiver sites, throughout the city. These receivers relayed the radio signals from the patrol cars and sent them to the main repeater, thereby ensuring radio communications between officers throughout the city. The old VHF radios had only four-channel capability, while the new UHF transistorized radios were capable of operating with 12 separate channels. The department, however used only six of them. The first hand-held, portable radios also came along at this time.

Des Moines' tallest building in 1983, the Ruan Financial Center, had radio antennas installed on its roof for the two primary police radio channels. The old antenna on the roof of the police station then became a standby antenna. Late in 1984, the department installed a new radio communications center that replaced the old electronic relay dispatch consoles with advanced microprocessor consoles.

Advanced microprocessor radios began appearing in patrol cars in 1990. Currently, we use advanced Spectra radios in squad cars that are capable of containing 128 separate channels, and are one-fourth the size of the previous radios. Today, we are licensed to operate on seven separate police channels, one of which is used by the Animal Control Unit.

Police communications have indeed come a long way from the written notes and call boxes that were used by officers at the turn of the century. ✪

THE ACADEMY

BY SPO CHARLES GUHL AND
RICHARD CROOK

As recently as the late '20s, the Des Moines Police Department was still training its officers by issuing them a billyclub and a little book with various city ordinances printed inside, and turning them loose (usually on the same day they were hired) to walk a beat or go on motor patrol with an more experienced officer. Sometimes the pairing lasted only a few days, sometimes a few weeks. It all depended upon whether or not there was another beat out there that needed a body.

By the time World War II came around, it was well recognized that the DMPD's new recruits needed some formal training. The Iowa Highway Patrol had already set up a law enforcement training program with facilities at Camp Dodge and Iowa City, but there was still very little training being provided by the City of Des Moines. A few indoctrination and familiarization courses were taught to new DMPD recruits by a rotating cadre of police officers. The classes were small and the course material very basic: reading city and state ordinances, firearms familiarization, the DMPD organization chart, what fingerprints looked like, that sort of thing. The courses lasted a few days and then the new recruits were shuttled off to the street.

In 1944, with so many men off to war, the department was forced to hire what were called "Duration" officers whenever there was a need for new men. "Duration men" were hired with the understanding that they were only on the job temporarily, only there until the officers who had been taken by the various services came back home. "Duration men" were provided with very little in the way of training.

Late in 1950, someone decided that the city should appropriate funds to set up its own training facility. Renovations to the police station were completed early in 1951, and the first class began its training in the third-floor classrooms that March. There were eight officers in that group, and it included future Assistant Chief Tom Teale. The classes were

scheduled to last five weeks until mid-April. The chief at the time was Frank Mabee and the training commander was Capt. O.A. Kettells; recruits called the new training program "Captain Kettell's College." New DMPD recruits would receive their initial training on the third floor for the next 22 years.

For the first nine years, the emphasis was still on-the-job training. Classroom work, more or less full-time for those five weeks, was still considered to be merely familiarization time. The real training actually started when the new troops got out on the street. One innovative technique that was introduced by

Front view of the Police Academy

Mabee and Kettels was to rotate the street assignments of the new recruits. New officers now were to stay only a few days with any one veteran officer, and they were to spend some time on every beat that the department had before their training was completed.

In early 1960, after some determined pushing and shoving by Sgt. Harold Fryman, the department was finally convinced that it should expand the training program and intensify the classroom instruction. The recruit training period was extended to nine weeks and the curriculum broadened to include typing and spelling. Mandated administrative courses were introduced for senior officers in 1960, as well. Those courses were held twice a week and lasted for five weeks.

The 16th academy class graduated in July, 1962. Of the five members of that class, one

remains: Det. Clifford Claycomb, the department's senior officer.

In 1962, new officers were required to furnish their own uniforms and firearms. In order to be able to report to work fully uniformed and armed, new recruits often had to take personal loans from family, friends, banks or whomever they could find to provide money for them to pay for their initial purchases.

As a matter of fact, there were only two pieces of personal gear that the department did furnish to its new officers at that time. One was a brass call-box key for use in the telephone call boxes that were scattered around the city. Call boxes were used primarily by foot beat coppers to report in to division offices or to call in reports to the dictaphone operator. Any officer who lost his key was charged a dollar for its replacement.

The other was the wooden billy club that was carried by the foot beat patrolmen. If an officer wanted a leather carrying strap attached to the club that he'd been issued, he had to provide it himself. It hasn't been recorded whether or not officers got to keep that strap when they turned the clubs back in to the department.

By 1964, the curriculum at the academy had changed again. Recruits spent their first four weeks in the classroom studying report writing, English, the Code of Ethics and law. They were then assigned to three-wheel motorcycles and sent to traffic duty.

After a short time on the street, they returned to school for another nine weeks to study more

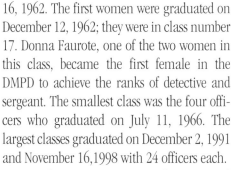

PHOTOS BY MARTY BOYD

English and law, but this time their schooling included boxing, baton training and firearms instruction. Then back to the street for one more week with a veteran officer, and finally they were on their own. Recruits were considered to have satisfied a probationary period after they had served for six months.

Recruit Class #24 graduated in August, 1967. The domestic civil unrest associated with the war in Viet Nam and with the latter part of the civil rights movement had just taken a grip on the country, and Des Moines found that it wasn't immune to the problems of the day. New recruits were sworn in on their first day, just in case extra bodies might be needed to help contain disturbances.

The curriculum at the academy was cut back to nine weeks, but remained otherwise essentially unchanged. Judo classes were added to the physical training. Those who went through the academy in 1967 clearly remember getting a harder workout carrying the gym mats from the basement of the station house to the third floor than they ever got practicing judo.

In 1971, the Des Moines Police Academy was certified by the State of Iowa as a regional police academy and plans were drawn up for a new building. In 1973, the Des Moines Police Department unveiled their

Left to right: **SPO Richard Roland and Capt. Jack Morton**

new training facility on Army Post Road: a 12,000 square foot, one-story concrete building set on city property that had been deeded to Des Moines by the federal government, 93

The Honor Roll Memorial at the Academy

acres of gently rolling meadowland and woods. The regional academy concept was developed by the Polk County Law Enforcement Advisory Council and funded in part with federal and state monies.

Over the years there have been a number of "firsts" for the academy. The first African-American officers to have been trained there graduated in the 15th academy on February

16, 1962. The first women were graduated on December 12, 1962; they were in class number 17. Donna Faurote, one of the two women in this class, became the first female in the DMPD to achieve the ranks of detective and sergeant. The smallest class was the four officers who graduated on July 11, 1966. The largest classes graduated on December 2, 1991 and November 16,1998 with 24 officers each.

In early August in 1998, the Regional Police Academy's 57th class was in its fifth week of training. In very many ways this class was probably much like most of its predecessors. It was made up of 24 police officers-in-training, 20 of whom are slated for service with the Des Moines Police Department; two will be going to West Des Moines and two to Windsor Heights. The youngest was 21, a fresh-faced young woman newly graduated from college; the oldest, at a grizzled 39 years old, was a 20-year Marine Corps veteran. Three of the recruits had some amount of law enforcement experience and seven are ex-military.

I was given the opportunity to talk at short length with four of these recruits: Denise Schafnitz, Lori Hickman, John Poplowski and Brad Kress, on a pleasant summer afternoon while the class was in the middle of physical training. I'd originally intended to talk with them merely to try to get some basic statistical-type bits of information—age, level of education, that sort of stuff.

Old Academy classroom

207

I did get all of those things. All four have some college, as all police recruits are now required to have. Two have already earned their Bachelors degree and one has some work toward a Masters degree. Two of the four have had some prior exposure to police work; one is married to a current Des Moines police officer, and the other is a former Colorado State Trooper. Three of the four are originally from somewhere other than Des Moines. They've chosen the Des Moines Police Department because they believe that it's a better place to work than other agencies with whom they've spoken. Although rookie police officers are all assigned to the Patrol Division immediately after graduation, these four expressed interest in becoming involved in police work that is slightly more focused

guess if I'd thought about it at all, I'd have expected to see a certain level of enthusiasm in them; but the extent to which these four wanted to do well, both for themselves and for the class as a whole, surprised me. They wanted to be police officers. They wanted to be able to live up to their department's expectations of and for them. They wanted to serve. I believe what they've told me. I did not necessarily know that I would.

They're only a quarter of the way into their training but they already know exactly why they are where they are. I've been assured that these four are no different than any of the other 20 in their class. For the rest of their lives, a certain amount of pride will stay with these 24 people because of the fact that they went through this training.

help them write intelligible, thorough reports. The training has also been designed to instill a sense of self-confidence and self-discipline into the recruits. Captain Jack Morton, the academy commander, described this aspect of the Regional Police Academy training to me. It is specifically designed to give the new police officer the confidence to deal with all those different situations out on the street that he or she is certain to run into, and to allow them to do so without feeling that they have to do it while wearing a "ten pound badge." They're learning how to deal in a professional manner with all sorts of people who might have all sorts attitudes. Dealing reasonably with a person out on the street who has an attitude is an important part of the job.

The first indoor "two-holer" pistol range

The 1950s indoor range with manual cranking retrieval at the City Armory.
Sitting at table front to back: **Joe Couch, Wallace Sidmore and Hasbrouck Henry**

than patrol: narcotics, canine handling, the Tactical Unit or homicide.

However, I came away with much more than basic statistics. Talking with police recruits about their jobs is, I suspect, not quite like talking with a group of retail clerks-in-training or construction-industry cubs. The recruits seem to maintain a certain level of enthusiasm that probably just isn't there with trainees in other fields. In talking with each of these four I was left with the impression that they had a sense of dedication and commitment to an extent that I hadn't expected. I

The training that police recruits go through has, to a certain extent, been patterned on military training curricula. I say "to a certain extent," because it isn't the sort of training that one might associate with the Marine Corps of 20 years ago, but it's not like being in college, either. It's sort of a combination of the two, I suppose.

It's true that police training curricula have been developed to teach recruits certain technical skills. As a matter of fact, one of the courses taught at the Regional Police Academy is English composition, designed to

Every law enforcement officer in the state of Iowa is required to complete a minimum amount of training. The Iowa Law Enforcement Academy (ILEA) requirements for certification are:

- 22 hours of general administrative instruction.

- 65 hours of patrol and traffic instruction. The 14 mandatory courses in this category include, among others: accident investigation, hazardous materials handling and OWI investigation.

- 141 hours of officer survival training that

Above, left: **SPO Todd Taylor,** right, **Capt. Drew Burham**
Right: **Capt. Drew Burham**

Above, wearing glasses: **Firearms instructor SPO Charles Guhl and recruit officers on the firing range**

Above, left: **Recruit Officer Amy Parsons,** right, **Officer Tracy Rhoades**
Left: **Recruit Officer Scott Fisher**

209

includes firearms instruction, defensive tactics, general physical training and use of chemical agents.

- 40 hours of miscellaneous skills training, fingerprinting, interrogation, crash injury management and crime scene management.

- 25 hours of investigative techniques for specific crimes.

- 65 hours of law, and

- 30 hours of human behavior skills including stress management and ethics.

However, the DMPD Regional Police Academy training program goes well beyond these basic twelve weeks of instruction. In their very first week, recruits are given 16 hours of familiarization and general administrative classroom training. Another 38 hours of administrative courses are interspersed throughout the 20 weeks that they spend at the academy.

Also beginning in the first week of training and continuing through many of the following five months, recruits are given 67 hours of basic academic instruction in such disciplines as composition, spelling and report writing.

Physical training also begins in that first week. During the 20 weeks that recruits spend with their instructors at the academy, a large share of time is spent in the development of physical skills, among them: firearms training, defensive tactics and defensive driving.

Starting in week six, recruits begin 80 hours of classroom instruction in criminal and constitutional law. That is merely the first step in a life-long learning process. Oddly enough, the least intensive curriculum that recruits are required to complete is that relating to traffic procedures. The mere 37 hours of instruction that are provided in this discipline

Pursuit Intervention Technique training on the driving range

make up less than five percent of the total time that they spend in their initial training.

On the other hand, beginning in the first week of training, recruits spend a total of 196 hours of instruction in patrol procedures and in the investigation of specific crimes such as forgery, vice, homicide and arson. By the time they graduate from the academy, they are as well prepared to go out on the street as classroom instruction can make them.

In week four, each recruit spends a full 40 hours on patrol with a Field Training Officer (FTO). Field training officers are veteran police officers who have expressed some interest and had instruction in training new officers. FTOs guide and evaluate new police officers during an additional seven-week period after graduation. The rookies' training is not

considered complete until they have spent this time with their FTOs.

Currently, there are several training programs being provided at the academy in addition to those provided for new recruits. There are, of course, several in-service courses for veteran officers. All departments within the state of Iowa must provide officers with at least 24 hours of in-service training each year.

New jailers are trained at the Regional Academy as well. Jailers are not sworn personnel and their responsibilities are significantly different than those of regular police officers. Their training lasts for eight weeks instead of 20, and includes classroom work in city and state regulations governing the handling of prisoners, use of force and defense techniques, report writing, and use

Felony stop training for recruit officers

Reprint: *The DM Register*, February 12, 1999

POLICE 'MASCOT' HAS LOTS OF STORIES TO TELL

BY TOM ALEX

of restraining equipment.

The academy also trains police cadets, young people who have expressed a high degree of interest in becoming police officers. Cadets are full-time, paid city employees with full benefits. They have limited police responsibilities: they issue parking tickets, direct traffic, take certain reports, help maintain the police property inventory and work in administration. They must become eligible to be officers and be selected for regular duty within five years of entering the program.

In 1992, a Citizen's Academy was initiated by Chief William Moulder. Citizens' Academy is a police familiarization program available to any citizen who would like to attend. Two such courses are offered per year and they consist of a few of the same sorts of classes that recruit officers are required to complete. The training is for nine weeks, one evening per week and includes firearms instruction, crime scene investigation techniques, and some live-action scenarios, such as traffic stops and building entry.

Reserve officer training is a program for para-professional officers, civilians who are provided with limited police powers and who assist regular officers out on the street. Reserve officers are paid one dollar per year and they must satisfy the same hiring requirements as regular officers.

The Des Moines Police Department's Regional Police Academy is a first-rate facility, the instructors and training officers are some of the best available anywhere, and the product that they turn out is as good as any being put on the street anywhere in the country. Their academy is a facility of which the department is very proud—justifiably so. ✪

Sixteen-year-old Marye Peel was ushered into the office of the Des Moines police chief.

"The boys tell me you have a boyfriend," the chief said.

She did not deny it.

"Tell me about him," the chief said.

So she told Chief Henry Alber about John Dusenbery Jr. What she didn't know was that the chief had already had him checked out to make sure he was suitable for Marye, the police department's "mascot."

More than 60 years later, Marye Dusenbery, 76, is a member of a committee compiling a history of the Des Moines Police Department. She has plenty of stories to tell, having grown up in a house next to the police department in the 1930s. She was the proverbial mouse in the corner of the police station, hearing and seeing much of what occurred at the station during the Great Depression.

Marye Peel married John Dusenbery Jr., in 1942 and then worked for the police department and later at City Hall until her retirement in 1984. And because she is a walking history of the department and the officers who served there, authors of the stories for the book sometimes check with her for accuracy.

The story begins in 1933 when 11-year-old Marye Peel

Marye Dusenbery, 1957

moved into the house just south of the police station.

To even speak to a girlfriend, she had to work up the courage to enter the imposing police building and use the public telephone.

About a year after moving in next door, Peel was befriended by some officers in the building. And gradually she became part of the police family, even getting one of the nightly pints of free ice cream delivered by a local dairy.

Officers working at circuses and other major events often ushered her inside with a wink and a smile, no ticket necessary.

Because she was something of a tomboy, officers began caller "Tommie." And as the years went by she acquired other nicknames, like "Sweetheart" and "The Mascot."

"Working on the police history book has stirred so many old memories, Dusenbery said. "How many children were fortunate enough to have that many guardian angels?"

She added: "At the time I didn't really realize how special it was."

The officers' affection for Dusenbery was so strong that in 1940, when the North High School formal dance and January graduation were approaching, police officers passed the hat and came up with enough money to buy her a formal gown, shoes, another dress, silk stockings and a pair of silver sandals. A judge contributed a silver purse.

Dusenbery's first job, clerical work in the police traffic unit, paid $18 for 60 hours a month.

Later, she worked for the telephone company for $13 a week. On Aug. 1, 1943, Dusenbery signed on full-time with the police department as a switchboard operator.

In 1968 she moved over to City Hall to work as a receptionist and telephone operator.

After 44 years of marriage, John Dusenbery, the guy who was investigated by police for dating their beloved Tommie, died in 1986. They had two children, Dan and Vicki, and later six grandchildren and two great-grandchildren.

Since 1971, their son Dan has been a Des Moines police officer. ✪

GENERATIONS

BY RICHARD CROOK AND JAN WALTERS

In most cases the familial experience with the DMPD is relatively recent, but in some cases there is a connection that stretches unbroken for nearly one hundred years. There has been a member of the McCarthy family in the Department continuously since 1910. There were Scarpinos in the Department around the turn of the century. There have been at least four sets of grandfathers, sons and grandsons in the Department since the 1930s.

Because of space limitations we're not able to include material on all of the family pairs that have been with the Department over the years. For those of you who might feel as though you or your family has been left out, any omission that we've committed hasn't been deliberate.

Assistant Chief William McCarthy, 1999

SPO John Scarpino, 1999

Con McCarthy and George Scarpino, 1918

McCarthy

In the days around the turn of the century, four of the eight siblings in the McCarthy family of Chicago, Illinois worked for the Chicago Police Department.

Around 1905, Patrick got tired of life in the big city and emigrated to Des Moines. He went to work for one of the local meat packing companies, and in 1907, his brother, Cornelius joined him. Cornelius (Con) went to work as a detective at the meat packing company where his brother worked.

In 1910, Con McCarthy decided to take the DMPD test for patrolman. He passed with one of the highest scores of the period and was appointed to the department the same year.

By 1919 Con had been with the Des Moines Police Department for nine years and promoted through the ranks to Detective. The thing that Katherine worried most about every day when Con went off to work happened early on the morning of September 27, 1919. He was shot and killed while trying to apprehend a prowler near 9th and University.

In 1928, with the sponsorship of William Walker, the Des Moines Commissioner of Public Safety and a close family friend, Katherine was appointed to a position as matron with the DMPD. She was issued Police Matron badge #1. Katherine remained with the department until her retirement in January 1953.

Katherine and Con's daughter, Helen, was appointed to the DMPD as a radio operator in 1948. Their oldest son, Edward, had come onto the force in 1941. Edward remained with the force until his retirement as Chief of Detectives in 1964. Katherine and Ed were the first mother/son pair employed at the DMPD.

In 1970 Katherine and Con's grandson, Bill, joined the force. Bill is the son of James McCarthy, one of a set of twin boys who were barely two years old when their father was killed. Bill McCarthy has held every rank available in the department during his 28 years of service. He currently holds the rank of Assistant Chief of Police and, until early in 1998, held the position that his uncle held in the 1960s, that of Chief of Detectives.

SCARPINO

On May 1, 1898 Des Moines Mayor John MacVicar appointed George Scarpino to the Des Moines Police Department. He began a stay with the Department that was to last for the next 37 years. He was 32 years old when he joined the department.

During his 37 years of service, George held a number of positions with the force: roundsman (patrol sergeant) and detective, but he spent by far the longest time as a beat patrolman. For fourteen of those years he was on foot patrol in the downtown area, regularly walking the beat between 1st and Walnut and 6th and Grand.

George died on August 5, 1935 while walking his beat downtown, just a few days after his 69th birthday. Over the years he'd declined retirement from the force and by the time of his death was the oldest active police officer on the force, and was likely one of the oldest ever to have served on the DMPD.

On March 19, 1923 George's second oldest son, William, joined the department. Bill was not to follow in his father's footsteps, however. He left the DMPD in 1926 and went to work as a clerk in the Polk County Circuit Court.

On August 18, 1978 George's great-grandson, John, joined up, following his great-grandfather and his great-uncle onto the force. John Scarpino is currently a sergeant

Steven Walters Sr. and Steven Walters Jr.

in the Patrol Division and in addition to his 13 years in Patrol has spent three years with the Tactical Unit, nearly five years in Vice/Narcotics and a year in the Administrative Division

Like most other police officers in the Department, John originally joined the force in order to make a difference for society. He still believes this is true. He does not, however, lay claim to any ambition to stay with the force until he gets to be the age that his great-grandfather was. It is unlikely that anyone else will, either.

BROPHY-WALTERS

The Brophy connection with the Des Moines Police Department (DMPD) began with John A. Brophy Sr. John's parents immigrated from Ireland in the late 1840s and originally settled in the Chicago area. John married Nora O'Shea in 1875, whose parents were also Irish immigrants, and moved to Des Moines in the late 1880s.

Settling on the east side of Des Moines, John and his wife raised seven children, including their youngest son John Brophy Jr. (Jack), who would go on to serve on the police department. John Sr. joined the DMPD in 1897 and retired in 1917 as a patrolman. He passed away at the age of seventy-three in August 1925.

Jack Brophy was born in 1890. While attending East High School from 1907-1910, Jack excelled as an all-round athlete. He was

the first freshman in the history of the school who made the varsity football team. He was an all-state fullback in 1909 and captain of the East High football team in 1910. He also participated in track and baseball.

He joined the DMPD in 1912. This was the start of a distinguished, yet tumultuous career.

Jack volunteered to become one of Des Moines' first motorcycle officers. During a chase on icy, brick streets, he lost control and crashed. His face sustained severe cuts and scrapes, enough to terrify his young daughter.

In 1924, after one of several encounters with the Public Safety Superintendent, John W. Jenney, Jack was fired due to a disagreement over policy and was ordered to turn in his badge. While his case was under appeal, Jack informed his superiors that he would continue to report for duty. Even though he couldn't ride in a patrol car or do any type of police work, Jack walked the streets surrounding the police department and carried out police duties. He continued to make arrests, much to the chagrin of his superiors. Jack was eventually reinstated and back pay restored.

During his 40 years of service with the DMPD, Jack held the title of Assistant Inspector, Captain of Detectives (1930s) and Assistant Chief of Detectives. Jack was also named Chief of Police from January to August 1947 when the City Council took control of the Police Department from the Department of Public Safety. This controversial move was the result of several factors. For several months, the Public Safety Superintendent had failed to name a permanent police chief, though Floyd Hartzer was the acting chief. Polk County Sheriff Reppert wrote a letter to the city council indicating that his deputies would move on gambling establishments within the city limits if the police didn't do their jobs immediately. There were also complaints from local citizens concerned about the rising crime rate. Once he was sworn in as chief, Jack immediately declared war on gambling and vice.

Jack's tenure as chief was overturned eight months later when the public safety superintendent filed an appeal over the city council's action. The court ruled that the city council had exceeded their authority. After the court ruling, Jack finished out his career in 1952. Retired, he continued to live in Des Moines until his death in September 1967.

In 1970, Jack Brophy's great-grand daughter married Steven W. Walters Sr., who joined the Des Moines Police Department in 1971. Steve's interest in law enforcement began in the mid-60s when Tech High School developed a program to recruit police officers for Police Department. During his 26 years of service, he worked narcotics, radar, and the airport. He was also the first officer to walk a beat in downtown Des Moines after foot patrols were reintroduced in the early '80s. He spent 15 years patrolling the south side of Des Moines and held the classification of senior patrolman until his retirement in early 1997.

Steven W. Walters Jr. began working for the Des Moines Police Department as a police cadet in 1995. In November 1998, he graduated from the Des Moines Police Academy. Choosing a career in law enforcement was a foregone conclusion for Steve. He grew up listening to his great-grandmother tell stories about Jack Brophy and on occasion, riding with his father while on duty. As a patrolman for the DMPD, Steve is looking forward to serving the citizens of Des Moines in the

tradition of his father and great-grandfather.

HARDENBROOK - DAWSON

Lew Hardenbrook needed a decent job. He and his wife, Mary, had eleven children and Lew needed to make a lot more money than he'd been able to before. He was thirty-nine years old and it was the summer of 1918. If he didn't get cracking pretty soon, he was afraid he'd never be able to find something better than the work that he'd been making a living at earlier in his life. He'd tried barbering, the photography business, he even tried the restaurant business. He and his wife opened a restaurant in a tent at the state fair near where the cattle barn is currently situated. That was only good for about two weeks in the summer, though. Nothing permanent had seemed to work real well so far.

That August, Des Moines' Chief of Police Charles Jackson decided to relax the age requirements for joining the department because so many of the area's younger men had gone off to the war in Europe. Lew decided he'd give the police business a try; he didn't have anything to lose and, who knows, he might get lucky. He did.

Lew was invited to join the Des Moines Police Department later in the month. He was to stay on the job for the next 21 years, one of the oldest officers on the force when he joined and one of the oldest when he retired early in 1939. Over the years he'd held down nearly every job and earned every rank the department had to offer: beat patrolman, jailer, detective, supervisor of the traffic and liquor squads, sergeant, lieutenant, and inspector. He made captain in 1935 after Captain Steve Howard was killed during a robbery at a bar on the city's east side. It was the rank Lew would hold until his retirement four years later.

Lew had been on the force only about nine months when he had his first encounter with armed robbers. He was walking his beat downtown when his supervisor asked him to

go to the scene of an armed robbery at a grocery store at 15th and Maple, the western edge of the old White Chapel district. When they got to the store the officers found that they'd walked into the middle of a real wild west shootout. The building had been surrounded by police but the thugs inside refused to surrender. They were taking pot shots at anything that moved outside and had already wounded the owner of the grocery and one police officer.

Lew was sent to the rear of the building in case the robbers tried to escape out the back. Sure enough, a few minutes after stationing himself near the rear door two of the desperados came bursting through, blasting away at anything they could see. Although he wasn't the only officer there, Lew felt as though all the gunfire was being aimed exclusively at him. He'd never been in a gunfight before. He caught a glimpse of a dim figure lurching toward him in the street and snapped four shots in that general direction. The man stumbled and fell right at Lew's feet. He later claimed that he wasn't sure whether or not any of his shots had hit the man and he didn't want to know. He didn't want to think he'd actually killed anyone.

For awhile during Prohibition, Lew was the commander of the Big Four, a squad of officers who were assigned especially to investigate violations of the Volstead Act. In several pictures in the Des Moines Register from that period, Lew and several of his brother officers, looking much like refugees from an old "Untouchables" show, are shown standing over the ruins of stills taken in raids around the city.

In January, 1939 Lew Hardenbrook suffered a heart attack and was confined for a time in his home to recuperate. He suffered a recurrence of the problem the following month and was voted a disability pension early in the spring. He suffered another relapse in March and passed away at age 62. A man of many interests, Lew is credited with having written several popular songs, the best known of which was one about his home state; "We're from Ioway. Ioway. That's where the tall corn grows"

In 1925 Lew's son, Louis Orlin, joined the DMPD, the only one of Lew's children to have followed him into law enforcement. Louis retired from the department in 1952 and passed away four years later.

In about 1925 Lew's daughter, Ferne, married Walter Dawson, a detective with the DMPD. When Walter retired from the department in about 1950 he became a special investigator for the Polk County Attorney.

Ferne and Walter's son, Carroll, joined the force in 1949, the third generation (albeit once removed) to have done so. Carroll retired from the force in the '70s after attaining the rank of captain.

The restaurant that Lew and Mary opened in 1911 is still in the family, being run by the third generation of Hardenbrooks to have been involved each summer in the operation of the Hardenbrook Cafe`at the state fairgrounds.

ROUNDS

In 1937 Thomas Rounds went into the service station business, taking a lease on the Shell station at E. 22nd and University.

In late 1939 Tom decided to give up his station and try for a job with the Des Moines Police Department. When he was appointed on March 1, 1940 he and his wife, Edna, bought a home of their own at 2338 Lyon Street. Tom would live in the home until his death in 1975.

After a stint as a detective in the '40s. Tom was back in the Patrol Section by 1950. One of his early assignments was as a motorcycle officer, riding around on one of the old two-wheel traffic cycles that the department had in service for a time after the War. His days as a motorcycle cop were cut short when he swerved to miss a dog one day, upset his cycle and broke his leg.

Tom was promoted to sergeant in 1960 and

retired from the force in 1967 with 26 years of service behind him. He died of cancer in 1975.

In August, 1941 Tom and Edna's son had a son, Peter. Pete followed his father to East High School, graduating in 1959. He began his college work in 1960 and would spend the next three years in school at the University of Iowa and Simpson College, working as a laborer during the summers. In 1962 Pete followed his father onto the Des Moines Police Department.

Pete's first assignment after his promotion to detective in 1968 was to the Juvenile Bureau as a liaison officer at Washington Irving Junior High School. Two years later he was promoted to sergeant and shortly afterward was given the first of three assignments to the Police Academy.

As a lieutenant Pete spent three years commanding the Tactical Unit and another three years commanding the Vice/Narcotics Unit. He was then was assigned to the Academy again. He would be there for four years this time.

Over the years Pete, earned his undergraduate degree from Drake University and in 1988 completed the Master of Public Administration program there. Shortly afterward. he was promoted to captain and given command of the Academy.

Pete retired with the rank of captain in August, 1996. Ironically, the only time he ever had the opportunity to spend any time on the street with his father was after Tom had retired. The two had gone to a local restaurant for dinner one evening. A short time after they got there a fight started in the parking lot and the father and son went outside together to break it up. They ended up arresting two of the men.

After his retirement, Pete spent two years as a Special Deputy Marshal with the U.S. Marshal Service in Des Moines. He is currently an investigator for the Polk County Attorney's office.

Pete's son, Scott, followed his father and grandfather onto the force in 1988 after

spending a short time as a counterman at a local auto parts store. The whole thing came as a complete surprise to his parents; he'd never expressed much interest in police work to either of them.

Scott was promoted to sergeant in 1997 and is currently assigned to the Patrol Division. By the time he retires, likely around the year 2025, there will have been at least one member of the Rounds family on the Des Moines Police Department for 85 years.

BAKER

When Dennis Baker was a child, his father, Ralph, would take him for a short ride every afternoon down into the police garage on the back of the elder Baker's three wheel motorcycle. That was when Dennis decided that he wanted to be a policeman, too. Ralph's assignment in those days was to the DMPD's Traffic Division; he was a motorcycle cop.

Ralph Baker was born in 1922 - just the right year to have become eligible to participate in World War II twenty or so years later, he went off to the Navy in 1943.

After he was discharged from the Navy, Ralph took a number of jobs to support his family: hospital technician, credit investigator, he even had a brief stint as an Iowa Highway Patrol trooper from August, 1947 to July, 1948. In June, 1951, however, he began with the DMPD and the Department would be his only employer for the next 27 years.

During those years Ralph served on the force in a number of capacities. In addition to his time in Traffic, he was also one of the department's first public relations officers. He also started a neighborhood watch program called Blue Star and was instrumental in generating donations from the Iowa Association of Independent Insurance Agents to use for "drug buy" money. Ralph retired as a lieutenant in 1978.

In September 1971, Dennis realized his boyhood dream and was appointed to the Des Moines Police Department. Like his father, he had spent a tour in the U.S. Navy, receiving a 90-day "early out" in June of that year to become a police officer. He was 23 years old when he was appointed.

After being sent to the FAA Airport Training School in Tulsa, Dennis spent 16 months with the airport security detail. However, he spent the largest share of his time on the force in accident investigation. He was one of the investigators on an accident that caused one of the largest amounts of property damage in the city's memory. A loaded gasoline transport was involved in an accident with another vehicle near Southridge Mall on the city's south side. The truck overturned and the transport tank ruptured sending gasoline gushing through a building housing a branch bank. The fuel ignited and destroyed the building, but no one was injured. The accident happened in the early evening; the bank had been closed for several hours. There was, however, in excess of $750,000 in property damage to the truck, several cars that were parked in an adjacent parking lot and to the building itself.

One evening in October 1995, Dennis was in pursuit of two men in a pickup truck who were wanted in connection with the theft of a snow blower. The thieves drove their truck over a ten foot embankment but Dennis, following closely behind, never became aware of the drop-off until his squad car hit the bottom of the shallow ravine. He sustained several injuries including a shattered knee. The injury was permanent and necessitated his eventual retirement from the force in November, 1996. He is currently the owner/ operator of a funeral escort service in Des Moines.

Scott Baker followed his father and grandfather into the department in 1990. After his graduation from East High School in 1987, he worked as a convenience store manager and a photographer for three years before joining the force. In 1993 Scott and his partner went into the flood-swollen Des Moines River to pull out a suicidal man who had jumped into the water. Coincidentally, his father had done the same thing twenty years earlier when a suicidal woman jumped from the University Avenue bridge.

Scott has been assigned to the Vice-Narcotics Unit since 1998. Like his fellow officer Scott Rounds, if Scott Baker stays with the department until his retirement in about 2025, there will have been members of his immediate family in the Des Moines Police Department for the better part of a century.

BEARDSLEY

Omar Beardsley moved to Des Moines as a teenager where his mother remarried. He earned his high school diploma in 1915 and worked for a time at the Empress Theater after graduation, waiting for something better to come along. In 1921 something did come along. He found what he hoped would be a permanent job at the Ford assembly plant at the corner of 18th and Grand. But in the early '30s, the Depression caught up with Ford and with Omar as well. The Des Moines assembly plant was shut down and Omar, along with several hundred of his fellow workers, was out of a job.

After another extended period of unemployment Omar got lucky once again. In 1934 he was appointed to the DMPD. He began in the Patrol Section, walking a beat downtown from 8:00 at night until 4:00 in the morning.

He retired in 1955 at the rank of detective after 23 years on the force, then went to work as Chief of the Polk County Sheriff Department's Criminal Investigation Division. He retired from county service in 1970 and passed away on November 26, 1973.

Omar's brother, Walter, moved his wife and son, Jim, up to Des Moines from the coal fields in 1929. Omar found Walter a job at the Ford plant and Jim set out to finish school. Jim would follow his uncle onto the force in 1944, where he spent the next 27 years on the DMPD. He retired to a cabin in Minnesota in 1971. He passed away July 17, 1989.

In the late '30s a cousin from the Beacon area, Wendell Nichols, was persuaded to move to Des Moines. Jim Beardsley was working at one of the city's packing houses at the time and Wendell's first job in Des Moines was alongside his cousin. Wendell didn't last long in the meat-packing business, though. He would join his two cousins, Omar and Jim, on the police force, eventually rising to the position of chief of police.

Omar's son, Jack, joined the DMPD in November, 1952. He was 22 years old at the time of his appointment and would work his way through the ranks of the department for the next 35 years and three months.

During his years on the job, Jack would become acquainted with many nationally and internationally known figures. He was in charge of security for Elvis Presley's visits to the city in the '70s. He was on security details during visits by Richard Nixon, Lyndon Johnson and Ronald Reagan. He ran Janis Joplin and her groupies out of town back in the '60s and met Glen Campbell, Julius LaRosa and Andy Williams when they came to town to perform. When Nikita Khrushchev visited in the '50s, Khrushchev's wife presented Jack with a peace medal and the Russians' KGB bodyguards gave him one of their medals, as well.

Jack Beardsley retired from the DMPD in January, 1988 with the rank of captain. He is now a Court Security Officer with the U.S. Marshal Service. Jack's son, Jack Jr. (Chip), joined the force in August, 1988, seven months after his father retired. Chip has worked in the Crimes Against Persons Section and is currently a sergeant in the Administrative Services Division.

Wendell Nichol's son, Doug, is currently an Assistant Chief at the department. Chip and Doug are the last of six members of three generations of DMPD police officers. Like the Rounds and Baker families, the Beardsleys and Nicholses will have had family members on the force continuously for some 85 years by the time the latest generations retire. ✪

Des Moines Policemen Through the Ages

A

Last	First
Ablett	Leon
Agan	Michelle
Aiello	Albert
Aiken	William J
Alber	Henry A
Albright	Robert M
Aldred	Krista
Aldrich	Jeffrey M
Alexander	
Alexander	Charles B
Aliber	Harriet
Allbright	E H
Allen	Carol
Allen	Edgar D
Allen	Frederick L
Allen	Helen
Allen	Herbert M
Allen	James S
Allen	Thomas H
Allen	William A
Allison	Misti
Allsup-Stauble	K
Alvord	Irene
Amber	Brenda
Anderson	Charles H
Anderson	Claus
Anderson	Dale L
Anderson	Donald K
Anderson	Hans C
Anderson	J W
Anderson	Mary L
Anderson	Reuben W
Anderson	Richard T
Anderson	Scott H
Anderson	Steven
Anderson	Troy D
Andre	Gina A
Andreano	Anthony
Andreano	Charles T
Anser	Lloyd A
Antrim	Charles T
Antrim	Mrs. Charles
Applegate	L
Arlaud	Jack S
Armstrong	Irene
Armstrong	Walter I
Arnold	Barry
Arnold	Dennis G
Artuscheske	Gustave
Aschim	Kenneth R
Atkins	Debra F
Atmare	E
Atwood	Myrle J
Aughe	Bill
Aylesworth	C M

B

Last	First
Babb	Ronald C
Babcock	L L
Bachman	Richard
Backstrom	CharlesE
Badgley	Frank E
Bagley	David N
Bahler	William
Baied	Denise Almo
Bailey	Donald
Bailey	Meta D
Bailey	Wendell L
Bailey	William
Bain	James G
Baker	Arthur P
Baker	Dennis L
Baker	Dennis S
Baker	Ralph E
Baker	Robert S
Baldwin	John E
Baldwin	L T
Baldwin	William E
Balius	W R
Bane	Roscoe P
Banks	E F
Barber	Jeffrey V
Barkhaus	Donald W
Barkley	Anita
Barkley	Paul K
Barnes	Edward W
Barnes	G M
Barnes	James
Barnes	Paul S
Barnes	Stewart Mark
Barnhouse	Connie
Barrett	C H
Barron	Bradley C
Barron	Glen W
Barron	Matthew
Barron	Xavier Lee
Bartholomew	Arthur A
Barton	Robert O
Barton	Tina
Bassett	Willis
Batchelor	George H
Battani	Eugene
Batts	Herman D
Bauer	Melanie
Baumann	Scott A
Bean	Benjamin A
Beard	Connie R
Beardsley	Jack R Jr.
Beardsley	Jack R Sr.
Beardsley	James L
Beardsley	Omar
Beau	B A
Becker	August C
Bedford	Lawrence G
Beechum	Hurl
Beener	Robert L
Beers	Arthur D
Beghtel	Nancy
Belieu	Harold R
Bell	Geneva
Bell	Janet R
Bellizzi	Nicola
Bemis	Charles P
Bender	Kimberly
Bender	Kurtis J
Bennett	Dennis Wade
Bennett	Jason Allen
Bennington	C E
Berg	John
Berk	Shamin
Berkland	Mildred A
Berkley	Emma
Berlovich	Edna
Berry	Raymond
Betts	Jeremy
Bevel	Walter V
Bice	Clyde
Bice	Raymond
Bickel	Christopher
Biddle	James W
Biddle	Ken
Bierma	Donald R
Bierman	Carla L
Bird	Larry C
Bird	Warren W
Bishop	Benjamin
Bishop	David G
Bixby	Cheryl
Bjornson	Rahn G
Bjurstrom	Bruce J
Bjurstrom	Darren M
Bjurstrom	Jan
Blachley	Harry S
Black	Earl H
Blacksmith	Tony E
Blad	Larina F
Blake	Tom J
Blanchard	Clay D
Blanchard	Tammy
Blankenship	E F
Blattel	Leonard W
Blaylock	David
Blaylock	Robert J
Blee	James
Boal	Douglas E
Boesen	Lucy
Boggs	William F
Bogle	Stephen
Bognanno	Joseph M
Bolen	Ephraim C
Bonner	William W
Bonwell	Jams P
Booth	Karon S
Booth	Robert L
Booton	Harry L
Borre	N H
Botkin	A H
Boulger	D
Bowen	David A
Bowers	Willis A
Bowersox	James F
Boyce	Mary E
Boyd	Mary A
Boyd	Robert C
Boyers	Irene
Boysel	Joyce
Brackett	Andy B
Braden-Harrari	Marilyn
Bradford	Robert E
Bradley	John
Bradshaw	Judith A
Bradshaw	Louis H
Brafford	Everett
Brafford	Richard J
Bragg	C
Brannan	Hugh
Braud	Loren
Bray	George
Breeding	Jeff G
Breese	Edward
Breining	James E
Breman	William E
Brenda	Laird
Brewer	Donna
Brewer	Marvin Lee
Brewer	Melva
Brewer	Richard D
Briggle	Marvel I
Briggs	Richard E
Briggs	Timothy W
Brightman	Hubert R
Brightman	Martin B
Brimley	J
Brindley	Joe B
Brinker	Charles
Britton	Chester F
Brockmeier	Marie Olivia
Brockway	Nathaniel
Broich	Richard A
Bronson	W
Brooks	Ronald E
Brophy	John A Sr.
Brophy	John A Jr.
Brophy	Ralph W
Brothers	Frank
Brown	A C
Brown	Bruce W
Brown	David F
Brown	Dorthea
Brown	Douglas Mark
Brown	Eric C
Brown	Kenneth R
Brown	Kevin Alan
Brown	Larry Ray
Brown	Lloyd A
Brown	Nickolas S
Brown	Rex D
Brown	Steven
Brownson	William N
Bruce	Lloyd J
Brundige	Lewis Frank
Bruner	James M
Bruner	Joseph E
Bruner	Ronald R
Brunnemer	Arcus
Brunotte	Jack E
BrunsKelley	Lee
Bruton	James F
Bryan	Anderson
Bryan	Garey Allen
Bryan	Garey A
Bryan	P L
Bryant	C E
Bucey	A C
Buchanan	Ronald L
Buckroyd	Robert R
Bunce	D W
Buntz	Frank J
Burcombe	George F
Burgess	William
Burham	Drew C
Burham	Janet
Burke	Kevin Ernest
Burnett	Marcus
Burns	Patrick
Burns	Robert M
Burns	Robert L
Burress	William Earl
Butin	Authorius J
Butler	James L
Butler	Leon L
Butler	R Dale
Buzynski	Mark J
Byers	Julie Ann
Byers	Kevin L
Bywaters	George W

C

Last	First
Caboul	A
Caddell	Randolph
Cade	Paul
Cady	Frank W
Cady	William
Cahmplin	Mildred H
Cahoon	Jerry
Cain	Mary
Caliger	Roger K
Callender	William
Campbell	Emanuel Luther
Campbell	Glenn Francis
Campbell	Wilbur
Cannon	Rollie
Canova	Addie
Cansdale	William H
Cantrell	David
Cardona	Angel Manuel
Carey	J H
Carlson	Claude Gene
Carlson	Ernest A
Carlson	Lloyd
Carlson	Robert E
Carpe	Albert K
Carpe	Lawrence L
Carpenter	Daniel
Carpenter	Larry
Carr	Jake B
Carrington	Raymond
Carroll	Thomas J
Carson	Frederick Victor
Carson	Samuel H
Carter	A
Carter	Francis W
Carter	J F
Carter	Otis
Carter	Vincent C
Cartwright	Raymond E
Cason	John E
Casper	L C
Castelline	Paul J
Castigan	D F
Catalfo	Daniel B
Catron	Gregory A
Cavender	Gladys
Cavender	James
Cavender	Philip D
Cavil	Pauline
Cessna	George C
Chamberlain	Roy J
Chamberlin	R L
Chambers	Harry W
Chambers	James S
Chaney	Jean M
Chanly	John
Chapman	Steve Elliot
Christ	George W
Christensen	Gilbert
Christiansen	Martin E
Christie	Archie L
Clancy	W J
Clapper	Nels
Clark	Barbara
Clark	Carla
Clark	David Glenn
Clark	Gary Lee
Clark	Joe
Clark	Leslie H
Clark	Robert David
Clarkson	Roy E
Clary	Andrew W
Clausen	Deanna Lynn
Claycomb	Clifford M
Clayman	Mose
Cleary	A M
Cleary	Ed
Clemens	Charles L
Clemens	Dick J
Clemens	Jeffrey T
Clemens	Leon J
Cleveland	Max O
Clifford	W D
Cline	Daniel
Cline	John L
Cline III	James
Clock	Robert Merle
Clossen	Kern C
Cloyed	Wilbur Carl
Coalson	Mary
Cohen	Harry L
Colavecchio	Mary
Cole	Donald R
Colee	Pamela Rae
Colflesh	Allen
Colley	A
Collins	Frank
Collins	J J
Collins	James Lester
Collins	Lynette Ann
Collins	Marvin L
Collins	Mary L
Collins	Nathan P
Colville	Sharon Leigh
Conner	W A
Connolly	Joe C
Conrath	Barbara
Cook	R B
Copeland	Dan
Copic	Robert Lesli
Cordray	A E
Cornwell	Darren Mason
Cornwell	Robert W
Cortese	Benjamin
Cose	Donald
Cota	Gordan S

Couch	Joseph A
Couch	Raymond W
Coughlin	Michael R
Courtney	Jeremiah
Courtright	E V
Covell	Charles L
Cowan	Richard
Cowart	James J
Cowger	Gary Lynn
Cox	James E
Cox	Melvin
Coxe	Donald J
Coy	David Lance
Craig	Michael L
Craig	Worthy S
Cram	Edith R
Cramblit	Loren P
Cramer	Charles Larry
Crawford	Ed
Crawford	Glen L
Crawford	Jolene Rae
Crawford	Ronnie G
Crawford	Ruth E
Crawford	Urban L
Creamer	Carl J
Cretsinger	Sean
Criswell	Bradley
Cronin	Glenn
Cronin	Jeffrey
Crosby	Albert C
Crosby	W
Cross	Glen W
Cross	Philip J
Cross	Thomas R
Crouse	Robert L
Crowley	Scott E
Crozier	Edward Ernest
Crozin	Shirley
Crum	Alfred H
Crumbaker	James W
Crydeler	W H
Cully	J G
Cunningham	Clifford D
Cunningham	H A
Cunningham	Harold W
Cunningham	Timothy
Curtis	Brent Alan
Curtis	Christopher
Curtis	Donald
Curtiss	Robert W

D

D'Ostilio	Patrick W
Dahlen	Mathieu
Dahlstrom	Scott
Dailey	John M
Dailey	Malcom N
Dameron	Virginia
Daniels	Floyd A
Daniels	John W
Danner	Brian K
Dare	Raymond J
Darr	Connie
Daugherty	John
Daugherty	William H
Davey	James
Davey	Larry D
Davidson	Glenda Jean
Davis	Arnett Douglas
Davis	Charles
Davis	Fred E
Davis	Jon L
Davis	Leo V
Davis	Richard Wayne
Davis	Rolland F
Davis	William C
Dawson	Carroll W
Dawson	Craig
Dawson	L E
Dawson	Randy
Dawson	Walter L
Day	Albert H
Deane	B H
Dearinger	David
DeBonis	Joe
Decker	Jerry
DeFord	Ed N
DeFord	Nelson
DeHaven	
DeJoode	Richard
Delaney	John H
Delaney	Michael F
Delmege	Frank R
Delmege	Sherman E
DeLong	W
Demory	Stacey J
DeMoss	S W
Dempsey	Judd G
Denholm	Thomas
Dennis	Barbara Jean
Denny	Austin E
Denny	Jack
Deremiah	Wesley L
Derrick	Wilbur J
DeVies	W H
Devine	Galyn Aubrey
DeVore	George M
Dickel	Gregory M
Dickerson	Max Edwin
Dickey	George W
Dietsch	Ronald
Dillinger	J G
Dingeman	John
Dockstader	H L
Dodson	John
Dodson	Joleen
Doescher	Lorre A
Doherty	Elbert L
Dolan	John P
Dolley	Gordon W
Domenig	Paul
Donahue	Cynthia M
Donahue	Melanie
Donahue	Patrick
Donaldson	Howard K
Donoghue	G
Donoghue	M Joe
Donohue	John
Dorman	W L
Dorsey	D C
Dougherty	Frank
Douglas	B B
Douglas	James
Douglas	Vear V
Dove	Charles E
Dowie	Julianne L
Downing	Isaac T
Drady	William
Drake	Stewart
Dreyer	Scott L
Dubois	David E
Duffy	Shannon
Dugan	Patrick
Dunagan	C A
Dunagan	Carl D
Dunagan	John
Dunham	Joseph
Dunn	Gail A
Duquette	John J
Durham	Douglas F
Durrance	Grady B
Dusenbery	Daniel A
Dusenbery	Marye V
Duteau	Joan K
Dutton	F E
Duvall	John F
Duver	Henry L
Dyer	Bruce
Dyer	Robert
Dykstra	Todd T

E

Easley	Loretta A
Eastman	Robert S
Eaton	Jack H
Eaves	Elizabeth
Eckels	J O
Eckhardt	Ralph A
Edwards	Annette
Edwards	Bernel L
Edwards	Diane R
Edwards	Etta
Edwards	Jeffrey D
Edwards	Larry E
Edwards	Frank
Eggleston	Howard R
Eide	L L
Eklund	John
Ekroot	Laura L
Ekstrand	Thomas
Elliot	Ilda
Elliott	Winton C
Elliott	Ann
Ellis	Jack
Ellis	Robert H
Ellis	Tammy
Elrod	Bruce E
Elwell	Richard L
Emary	Dean W
Emrich	James O
English	K
English	T W
English	Thomas W
Erickson	Ellen L
Ervin	E W
Ervin	James T
Ervin	Robert R
Espinosa	Elva
Evans	Donna S
Evans	Kelly M
Eveland	Richard D
Eveland	Sadie S
Exline	Hubert C

F

Fagen	Clarence E
Faith	Clifford W
Farrell	Debra S
Farrell	Michael L
Farrell	Patrick J
Fedson	Richard
Feeley	A J
Feeley	Eamon E
Feeney	J P
Ferguson	Arthur W
Ferguson	Melvin
Ferguson	Robert C
Fetters	Walter W
Fever	Pearl T
Fever	Pearl K
Finkelstein	I
Finn	Thomas
Fish	G
Fisher	Jerald D
Fisher	Scott Allen
Fisk	Walter W
Fitzgerald	James
Fitzgerald	William Lee
Fitzpatrick	Anna
Fitzpatrick	Hugh
Fitzpatrick	Laura Karen
Flannery	John J
Flickinger	Steven Alan
Floyd	J
Flynn	Dustin R
Fogel	Bernie
Fogle	Elwood Elton
Fogle	Peggy
Foley	Patrick J
Follett	Thomas D
Fontana	Donna
Ford	Daniel
Foreman	David A
Foster	L T
Foster	Ronald K
Foster	V F
Foster	William B
Foust	Robert Eugene
Frace	Thomas M
Franey	James M
Frankford	Joseph
Fredregill	Carl J
Fredregill	Frank
Fredregill	Roscoe T
Freeman	
Freeneire	H
French	Roger Leiton
Fridl	Cheryl
Fristo	Billy Wayne
Fronsdale	C A
Frost	Douglas W
Frost	Herman L
Frowick	E J
Fryman	Harold U
Fuller	Donald
Fuller	H E
Fuller	Steven Craig
Funaro	Samuel
Fusaro	Joseph Anthony

G

Gagen	Frank A
Gallardo	Raymond
Gallispie	Thomas
Galloway	
Gamboa	Victor S
Gansley	Charles F
Gant	Floyd E
Ganzley	Charles F
Garanson	Donald L
Gardner	
Garland	L A
Garlock	Frank
Garrett	William H
Garrison	Jinny Gail
Garrison	Mary K
Garritt	W H
Garvey	Michael Owen
Gass	Carol
Gates	Richard Alan
Gathercole	John G
Gavin	Thomas M
Gay	Marvin
Geager	
Gearhart	E G
Geneva	John T
George	John
Gerde	Rasmus
Gerhart	
Geyer	Stanger B
Gibson	Daniel A
Gibson	Samuel
Gilbert	Orris E
Gilespie	Thomas
Gill	John Patrick
Gill	Seymore T
Gillispie	Paul Hoyt
Gillispie	Thomas
Gladdon	Joseph
Glade	Richard R
Gladson	Albert D
Glann	Harold R
Glasco	Charles W
Glascock	Alva H
Glassburn	Hugh S
Glenn	Holly
Godfroy	Joseph Lee
Goelz	Donal C
Goff	Carrie
Goldenson	Sol
Goldsbury	Diane I
Goldsmith	Samuel J
Goldstein	Dana
Gomez	Anthony J
Gonzalez	Joe A
Gonzalez	Mike
Good	Daniel W
Good	Herbert Dale
Good	Robert Harold
Gordon	Dolley
Gordon	Russell
Gore	Andre
Gorsuch	Bobbi
Goulden	Raymond Joseph
Gourd	Gregory
Gowen	Jeffrey P
Grabau	Marshall
Gracey	Judith
Gran	T F
Grant	John
Grass	Amy Jo
Grasso	Michael T
Graves	H H
Gray	Daniel
Gray	George B
Green	L H
Greenfield	Jerry
Greenfield	Lonnie Lee
Greenlee	Gerald S
Gregory	W J
Griffith	Douglas L
Griffith	George
Griggs	M
Griggs	Walter K
Griglione	James R
Griglione	Richard J
Grimes	Ed
Groff	Gus
Gross	S L
Grossnickle	Harold J
Grove	Chester
Grove	Michael
Groves	Jack
Groves	William Roger
Grubb	Robert W
Guhl	Charles W
Gustafson	Roger
Guthrie	Daniel
Guy	Equinsia

H

Haag	George W
Haas	Margaret
Hafner	Adam
Hainlin	Sheila
Hale	Allen
Halifax	Jason
Hall	A C
Hall	Charles B
Hall	Tawnson
Hall	William
Hallett	George
Hallett	William A
Halliday	
Halverson	Max
Hamborg	Constant
Hamilton	Arthur M
Hamilton	Craig
Hamilton	Donna Lea
Hamilton	Dwayne J
Hamilton	James
Hammell	Barney
Hammond	Florence
Hammond	John B
Hammond	William Mckinley

Last Name	First Name
Hancock	Alan Eugene
Hand	Christopher
Hanger	William
Hansen	Eugene Kay
Hansen	Gregory T
Hansen	Herman C
Hansen	Robert Lloyd
Hansen	William G
Hanson	Hans Mikkel
Hardenbrook	Lewis O
Hardenbrook	Louis W
Hardiman	Thomas P
Hardin	Eli
Hardin	John C
Harding	Clarence
Harding	Tyler
Hardy	Chris
Hare	Rosemary S
Harkin	James J
Harkin	Matthew J
Harkin	Anne
Harlan	Edgar Leroy
Harmon	Frank
Harper	Bonita
Harper	Charlene Ann
Harrigan	William
Harris	Brent A
Harris	Donald Wayne
Harris	Judy A
Harris	Keith
Harris	Larry D
Harris	Tony Paul
Harrison	Mary
Hart	Jess R
Hart	Robert R
Harter	James
Harter	Robert
Hartline	Donald Ray
Hartman	John
Hartman	Robert Joel
Harty	Frank J
Hartzer	Floyd
Hartzler	
Harvey	Douglas M
Hathaway	
Haubert	Henry J
Havaland	G
Havens	J
Haviland	David Lyle
Havran	Paul Francis
Hawkins	S E
Hayes	F Charles
Hayes	William R
Hays	Floyd
Hayworth	Samuel T
Healey	George E
Hearshman	Lori J
Heath	William
Heaton	Elza G
Hector	Isaac J
Hedberg	L
Hedges	Deanna
Hedrick	George
Heefner	J C
Heffelfinger	James
Helle	Lorna
Heller	Charles Edward
Heller	John Jenson
Heller	Judy Marie
Heller	Thomas R
Heller	Thomas H
Henderson	Cecil P
Henderson	Charles D
Henderson	Robert A
Hendrix	William H
Henry	Hasbrouck H
Henry	Phyllis
Hensen	Andrew
Herink	Dennis D
Herschberg	Marion
Hessler	George
Hethershaw	Nile
Hewitt	Edward C
Hewitt	Harry
Hiatt	E
Hiatt	Robert V
Hiatt	Walt R
Hiatt	Willis E
Hibbs	George Donald
Hickey	Patrick Edward
Hickle	Richard V
Hickman	Lori Ellen
Hicks	John B
Hildreth	Georgia E
Hildreth	Richard
Hildreth	Roger R
Hill	Colonel W
Hill	Dennis E
Hill	Earl
Hillhaugh	F L
Hines	Evan Athen
Hines	Ione
Hobart	Bryan
Hobart	Byron Joseph
Hoblik	W L
Hoblit	W D
Hoblitt	N D
Hobt	Terry F
Hockersmith	Jon S
Hodges	Shelley
Hoferman	Keith Jerrod
Hoffman	August
Hoffman	H
Hoffman	Roland
Hofmann	Michael
Hogate	Clark W
Holeman	James E
Holland	George Arthur
Hollibaugh	F L
Hollibaugh	J J
Holt	August J
Hommer	Bren A
Hooper	Thomas
I lopkins	Laurie
Hopkins	Rober B
Hoppie	Charles
Horsburgh	James G
Hoskins	James E
Hoskinson	Linda Lee
Host	Rick L
Houghton	Allen
House	Garth L
House	James E
Houston	Gaylord
Howard	Albert R
Howard	Irene
Howard	Robert
Howard	Steve T
Howell	Stephen K
Howland	Margaret Ann
Hoyla	Anthony Albert
Hoyt	George
Hubbard	T Jay
Huberty	David
Hudson	Sharon
Huffman	Christopher
Hughes	Wilson
Hulgan	Oma
Hull	Austin W
Hume	William P
Humphrey	Howard W
Hunt	Charles Edward
Hunt	Ed
Hunt	Raymond
Hunt	William A
Hutchinson	Gene A
Hutson	Joseph
Hutzel	Larry J

I

Last Name	First Name
Ihrig	Lawrence
Ingle	Brenda K
Inman	William F
Irvin	Franklin K
Irwin	Marshall T
Iseminger	G
Ives	Max B
Ivie	Cheril Diane

J

Last Name	First Name
Jackson	Charles C
Jackson	Lauryn
Jacobs	J A
Jamess	Robert Vance
Janson	Donna Lee
Jardine	Mary
Jarvis	Albert
Jeannin	Jesse A
Jefferson	Sandra
Jeffries	Ben
Jenkins	W C
Jenney	John W
Jennings	Sharon
Jennings	Sue Ann
Jennisch	Bernard J
Jergens	George
Jerome	Henry E
Jobe	Clarence
Joelson	Deloris
Joelson	Iner C
Johansen	A Marguerite
Johnson	Adolph E
Johnson	Alfred
Johnson	Arthur A
Johnson	B L
Johnson	Fred
Johnson	George H
johnson	John W
Johnson	Nolan
Johnson	Otto P
Johnson	Timothy A
Johnson	Wade Bruce
Johnson	Walter E
Johnson	William L
Johnson	William A
Johnston	Andrew Carl
Johnston	August
Johnston	E E
Johnston	Larry Lee
Jones	Aaron
Jones	Frank
Jones	Ivory M
Jones	James Wilson
Jones	Jennifer
Jones	Jerry A
Jones	John F
Jones	John L
Jones	Judith Kay
Jones	Kelly Dee
Jones	Minnie
Jones	Patricia L
Jones	Richard L
Jones	Sharon
Jones	Wanda Della
Jones	William R
Jordan	Charles T
Jordan	Daniel Charles
Joss	Dennis Howard
Judkins	Larry Leroy
Judkins	William Darryle

K

Kachelhoffer	George E
Kail	Richard William
Kaiser	Fran W
Kamerick	Jack Dean
Kane	Dan
Kastler	Ray G
Kauzlarich	Daniel Louis
Kavanaugh	Edgar
Keahna	Betty
Keeley	John H
Keely	James H
Kees	Steven E
Keffer	W B
Keller	James H
Kelley	Daniel
Kelley	George P
Kelley	William L
Kellogg	Lester L
Kelly	James
Kelso	Guy
Kemp	Terry Eugene
Keppel	George H
Kern	Cole Edward
Kern	William
Kerpon	Nick
Ketchum	Dani
Kettells	Dorothy Pauline
Kettells	Orin A
Keul	Sandra Kay
Kihlborn	Otto
Kilgore	Dennis John
Kilgore	Galyn M
Kilgore	Rolla G
Killin	Edward D
Kimble	Laverne
Kimes	Jesse
King	Hugh A
King	Robert L
Kingery	Anna
Kinney	Philip James
Kinsey	Al
Kircher	Louis M
Kirk	Charles W
Kirkman	Amy
Kirkman	Edward Patrick
Kittleman	H B
Klein	E
Klein	Ross
Kline	Kenneth Eugene
Klingaman	Bruce Lawrence
Knight	Albert LeRoy
Knight	Jay F
Knolton	Lyman
Knox	Donald E
Knox	John
Knox	Tony D
Koons	John C
Kooyman	Donald F
Kracht	Edwin A
Kramer	Timothy D
Kramme	Clark Alan
Kramme	Robert
Krehbiel	David
Kress	Bradley Ray
Kubick	Mark
Kubik	Mary Jay
Kuehner	E C
Kuehner	Harry
Kueny	Carol J

L

Last Name	First Name
Labus	Eugene
Laferty	J E
Laird	Brenda
Laird	Jacob
Lalley	James
Lamasters-Kappel	Nancy
Lamb	Richard Charles
Lane	C C
Lane	Sharon
Lang	W M
Langbein	Donald Joseph
Langstaff	George
Lannon	Jan
Larson	Paul F
LaRue	Earl Dean
Latham	John J
Latimer	John L
Lavender	Lori Jo
Law	Randy E
Lawman	Carol
Lawman	Carol Rae
Laws	Thomas
Layton	Clifford E
Layton	Steven
Lazarus	Jack
Leahy	Benjamin D
Leaman	Fred
Leaming	Cleatus M
Leaming	Craig M
Leaming	Derald R
Leasure	Robert M
LeCroy	Jack
Lee	E Leslie
Lee	Edmund M
Leeper	Michael L
Leighter	Neil A
Leighter	Steven
Leighton	June
Leinen	Jack L
Leitzke	Lawrence E
Lemon	Kevin
Leo	Joseph M
Leon	Soloman
Leporte	John
Leseney	Mary Jo
LeVere	John F
Lewellin	Lisa
Lewis	Bridget A
Lewis	Charles D
Lewis	Clay H
Lewis	Cleo E
Lewis	Edward
Lewis	John
Lewis	John F
Lewis	Robert
Lewis	Russell
Lewis (Schneider)	Deborah I
Lieber	A J
Lillard	David O
Limke	Gerald R
Lindley	T D
Lindquist	Charles A
Link	Noel E
Lint	Lloyd C
Little	Paul J
Livingston	James L
Lockard	William
Loeffler	Andy W
Loehr	Joseph F
Logan	Paul S
Lohrman	Matthew
Lohrman	Robert C
Lomen	John
Long	Esther R
Lor	Doua (Bruce
Lor	Toua
Lord	Philip W
Losee	Lonnie L
Lovejoy	Emerson
Lovejoy	Gerald R
Lovejoy	John
Lovejoy	Richard
Lovejoy	W E
Lovell	Grace
Lower	Edwin C
Ludwig	Anne Marie
Lumley	William D
Lunders	Terry
Lunders	Wayne L
Lundholm	Gary L
Lutz	Kenneth E
Lynch	Deborah A

Lynch	Timothy A	McGilvra	Dennis	Moody	William J	Nicholls	Enoch	Patchen	William M
Lyon	Robert	McGinn	A J	Moomey	Wayne L	Nicholls	Nolan J	Pattee	W W

M

Mabee	Frank C	McGoldrick	Hugh	Moon	Gary R	Nicholls	Roland E	Patterson	J G
MacDonald	James	McGowan	William	Moon	J A	Nichols	Carrie	Paul	Richard Ray
MacDowell	W E	McGrath	John S	Moon	Kenneth E	Nichols	Wendell E	Paulsen	Kenneth
Mackey	Robert E	McGuire	James L	Moore	Carl	Nicodemus	Harold E	Peairs	Elizabeth
Mackintosh	G R	McInnis	William L	Moore	Nellie	Nicodemus	Melvin A	Peak	Timothy R
MacVicar	John	McIntire	J R	Moore	Oscar	Nielsen	Holly B	Pearce	Sidney H
Maddison	Robert T	McIntosh	G R	Moore	Ronald	Nielsen	Merlin Dale	Pederson	A H
Madero	Gerald	McKercher	Jesse	Moore	William H	Noble	Larry D	Pehl	Mark A
Mahaffey	Lawrence A	McKinley	Ralph E	Moorman	Eric Scott	Noble	Robert C	Pendarvis	Larry
Maher	W J	McKinney	James	Moran	Camden J	Noel	David D	Pendland	Melvin Boyd
Mahlstadt	Chris	McKinney	Loretta J	Moran	James Lewis	Nolan	John	Pendleton	Dennis W
Maitland	W T	McKinney	Mark Allen	Morgan	Dennis P	Nordaker	Vance Robert	Penland	Larry K
Malm	Charles	McKircher	Jesse	Morgan	Douglas	Nordaker	Vance A	Penland	Robert Howard
Manbeck	Jennie	McKirscher	Jesse	Morgan	George P	Nordyke	John David	Penn	J W
Mangra	Ramkishore	McLain	Alonz C	Morgan	Joseph Patrick	Northup	Daniel	Penn	John O
Mann	Gary G	McLaughlin	Wendell W	Morgan	Mark S	Norton	Warren K	Penney	Clarence R
Manning	Kimberly	McMains	Ronald D	Morgan	Tim	Novak	Edward	Pennington	William L
Manny	Faye	McMickle	G W	Morgan	Timothy	Novinger	William D	Perkins	Cynthia M
Manny	Frank C	McMillen	Harry L	Morris	Gale B	Nutt	Janet	Perry	A
Marasco	Nat	McMurray	Starla Marie	Morris	Harry M	Nye	William P	Perry	Herbert W
Marasco	Paul J	McNamara	Daniel	Morris	Sandra	Nystrom	Janice	Persons	C D
Maring	Joseph L	McNamara	Tim	Morris	Steven			Petersen	Loren
Marker	Gary	McNerney	Timothy	Morris	William	**O**		Peterson	Alycia
Markey	John J	McNutt	George W	Morse				Peterson	D P
Marks	Lewis	McQuerry	Charles	Morse	Gregory V	O'Brien	Robert E	Peterson	John A
Marlette	Earl William	McRae	Fama	Mortenson	Lynn R	O'Connell	James J	Peterson	John P
Marohn	William E	McVey	Pearl E	Morton	Jack	O'Donnell	Dennis	Peterson	Ray O
Marquis	Ralph R	Means	William A	Morton	Jeffrey Howard	O'Donnell	James M	Pettit	Thomas W Sr.
Marshall	Thomas W	Medbury	Sheldon P	Mortoza	Rick G	O'Donnell	M J	Pettit	Thomas R Jr.
Martin	Roman G	Meeker	John H	Moser	Carol	O'Leary	John T	Pherrin	William M
Martin	Thomas M	Meholovich	Connie	Moses	Michael	O'Neal	Linda	Phillips	Jeffrey K
Martin	Walter T	Melendez	Rita	Moss	James Patrick	Odam	Terry	Phillips	Margaret Fern
Martin	Warren L	Mellon	H Edisco	Mould	Richard Dennis	Ofterdinger	Mildred	Phipps	Claude E
Marts	William	Melton	Brian C	Moulder	William H	Ogan	Phillip E	Phipps	Shawn Marie
Mason	Bobby R	Melugin	Steven Ray	Muelhaupt	Linda	Ogilvie	Harry	Pickering	J Elsworth
Matalone	Jerry	Mengus	Charles	Mueller	John	Ogle	James C	Pickett	C L
Mathis	Frank A	Messerly	Curtis	Muldoon	James	Ohlswager	Charles D	Pickett	Gerald D
Mathis	William	Messerschmidt	Carol	Mulford	David M	Ohnemus	Andrew J	Pierce	Charles E
Mattern	George W	Meyer	Pam	Mullins	William E	Olechnovics	Sandy	Pierce	Frank D
Mattern	Grace M	Meyer	William	Munger	Traverse D	Oleson	James D	Pierce	Roland V
Maxwell	A R	Meyers	Earl L	Murillo	David M	Oliver	John	Pierce	William John
Mayfield	Darryl	Mickelson	Steven	Murphy	James	Oliver	Steven	Pike	Christopher E
McAfee	Ed	Mihalovich	Anthony John	Murphy	Kenneth R	Olmstead	Farron	Pilcher	Michael
McBride	Arthur	Miles	Milton R	Murphy	P	Olney	Leo E	Pinegar	F
McBride	Michael J	Millard	Thomas	Murphy	Thomas	Olson	Harry W	Piziali	Elizabeth R
McCarthy	Con J	Miller	Albert G	Murray	Franklin	Olson	Steven Anthony	Piziali	Joe
McCarthy	Edward J	Miller	Carolyn	Murray	Leonard R	ONeal	Amy	Plaisted	Robert E
McCarthy	James	Miller	Charles	Myers	Nancy L	Ortman	Eric James	Plummer	A P
McCarthy	Katherine Marie	Miller	Glenn B	Myers	Rosemond	Osberg	Edward T	Plummer	Bert
McCarthy	Martin M	Miller	Harold A			Osborn	Ned	Poe	Jamie
McCarthy	William Michael	Miller	Herbert M	**N**		Osterquist	James	Polley	Martin L
McCauley	Cormick	Miller	Ira			Ouimet	Donald E	Pollock	Joanne M
McClain	A	Miller	James R	Nagle	Thomas	Outland	Forrest J	Pomeroy	James Adams
McClanahan	John N	Miller	Joel W	Namanny	Lonny L	Overton	Alvin Edward	Pontious	Earmel (Mike)H
McClanahan	Rodney	Miller	Loren O	Napoli	Philip	Overton	Sally	Poplawski	John Andrew
McClelland	J R	Miller	Marcellinus E	Nauman	Russell	Owens	Thomas J	Potts	George W
McClintic	Katherine	Miller	Mark R	Negrete	Charles			Powell	B W
McClure	Jack T	Miller	Marshall E	Nehring	Michael	**P**		Powell	Katherine Ann
McCollough	Deborah	Miller	Morris	Nehring	Richard W			Powers	Drue
McConkey	Ervin	Miller	Murial A	Nelson	Arthur W	Page	James S	Powers	William W
McConnell	Nancy Lou	Miller	Teckla Anne	Nelson	Arvene S	Palmer	Dann Norman	Priebe	William
McCord	H	Mills	James T	Nelson	Carolyn	Palmer	Darlene	Prothero	Judith Kay
McCown	James F	Milner	Gordon D	Nelson	Steven	Palmer	Louisa	Pugh	Frances M
McCracken	Albert C	Milton	Brian	Nesbitt	Mary Joanne	Palmer	Marilyn Joyce	Punelli	Frank J
McCurn	Myrna	Mingus	Charles	Ness	David Michael	Palmer	Paul Preston	Purcell	Earl
McDermott	David	Mishler	James	Ness	Jack Paul	Panor	Samuel	Purdy	William Edmund
McDivitt	Thomas R	Miskimmen	J	Nessen	Paul B	Parish	Sandra Jean	Pursley	Jacob
McDonald	James	Mitchell	Mae	Nesson	Paul B	Parizek	Paul E	Purviance	Michael
McDowel		Mitchell	Terry	Netherow	C	Park	Charles E		
McElderry	E R	Mogelberg	Emil C	Neumann	Verna M	Parker	Percy Richard	**Q**	
McEwen	Len P	Mogensen	Harold R	Nevins	Eric	Parkhurst	F		
McFarland	Myrna Lynn	Mohler	John C	Newcomb	S P	Parrish	R J	Queener	Mary Anna
McGavran	Warren	Mohr	Charles J	Newell	Joseph A	Parrott	Don	Quick	James A
McGee	Patrick	Monarch	John W	Newell	Lem V	Parsons	Amy Elizabeth	Quinn	
McGilvern	Dennis	Moody	Bert	Newman	John A	Paschal	Patricia		
		Moody	Michael R	Newman	Pat	Pascuzzi	Laura	**R**	
		Moody	Patrick J	Newquist	Charles D	Pastel	Nels		
				Nicholls	Charles A	Pasutti	Betty Jean	Rabbitt	Warren C
						Patch	Dale P	Radosevich	Frank C

220

Rains — Frank E
Rambo — J H
Ramirez — Cheryl
Ramsey — Edwin L
Ramsey — Leander G
Ramsey — Robert R
Rand — Edward J
Rasmussen — Kelly
Rath — Denise
Raudabaugh — Scott
Ray — George H
Rayburn — DeMoss W
Reaney — Robert R
Rebik — Diana
Rector — John D
Reed — Lester P
Reelitz — Daniel
Reese — Forrest E
Reese — William
Reeves — James
Reeves — William
Reich — Herman
Reiley — Thomas
Reints — William R
Renfro — Steven Dewayne
Renoe — James D
Resch — Michael J
Rex — W A
Rexroat — Raymond C
Rexroat — Richard
Reynolds — Kimberlee
Reynolds — Lawrence
Reynolds — Robert D III
Reynolds — Robert D Jr.
Rhinehart — E W
Rhoads — Tracy
Rhodes — John W
Rhodes — Lewis E
Riccio — Dominic
Riccio — James J
Rich — Ben
Rich — Dennis A
Rich — Harry H
Rich — Sandra
Richardson — Charles
Richardson — Debra
Richeson — Hazel B
Rickard — Charles
Rickert — Orville A
Rickman — Jack W
Rico — Jennifer
Riddle — J W
Riddle — William
Rider — Charles
Rider — John Wesley
Rieger — Susanne K
Riley — Asher S
Riley — William L
Rinker — Irene
Ripperger — Lance
Rivera — Rick
Rizzuti — Regina S
Robbins — Ida Sue
Robbins — Judy
Robertson — M M
Robinson — Gregory
Robinson — J
Robinson — Kayne B
Robinson — Kenneth
Robinson — Marvin
Robinson — Thomas Volineer
Robison — Byron F
Roddy — Joseph
Rodgers — Barbara
Rodgers — Stanton T
Rodine — James E
Roe — D E
Roe — Linda
Roe — Zell G

Roemer — Richard B
Rogers — Larry D
Rogerson — Jno R
Roland — Richard D
Rood — Joseph T
Roozeboom — Sandy Dawn
Rose — Bill R
Rose — Jack L
Rosecrans — J O
Rosen — Edward
Rosenberg — A B
Rosenberg — George E
Roske — Ronald
Ross — Sam
Rote — Robert D
Roth — Ralph
Rounds — Peter Willaim
Rounds — Scott
Rounds — Thomas A
Rouse — George R
Rousseau — Richard Ivan
Routh — Rhett R
Routt — Donald Dewey
Rowen — Larry
Rowley — James E
Rowley — Roger D
Ruopp — Dave
Rush — Michael D
Rushton — Janet
Russell — Charles F
Russell — Charles
Russell — M T

S

Saddoris — Eldon P
Salazar — Albert M
Saltzman — Bernice
Sample — George W
Sampson — H
Sanders — Charles S
Sanders — Richard L
Sanders — Roger W
Sanford — Bruce H
Sarchfield — John F
Sarcone — Anthony
Saunders — John F
Saunders — Roscoe C
Savage — E
Sawhill — William D
Scanlon — Morris
Scarberry — George W
Scarcello — Francis
Scarcello — Pat
Scarpino — Gabriel
Scarpino — George
Scarpino — John L
Scarpino — William
Scearcy — William Retauno
Schaffer — Richard
Schafnitz — Denise Linn
Schafnitz — Russell
Schane — Georg Wesley
Schaper — Nancy
Scharlach — William E
Schettler — Rodney A
Schieholz — William
Schinkel — George
Schinkel — Sharon
Schinkel — Steven
Schlachtenhaufen — Laurie
Schleuger — Mark
Schleuger — Peggy
Schmeling — Paul
Schmell — George M
Scholes — William E
Schooley — Robert
Schrader — Jerry L
Schroeder — Connie
Schuett — Richard L

Schumacher — Brittany Lauren
Schwery — Lyle
Scovel — J A
Seals — Nancy Marie
Seaman — Scott
Seehan — Leo J
Seib — Thomas E
Seibert — Martin E
Sellers — William J
Sellick — Fred
Sergio — Kathy
Seward — Benjamin F
Seward — Steve W
Seybert — David J
Shafer — Charles J
Shaffer — Ann
Shaffer — Charles J
Shaffer — Claude B
Shaffer — Glade B
Shaffer — Glen
Shaffer — Warren W
Shaklee — Lee
Shane — George C
Shanley — John
Shannon — Jeffrey B
Shapiro — Pamela K
Shaver — John M
Shay — Maurice
Shay — Michael M
Shea — James
Shea — John
Shepard
Shepherd — Rupert L
Sherwood — Stanley L
Shevokas — Paul E
Shipley — Jeanette K
Shivers — Thomas S
Shoop — Kelin E
Shores — Arthur D
Shortell — Ed
Shuck — George A
Shultice — Donald
Sickels — Harley J
Sickels — Ray
Sideler — Fred
Sidmore — Wallace
Siedler — Fred
Silcott — James R
Sillick — Fred W
Silver — Steven G
Simmer — George L
Simmons — Allen S
Simmons — Lupe
Simon — William H
Simpson — Bradley
Sims — L D
Sims — William D
Singleton — Richard
Sinram — Dana
Skain — E V
Skinner — John B
Skinner — Richard
Skinner — William
Skinner — Wilson W
Slader — C E
Slater — Joe H
Sloane — John
Slopie — K
Smallwood — Bert
Smiley — Larry D
Smith — Billy
Smith — Charlie N
Smith — Charmaine C
Smith — Clay W
Smith — David
Smith — Denise
Smith — Donavee
Smith — Dorin
Smith — Doris

Smith — Earl
Smith — F M
Smith — Frederick H
Smith — Hersel W
Smith — James L
Smith — James
Smith — John H
Smith — Loomis W
Smith — Maude
Smith — Pamela Kay
Smith — Sheila D
Smith — Terry
Smith — Thomas Claude
Smith — Victor T
Smith — W C
Smith — Willie
Snedden — John
Snethen — Frederick
Snider — Richard
Snyder — Ethel M
Snyder — Harry W
Snyder — Irene
Snyder — James
Snyder — Randy
Soderquist — Charles
Sommers — Harry D
Sommers — Joseph Carl
Sommers — William C
Sorenson — Dennis
Soule
Southwick — Carmel Sue
Spad — Linda
Spanswick — Lonnie R
Sparks — C E
Sparks — Rex Thomas
Speck — Harlan G
Speck — William Forrest
Spencer — Thomas V
Sprafka — Lynn
Sprafka — Robin A
Sprague — Jeremy
Springer — William
Squires — R Dale
Staats — Steven
Staats — Warren L
Stader — G E
Stafford — Lori
Staggs — James A
Standley — Robert E
Stanford — Marion M
Stanley — Bobby J
Stanley — Bryan
Stanley — James
Stanley — Judy
Stanley — Ronald A
Stanton — Robert
Staples — George W
Staton — Janis M
Steel — Moses
Steele — Joel P
Steiner — Raymond L
Steinkamp — Warren R
Stephenson — Albert J
Stephenson — John William
Sterzing — Ed W
Stevens — James C
Stevenson — John P
Stevenson — Thomas J
Stevenson — William T
Steverson — Michael
Stewar — Jim
Stigers — E E
Stiles — John W
Stiles — Roger
Stone — Melville
Stookey — Jackie L
Stookey — Marvin R
Stookey — Vicki R
Story — Joseph

Stotts — Ronald
Stougard — Larry D
Stout — Paul A
Strable — Connie
Strait — William
Strasburg — Richard W
Strasburg — Theodore E
Strawser — Michelle
Strawser — Stephen
Street — Jay
Street — Jerry
Street — Max A
Strickland — F B
Stropes — Susan R
Stueckrath — Michael
Stuempfig — Mark
Stuhr — Dean R
Stuhr — Kelly
Stutsman — Jonathan
Stutsman — Sol
Suits — Joshua
Sullivan — Thomas
Sumner — William H
Sundberg — Edward J
Swan — Jesse J
Swan — John
Sweeney — Dana K
Sweeney — Thomas
Swertfager — Charles W
Swigart — Cindy Sue

T

Taber — Angelica
Tallman — Ruth
Tarver — Carlton M
Taylor — Carolyn
Taylor — Charles W
Taylor — George
Taylor — Kathy
Taylor — Todd M
Teale — Thomas A
Tedesco — Charles
Tellis — Blaine E
Temple — Charles
Terrones — Philip J
Terry — William
Tesdall — James
Tesdall — Richard B
Thacker — Wilmer C
Theil — Fred
Thiel — Fred E
Thomas — Buddy C
Thomas — David F
Thomas — H D
Thomas — Janis Marie
Thomas — Jennie
Thomas — Millard
Thomas — Ollie D
Thomas — Owen
Thomas — Paul A
Thomas — Sara R
Thompson — Andrew
Thompson — Irvin E
Thompson — James P
Thompson — John
Thompson — Robert M
Thompson — Ronald
Thompson — Tammy M
Thompson — Virgil E
Thoren — John
Thornton — William Robert
Thurman — Donald
Tibben — Merlin
Tieszen — Paul David
Tigue — William
Timmins — John W
Timmons — Fred E
Tinker — John W
Todd — James E

Further information may be obtained from DMPD.

CONTRIBUTORS

GOLD BADGE
Des Moines Police Burial Association

SILVER BADGE
Mail Service, L.C.
Pioneer Hi-Bred
John Ruan Foundation Trust
Spain Electrical

BRONZE BADGE
Rich Barnes, State Farm Agent
Berger & Culp Law Firm
Bob Brown Chevrolet
Duffy, Spellman-Law Firm
Gilcrest/Jewett Lumber Company
Jerry's Homes, Jerry and Ron Grubb
HyVee Corp. Office
McCarthy Family
William H. Moulder
Norwest Mortgage Company
Operation Down Town
Polk County Savings Bank, Johnston
Scarpino Family
Townsend Engineering Company

CONTRIBUTOR
State Farm DM Area Agents
Jim Bagbey
Mark Courter
Sandra Gillespie
Elizabeth V. Hoak
Cindy Howell
Robert Joynes
Michael and Marjorie Leeper
Robert Smith
Alan Richardson
Steven Wayne Walters Sr.

INDEX